ColdFusion® 4 For Dummies

S0-CWR-970

Development Environment Check List

✔ Make sure ColdFusion Server is running on my workstation (check services in system tray) or connect to a server where it is running.

✔ Make sure the ODBC entries for my database have been created in ColdFusion Server Administrator.

✔ Make sure a Web server is running on my workstation or connect to a server where it is running.

✔ Create an RDS server entry in the Files tab of the Resources pane by selecting Allaire FTP & RDS from the drive list, and then right-clicking Allaire FTP & RDS and selecting Add RDS Server.

✔ Create Development Mappings from the Options dialog box (press F8, and choose Browse⇨Development Mappings).

Coding Errors Check List

✔ All tag attribute names must be contained in quotes (and the closed quotes must exist). Tag coloring in Studio helps make it apparent when closing quotes are missing.

✔ All start tags that take end tags must have them. Use Ctrl+M in Studio to find the matching tag. Check for end tags for every tag *before* the one that appears to be the problem. Mismatched tags earlier on can cause the problem.

✔ All tags must be valid. Use Ctrl+F4 in Studio to edit a tag and check that all attributes you list exist, or press just F4 to inspect the tag in the tag inspector. Using *database* (wrong) instead of *datasource* (right) as an attribute of the CFQUERY tag will cause all sorts of apparently unrelated errors.

✔ Variable to which you refer must exist. Check the scope and specify where appropriate. Use the IsDefined() function to test for the existence of a variable before using it in an IF tag or elsewhere, or use CFPARAM to create a variable with a default value for a variable when it does not already exist.

✔ Use the correct operator in the CFIF tag. CFIF takes the text abbreviation for logical operators such as EQ, GT, LT, and NOT, instead of =, >, <, and <>.

✔ Use single quotes in a SQL query instead of double quotes, in most ODBC databases. And along the same lines, do not use quotes around numeric and True/False values.

For Dummies®: Bestselling Book Series for Beginners

ColdFusion® 4 For Dummies®

Cheat Sheet

Tags and Commonly Used or Required Attributes

Database access tags

```
<CFQUERY datasource="dsn" name="query_name">
    . . . SQL statements . . .
</CFQUERY>

<CFINSERT datasource="dsn" tablename="table_name">

<CFUPDATE datasource="dsn" tablename="table_name" formfields="field1,
field2">

<CFMAIL query="query_name" to="to_address" from="from_address"
subject="subject" cc="cc_address" bcc="bcc_address"
server="mail_server_name">
    . . . content of message . . .
</CFMAIL>
```

Data display tags

```
<CFOUTPUT query="query_name">
        . . . output . . .
</CFOUTPUT

<CFTABLE query="query_name" colheaders htmltable border>
    <CFCOL text="#field_name#" header="caption" align="alignment">
    . . . additional CFCOL tags . . .
</CFTABLE>
```

Conditional processing and variables

```
<CFIF text_variable IS "value">
    . . . some processing . . .
<CFELSEIF True_False_variable>
    . . . other processing . . .
<CFELSEIF numeric_variable GT numeric_value>
    . . . still other processing . . .
<CFELSE>
    . . . default processing . . .
</CFIF>

<CFSET new_variable_name = value>

<CFPARAM name="variable_name" default="default_value">

<CFCOOKIE name="cookie_name" value="value" expires="days/date/now/never">
```

The IDG Books Worldwide logo is a registered trademark under exclusive license to IDG Books Worldwide, Inc., from International Data Group, Inc. The ...For Dummies logo is a trademark, and For Dummies is a registered trademark of IDG Books Worldwide, Inc. All other trademarks are the property of their respective owners.

For Dummies®: Bestselling Book Series for Beginners

ColdFusion® 4

FOR

DUMMIES®

by Alexis D. Gutzman and John Paul Ashenfelter
with Charlie Arehart

IDG Books Worldwide, Inc.
An International Data Group Company

Foster City, CA ◆ Chicago, IL ◆ Indianapolis, IN ◆ New York, NY

ColdFusion® 4 For Dummies®

Published by
IDG Books Worldwide, Inc.
An International Data Group Company
919 E. Hillsdale Blvd.
Suite 400
Foster City, CA 94404
www.idgbooks.com (IDG Books Worldwide Web site)
www.dummies.com (Dummies Press Web site)

Library of Congress Catalog Card No.: 99-66121

ISBN: 0-7645-0604-8

Printed in the United States of America

10 9 8 7 6 5 4 3 2 1

1B/SV/QR/QQ/IN

Distributed in the United States by IDG Books Worldwide, Inc.

Distributed by CDG Books Canada Inc. for Canada; by Transworld Publishers Limited in the United Kingdom; by IDG Norge Books for Norway; by IDG Sweden Books for Sweden; by IDG Books Australia Publishing Corporation Pty. Ltd. for Australia and New Zealand; by TransQuest Publishers Pte Ltd. for Singapore, Malaysia, Thailand, Indonesia, and Hong Kong; by Gotop Information Inc. for Taiwan; by ICG Muse, Inc. for Japan; by Intersoft for South Africa; by Eyrolles for France; by International Thomson Publishing for Germany, Austria and Switzerland; by Distribuidora Cuspide for Argentina; by LR International for Brazil; by Galileo Libros for Chile; by Ediciones ZETA S.C.R. Ltda. for Peru; by WS Computer Publishing Corporation, Inc., for the Philippines; by Contemporanea de Ediciones for Venezuela; by Express Computer Distributors for the Caribbean and West Indies; by Micronesia Media Distributor, Inc. for Micronesia; by Chips Computadoras S.A. de C.V. for Mexico; by Editorial Norma de Panama S.A. for Panama; by American Bookshops for Finland.

For general information on IDG Books Worldwide's books in the U.S., please call our Consumer Customer Service department at 800-762-2974. For reseller information, including discounts and premium sales, please call our Reseller Customer Service department at 800-434-3422.

For information on where to purchase IDG Books Worldwide's books outside the U.S., please contact our International Sales department at 317-596-5530 or fax 317-572-4002.

For consumer information on foreign language translations, please contact our Customer Service department at 1-800-434-3422, fax 317-572-4002, or e-mail rights@idgbooks.com.

For information on licensing foreign or domestic rights, please phone +1-650-653-7098.

For sales inquiries and special prices for bulk quantities, please contact our Sales department at 800-762-2974 or write to the address above.

For information on using IDG Books Worldwide's books in the classroom or for ordering examination copies, please contact our Educational Sales department at 800-434-2086 or fax 317-572-4005.

For press review copies, author interviews, or other publicity information, please contact our Public Relations department at 650-653-7000 or fax 650-653-7500.

For authorization to photocopy items for corporate, personal, or educational use, please contact Copyright Clearance Center, 222 Rosewood Drive, Danvers, MA 01923, or fax 978-750-4470.

is a registered trademark under exclusive license to IDG Books Worldwide, Inc. from International Data Group, Inc.

About the Authors

Alexis D. Gutzman is an E-Commerce Technology Consultant. She's also co-author of *The HTML 4 Bible* and author of *FrontPage 2000 Answers!* She's been in systems development in various capacities since 1986, when she graduated from Northwestern University with a B.A. in Computer Studies. She currently provides technology consulting including project management, needs assessment, systems analysis, systems design, and development for e-commerce sites such as Value America. Her musings on e-commerce and the technological underpinnings of it can be found in the E-Commerce Guide (`http://ecommerce.internet.com/solutions/tech_advisor/`), where she serves as the EC Tech Advisor. Mrs. Gutzman also holds a Masters in Public Affairs from the Lyndon B. Johnson School of Public Affairs of the University of Texas. When she's not working, she enjoys the company of her husband and two young daughters.

John Paul Ashenfelter is a Web developer, author, and educator. He is the author of *Choosing a Database for Your Web Site* and writes columns on Web database development for `WebReview.com` and *WebNet Journal.* He has been heavily involved in academic Web site development at the University of Virginia and at commercial sites such as `Exploremath.com` and is the founder of `webdatabase.org`. He currently writes, consults, and lectures about technology. Mr. Ashenfelter holds a B.S. in chemistry from James Madison University, an M.S. in physical chemistry from the University of Illinois, and a Ph. D. in science education from the University of Virginia. In his spare time, he hikes, cooks, and spends time with his wife and their dog and two cats.

Contributor **Charlie Arehart** is an experienced ColdFusion developer who's worked with the product since 1997. An Allaire certified instructor, Charlie is also a frequent presenter to user groups all over the country. He presented at the first CF Developer conference in 1998 at Fort Collins, Colorado, and he has taught or spoken to thousands of ColdFusion developers since joining this wonderful community. Charlie brings nearly 20 years of IT experience to his role, having spent the bulk of his career designing, programming, and administering very large-scale enterprise database management systems. This culminated in several years working on two of the largest databases in the world, at the Australian Department of Social Security and the U.S. Health Care Financing Administration. Charlie is also a frequent contributor to the *ColdFusion Developer Journal* and is tips editor for the *CFAdvisor*.

ABOUT IDG BOOKS WORLDWIDE

Welcome to the world of IDG Books Worldwide.

IDG Books Worldwide, Inc., is a subsidiary of International Data Group, the world's largest publisher of computer-related information and the leading global provider of information services on information technology. IDG was founded more than 30 years ago by Patrick J. McGovern and now employs more than 9,000 people worldwide. IDG publishes more than 290 computer publications in over 75 countries. More than 90 million people read one or more IDG publications each month.

Launched in 1990, IDG Books Worldwide is today the #1 publisher of best-selling computer books in the United States. We are proud to have received eight awards from the Computer Press Association in recognition of editorial excellence and three from Computer Currents' First Annual Readers' Choice Awards. Our best-selling ...For Dummies® series has more than 50 million copies in print with translations in 31 languages. IDG Books Worldwide, through a joint venture with IDG's Hi-Tech Beijing, became the first U.S. publisher to publish a computer book in the People's Republic of China. In record time, IDG Books Worldwide has become the first choice for millions of readers around the world who want to learn how to better manage their businesses.

Our mission is simple: Every one of our books is designed to bring extra value and skill-building instructions to the reader. Our books are written by experts who understand and care about our readers. The knowledge base of our editorial staff comes from years of experience in publishing, education, and journalism — experience we use to produce books to carry us into the new millennium. In short, we care about books, so we attract the best people. We devote special attention to details such as audience, interior design, use of icons, and illustrations. And because we use an efficient process of authoring, editing, and desktop publishing our books electronically, we can spend more time ensuring superior content and less time on the technicalities of making books.

You can count on our commitment to deliver high-quality books at competitive prices on topics you want to read about. At IDG Books Worldwide, we continue in the IDG tradition of delivering quality for more than 30 years. You'll find no better book on a subject than one from IDG Books Worldwide.

John Kilcullen
Chairman and CEO
IDG Books Worldwide, Inc.

Steven Berkowitz
President and Publisher
IDG Books Worldwide, Inc.

Eighth Annual Computer Press Awards ≥1992

Ninth Annual Computer Press Awards ≥1993

Tenth Annual Computer Press Awards ≥1994

Eleventh Annual Computer Press Awards ≥1995

IDG is the world's leading IT media, research and exposition company. Founded in 1964, IDG had 1997 revenues of $2.05 billion and has more than 9,000 employees worldwide. IDG offers the widest range of media options that reach IT buyers in 75 countries representing 95% of worldwide IT spending. IDG's diverse product and services portfolio spans six key areas including print publishing, online publishing, expositions and conferences, market research, education and training, and global marketing services. More than 90 million people read one or more of IDG's 290 magazines and newspapers, including IDG's leading global brands — Computerworld, PC World, Network World, Macworld and the Channel World family of publications. IDG Books Worldwide is one of the fastest-growing computer book publishers in the world, with more than 700 titles in 36 languages. The "...For Dummies®" series alone has more than 50 million copies in print. IDG offers online users the largest network of technology-specific Web sites around the world through IDG.net (http://www.idg.net), which comprises more than 225 targeted Web sites in 55 countries worldwide. International Data Corporation (IDC) is the world's largest provider of information technology data, analysis and consulting, with research centers in over 41 countries and more than 400 research analysts worldwide. IDG World Expo is a leading producer of more than 168 globally branded conferences and expositions in 35 countries including E3 (Electronic Entertainment Expo), Macworld Expo, ComNet, Windows World Expo, ICE (Internet Commerce Expo), Agenda, DEMO, and Spotlight. IDG's training subsidiary, ExecuTrain, is the world's largest computer training company, with more than 230 locations worldwide and 785 training courses. IDG Marketing Services helps industry-leading IT companies build international brand recognition by developing global integrated marketing programs via IDG's print, online and exposition products worldwide. Further information about the company can be found at www.idg.com.
1/24/99

Dedication

For my father and mother, who never doubted me

— A.G.

For Ann, my inspiration and true companion

— J.P.A

Authors' Acknowledgments

This book would not have been possible without the invaluable contributions of Charlie Arehart of Figleaf Software. Charlie didn't know what he was getting into when he signed on as technical editor of a book that changed versions in midstream, but we thank him for hanging in there with us and helping us make this book a useful tool.

We'd like to thank the entire editorial and production staff at IDG Books Worldwide, particularly Greg Croy, for seeing that it was high time there was a *For Dummies* book for ColdFusion, and Susan Pink, for tirelessly editing chapters. We sure hope she gets paid by the hour, not by the project! We'd also like to thank IDG's Heather Dismore, Carmen Krikorian, Marita Ellixson, and Megan Decraene for putting together the CD.

Thanks also to Carole McClendon of Waterside Productions for getting us this juicy title. We've written in ColdFusion for a long time and we're happy to be advocates for it.

Finally, we'd like to thank our families, without whose patience and support this book wouldn't have been possible — at least not in the 20th century. One husband, one wife, and two little girls suffered considerable neglect to see this book to completion. Thanks Constantine, Ann, Trianna, and Marika.

Publisher's Acknowledgments

We're proud of this book; please register your comments through our IDG Books Worldwide Online Registration Form located at http://my2cents.dummies.com.

Some of the people who helped bring this book to market include the following:

Acquisitions, Editorial, and Media Development

Project Editor: Susan Pink

Senior Editor, Freelance: Constance Carlisle

Acquisitions Editor: Greg Croy

Technical Editor: Charlie Arehart

Media Development Editor: Marita Ellixson

Associate Permissions Editor: Carmen Krikorian

Media Development Assistant: Eddie Kominowski

Media Development Manager: Heather Heath Dismore

Production

Project Coordinators: Maridee Ennis; Amanda Foxworth, Regina Snyder

Layout and Graphics: Karl Brandt, Brian Drumm, Barry Offringa, Tracy Oliver, Jill Piscitelli, Brent Savage, Brian Torwelle, Dan Whetstine, Erin Zeltner

Proofreaders: Laura Albert, Christine Pingleton, Marianne Santy, Charles Spencer

Indexer: Sherry Massey

General and Administrative

IDG Books Worldwide, Inc.: John Kilcullen, CEO; Steven Berkowitz, President and Publisher

IDG Books Technology Publishing Group: Richard Swadley, Senior Vice President and Publisher; Walter Bruce III, Vice President and Associate Publisher; Joseph Wikert, Associate Publisher; Mary Bednarek, Branded Product Development Director; Mary Corder, Editorial Director; Barry Pruett, Publishing Manager; Michelle Baxter, Publishing Manager

IDG Books Consumer Publishing Group: Roland Elgey, Senior Vice President and Publisher; Kathleen A. Welton, Vice President and Publisher; Kevin Thornton, Acquisitions Manager; Kristin A. Cocks, Editorial Director

IDG Books Internet Publishing Group: Brenda McLaughlin, Senior Vice President and Publisher; Diane Graves Steele, Vice President and Associate Publisher; Sofia Marchant, Online Marketing Manager

IDG Books Production for Dummies Press: Debbie Stailey, Associate Director of Production; Cindy L. Phipps, Manager of Project Coordination, Production Proofreading, and Indexing; Tony Augsburger, Manager of Prepress, Reprints, and Systems; Laura Carpenter, Production Control Manager; Shelley Lea, Supervisor of Graphics and Design; Debbie J. Gates, Production Systems Specialist; Robert Springer, Supervisor of Proofreading; Kathie Schutte, Production Supervisor

Dummies Packaging and Book Design: Patty Page, Manager, Promotions Marketing

♦

The publisher would like to give special thanks to Patrick J. McGovern, without whom this book would not have been possible.

♦

Contents at a Glance

Cartoons at a Glance

By Rich Tennant

page 353

page 101

page 7

page 201

page 281

Fax: 978-546-7747
E-mail: richtennant@the5thwave.com
World Wide Web: www.the5thwave.com

Table of Contents

Introduction

● ●

ColdFusion, the Web application server, is every bit as exciting a technology as the mythical energy-generating technology after which it's named. The days of building Web sites that just *sit there* are gone. If you're going to publish a Web site or you already have, you need to consider how to

- ✔ Have your Web pages talking to a database
- ✔ Get data from visitors who complete forms
- ✔ Display information from a database
- ✔ Accept payments
- ✔ Create a members-only site

How can you do all that? With ColdFusion. ColdFusion is a Web server, a scripting language (CFML), and a rapid application development (RAD) environment.

ColdFusion 4 For Dummies tells you what you need to know to have your Web site talking to your database using the ColdFusion Server. You discover the basics of the scripting language — ColdFusion Markup Language. And you'll see how to use rapid application development to create complete applications in no time flat; a trial version of the RAD environment is included on the CD in the back of the book.

With ColdFusion, your site can greet returning visitors by name. You can search your database and return the results that visitors request. You can accept forms that your visitors complete. You can send e-mail to visitors when they request it or to an entire list of e-mail addresses.

The most exciting part about ColdFusion is that it's not any more difficult to use than HTML. CFML is modeled after HTML, with tags and attributes, so it will look familiar right from the beginning. You can understand how to use ColdFusion quickly, which is good because you need to do too many other things in this Web-based economy. You don't have time to waste learning new technologies.

We've been developing dynamic Web sites since we worked together at the University of Virginia in 1997 and 1998. In our positions there, we evaluated Web database technologies for instructional and administrative use. ColdFusion consistently rose to the top of the rankings because of its ease of use and fast learning curve. We could quickly train other members of the University's professional faculty and staff to develop their own applications in ColdFusion.

The best part was that after the training was over, we didn't have to hold the hands of the newly initiated. They'd come to us only a week or two later to demonstrate the cool, new, dynamic sites they'd created. In short order, we had a vibrant community of ColdFusion developers whose real job titles were professor or administrator but who were producing impressive sites to meet the demands of their colleagues, students, and departments.

About This Book

This book is designed for four audiences:

- ✔ People who are thinking about putting up a site and want to build it the right way from the beginning

- ✔ People who have specific problems with their sites that they need to solve

- ✔ People who want to improve their sites with dynamic content without having to become programmers

- ✔ People like us — who already know a handful of technologies and programming languages — but want to find out what ColdFusion is all about

Regardless of which category you fall into, you'll find what you need between these pages. Our goal is to get you up and running as quickly as possible. The only thorny part is configuring your development environment, but we walk you through that slowly so you don't get lost. After your development environment is working, you'll be in clover. With the help of the Studio wizards, you'll marvel at the speed with which you can get database-backed sites up and running.

There has *never* been a better time to start developing in ColdFusion. ColdFusion Server is mature, robust, and full-featured. In addition to being available for Windows NT Server, ColdFusion Server is also available for Solaris, HP-UX, and Linux.

If you're not sure you want to commit dollars to your foray into ColdFusion, check out the brand-spankin'-new ColdFusion Express, which is the free version of ColdFusion Server with a few bells and whistles removed. Most of the material covered in this book can be executed with ColdFusion Express.

Foolish Assumptions

It's high time you open a book like this and start using ColdFusion. We assume you know the following:

- ✔ Enough HTML to create a simple Web page
- ✔ What a Web server is
- ✔ How to install software from a CD with an install wizard
- ✔ Something about databases and how they store data in tables
- ✔ How to use a Web browser (such as Internet Explorer or Netscape)

Conventions Used in This Book

You won't find anything surprising as far as book conventions go. If you've ever looked at another software or technology book, you've probably seen conventions similar to the ones we use here.

When you see something such as Alt+F, it means that while holding down the Alt key, press the F key. Although it looks like you'd probably have to hold down Shift to get the capital F, we tell you when you need to hold down the Shift key. (Don't think too hard, okay? This is a *For Dummies* book).

When you see Choose File⇨New, it means you should select New from the File menu at the top of the screen. If you see something like Tools⇨ CodeSweeper⇨Default CodeSweeper, you need to go down one more level in the menu structure.

We use *italics* in the regular text to introduce a new term or for emphasis. This is the stuff you would have highlighted in yellow when you were in school so you could find it again quickly.

When we refer to variable names or attributes in the text, we will use `monofont` so that they look sort of codey.

When you see single or double quotes in the code, leave them there. One common cause of program errors is unterminated quotes or missing quotes. Some authors use quotes to set things apart, but we use `monospace italics` for that. Quotes in the code are part of the code; don't monkey with them!

How This Book Is Organized

So that you can find what you're looking for quickly, we divided the book into parts.

Part I: Bare-Bones ColdFusion

In Part I, we tell you what ColdFusion is, how the scripting language (CFML) works, how to install the ColdFusion Studio, and how to install and configure ColdFusion Server.

Part II: Making ColdFusion Do Simple Stuff

Part II is comprised of four chapters that cover the tasks that people most want to do with ColdFusion: add records to a database based on form data received from visitors, display information from a database on a Web page, update data in a database based on form data received from visitors, and send mail from a Web page. We cover how to do these tasks both by hand and by using ColdFusion Studio (the rapid application development environment).

Part III: Creating ColdFusion Applications

If simple stuff isn't good enough for you and you want your Web site to act like a single unified application, you want to read Part III. Here, you discover how to think like a programmer, use the variety of variables available in the ColdFusion environment, handle security and maintain state, and select and present data in powerful ways.

Part IV: Serious about ColdFusion

Part IV takes you through the enhanced forms and form fields (such as a slider) that ColdFusion makes available through Java or JavaScript on your site. This part also handles troubleshooting for common problems and a ton of debugging tips and tricks!

Part V: The Part of Tens

Cut to the chase in The Part of Tens and read the top ten coding mistakes (that *other people* make), the ten best ColdFusion tags, and the ten best ColdFusion functions.

Appendix: About the CD

This appendix covers how to install the software on the CD cemented into the back of the book. We recommend *CD Removal For Dummies Books For Dummies* to learn how to extricate the CD without having to tear off the back cover.

Icons Used in This Book

To help you find particular content on a page or to draw attention to text that helps you work faster, we've included the following icons.

It's sometimes difficult writing a *For Dummies* book because we don't want to leave anything out. We include juicy, behind-the-scenes whys and wherefores by putting them under this icon.

Tips are great timesaving bits of advice that we've collected from years of ColdFusion development and teaching experience. You'll find some real gems here!

As you might expect, many ColdFusion resources are available online. We mention Web sites here.

This icon indicates that the next step you take may be a doozie if you don't follow the instructions precisely, or that the software has some quirky behavior that you might see. If you're in a jam with your code, see whether you can find a warning that tells you how you got there and how to get out.

When we discuss something on the CD, we tell you about it under this icon. Most code examples are on the *ColdFusion 4 For Dummies* CD.

This icon reminds you of terms you've seen before. Or it reminds you that for a particular procedure to work, you must complete something we told you earlier. We discovered these reminders the hard way!

 When we want to draw your attention to a particularly useful book, we use this icon.

Where to Go from Here

As impatient readers, we find it difficult to believe that you're still reading the Introduction and haven't jumped into the meat of the text yet! If you're the more circumspect type, you may be most comfortable reading this book one chapter at a time. That way, you won't worry about having missed anything.

If you don't know the first thing about ColdFusion except that everyone's talking about it, start with Chapter 1 and get acquainted. If you have a particular problem that needs to be solved *now*, go directly to Part II and see whether one of the chapters there doesn't solve a problem similar to yours. Note, though, that you probably have to go through Chapter 2 to configure your development environment; otherwise the examples in Part II won't work.

If you're a hard-core techie who's embarrassed to be seen carrying around a *For Dummies* book, get some brown paper and make a book cover. Then jump to Part III to read about creating ColdFusion applications. If you've already developed a bit in ColdFusion, and you've made a huge mess of your code, flip to Chapter 14 to read about troubleshooting and debugging. We've all been there!

After you wear the pages of this book thin from use and need more information, turn to one of the many ColdFusion support resources, such as the Allaire Support Forum, which is available at the Allaire Web site (http://www.allaire.com). Most major cities have ColdFusion Users' Groups (CFUGs); you can attend monthly meetings at no charge and see what Allaire is cooking up with ColdFusion. Also available are a plethora of resources, from the old-line House of Fusion (http://www.houseoffusion.com) to the newer ColdFusion Developers' Journal (http://www.sys-con.com/coldfusion/index2.cfm).

Finally, being a ColdFusion developer opens up career opportunities. In any given week, the ColdFusion jobs mailing list available from the House of Fusion has between 20 and 50 openings for ColdFusion developers all over the world — even for beginning and intermediate-level developers.

Part I

Bare-Bones ColdFusion

The 5th Wave   By Rich Tennant

NERD MOMS

Okay young man, it's time to wash your hands, brush your teeth, and defrag your hard disk.

Awwww, Mom.

In this part . . .

*I*f you're not excited about the prospect of finding out more about ColdFusion, you should be! Using ColdFusion is the easiest way to connect your Web site to a database. It's a language, it's a server — it's even a rapid application development (RAD) environment!

In this part, you jump right into the ColdFusion language (ColdFusion Markup Language) and see how similar it looks to HTML. You also get a chance to install much of the nifty software on the CD in the back of the book.

When you finish with this part, your local (or remote) development environment will be configured, you'll recognize ColdFusion when you see it, you'll be able to make a passable guess at which ColdFusion tag to use when you want to do something, and your database will be talking to ColdFusion Studio. Not bad for four chapters, eh?

Chapter 1

Basic ColdFusion

● ●

In This Chapter

▶ Understanding ColdFusion

▶ Using tags to perform actions against the database

▶ Processing data with functions

▶ Storing data with variables

▶ Displaying output on your page

● ●

*1*s ColdFusion a language? Is it a server? Is it an application? Yes!

✔ **A language:** ColdFusion Server processes the ColdFusion Markup Language (CFML).

✔ **A server**: ColdFusion Server typically resides on the same physical server as your Web server software.

✔ **An application**: ColdFusion Studio is a rapid application development environment (RAD).

ColdFusion is simply the best way to build a Web-based application. The learning curve is short, so you can have your Web site performing basic tasks, such as writing records to a database, in no time flat. The server is robust, the technology is stable, and the user base is large and growing. Allaire estimates that more than 200,000 developers are working in ColdFusion.

This ColdFusion might not turn water into energy, but it can turn your boring old Web site into the digital equivalent of a nuclear reaction. The results are fast and astounding. You can serve up dynamic data and collect form data from site visitors in no time. You can send e-mail confirmations and display the results of text files, too. With ColdFusion, if you can imagine doing it on your Web site, you can do it. It really *is* that good!

How ColdFusion Works

When you open your browser and load a Web page, what you see in the browser window is the result of instructions sent to the browser. The instructions are written in Hypertext Markup Language (HTML). For example, if you want to bold the word *house*, send the following text to the browser:

```
<b>house</b>
```

Note: We assume that you have a working knowledge of HTML. If you aren't already familiar with HTML, *The HTML 4 Bible* by Pfaffenberger and Gutzman (published by IDG Books Worldwide, Inc.) is the place to start.

If you want to send the same page to everyone who visits your site and that page will be the same every day, you don't need ColdFusion; HTML will do. If you want what appears to each visitor to depend on an action taken by the visitor or some other variable factor, you want to produce *dynamic output* for your visitor. For dynamic output, you need ColdFusion.

Here's how the process of sending a page to a browser works: When your visitor asks the Web server for a page written in ColdFusion Markup Language (CFML), the Web server software passes the page to ColdFusion Server. ColdFusion queries the database to get the data for the page. When the database returns the data, ColdFusion Server processes the CFML, which generally results in the creation of some HTML, and then passes the page back to the Web server software. The Web server then passes the HTML to the browser, which converts the HTML into what the visitor sees. All this happens in less than a second. Figure 1-1 shows this process visually. (For more on how ColdFusion works, check out Chapter 11.)

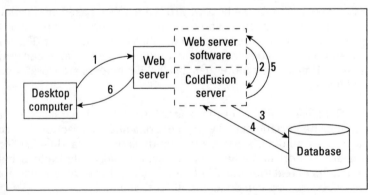

Figure 1-1:
Serving up a dynamic page to your visitor through ColdFusion Server.

ColdFusion Markup Language, unlike Hypertext Markup Language, is processed at the server. When you create a page, you can't see how it will look unless you run it through ColdFusion Server or through the single-user desktop version of ColdFusion Server available with ColdFusion Studio.

Forms: Where your visitor enters data

If you're like most folks, your first task for ColdFusion is to accept data that a visitor to your site enters on a form you provide. The form might be part of a survey, a newsletter subscription, a drawing for a prize, or a checkout sequence. In any case, the ease with which you can use ColdFusion to accept form data and write it to your database is partly responsible for the enormous success of the product and the assortment of awards it's won.

To collect form data from a visitor, you need a form. Makes sense. Figure 1-2 shows a standard form a visitor might use to sign up for a newsletter.

After you collect the data on the form, you'll probably want an acknowledgment page, such as the one in Figure 1-3. This page could certainly be fancier. We could thank the visitor by name, for example. And we could also confirm the types of information for which the visitor wants to be kept informed.

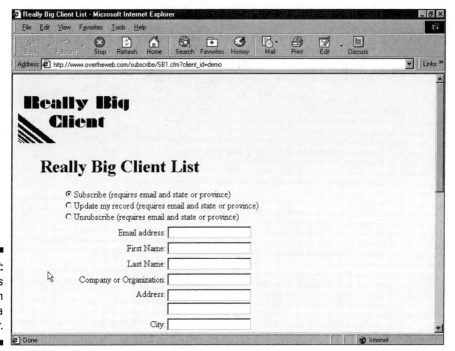

Figure 1-2:
Fill out this
form to sign
up for a
newsletter.

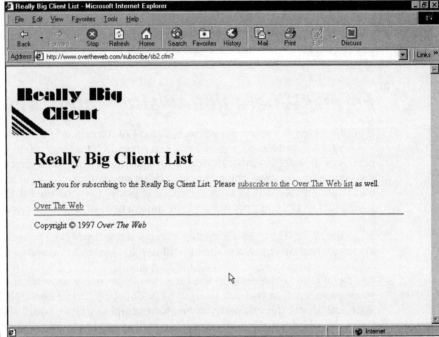

Figure 1-3:
The
acknowl-
edgment
page you
see after
completing
the form in
Figure 1-2.

Why have we kept the form so simple, when ColdFusion can do so much more? We want to emphasize the ease with which you can perform a common action. And that action requires only one line of CFML:

```
<CFINSERT datasource="newsletter"
        tablename="subscription_list">
```

One instance of one tag is all you need. You still need HTML to build the form and the acknowledgment page, but because you already know HTML, you need to master only one little tag!

In Chapter 5, we describe the CFINSERT tag at length. We also go through an example of creating a form, paying particular attention to setting it up correctly for use with CFINSERT. Even if your HTML isn't that strong, you'll be able to follow along.

The CFML is unfamiliar, so let's walk through the tag:

- ✔ CFINSERT, the name of the tag, is a command to ColdFusion Server to insert a row of data into the database.
- ✔ The `datasource` attribute tells the server what the database is called. In the example, the database is called `newsletter`.

> ✔ A database is usually comprised of many tables. As such, we need to indicate which table in the database we want to update. The table name is specified in the `tablename` attribute. In the example, the table is `subscriptionlist`.

In Chapter 4, we discuss how to set up data sources.

To Studio or not to Studio

Part of the magic of CFML is that it's all just text. To early developers of ColdFusion, that meant they didn't have to run out and buy expensive development tools. Any old text editor would do: NotePad, TextPad, WordPad, or even an obscure little editor named HomeSite, sold by a one-man company.

HomeSite was different than the other text editors because it had a few features built into it that made CFML development a bit faster. The most notable feature was a CFML toolbar. Allaire liked HomeSite so much, they acquired it.

The souped-up version of HomeSite is called Studio. Studio is a nice text editor with some toolbars for CFML development, some communications tools to help you access your data and write queries more quickly, a single-user desktop version of ColdFusion Server, and CFML wizards to make development a snap!

You can find 30-day evaluation copies of HomeSite, Studio, and ColdFusion Server on the *ColdFusion 4 For Dummies* CD. They're also available on Allaire's Web site.

If you have Studio installed, great. You'll find that it can save you time if you do a lot of CFML development. If you're still just dabbling with ColdFusion, work with whatever you use for text editing until you're hooked on ColdFusion and then check out Studio.

Studio comes with a single-user version of ColdFusion Studio, which is great for testing your applications on your desktop but won't provide a production-level solution for serving Web pages to the world. Check with your Internet Service Provider (ISP) or Web Presence Provider (WPP) to see whether they run ColdFusion on any of their servers so that you can serve ColdFusion pages on your Web site.

Both Allaire and The House of Fusion Web sites list ISPs and WPPs that support ColdFusion. Allaire is at `www.allaire.com`. The House of Fusion site also has a mailing list of job opportunities in ColdFusion and a vibrant community for discussing ColdFusion. Its address is `www.houseoffusion.com`.

Finding a ColdFusion-enabled Web Presence Provider

In the past, finding a Web Presence Provider that had ColdFusion installed was difficult. Today, however, lots of WPPs make ColdFusion a part of their development environment. Both authors of this book have used Minerva Network Systems (www.minerva.net), which is known for fabulous customer service.

When you call tech support, you talk to a network administrator almost every time, not a voice-mail system or a phone bank of people who know only a little bit about your server. They also permit RDS access, covered in Chapter 2, which is necessary if you're going to use all the features of Studio.

If you want to install the single-user version of ColdFusion Server that ships with Studio, you must have a Web server, such as the Microsoft Personal Web Server, installed. We provide Personal Web Server on the *ColdFusion 4 For Dummies* CD, to make configuration of a working testing environment easier.

Tags Make Things Happen

For almost everything you want to do with ColdFusion, you can use tags and functions. To pass data around, you also need to know a bit about variables: how to get data in them, how to get data out of them, and how to reference them. In this section and the next two, you find out about all three of these ColdFusion components. (Check out Chapter 17 as well for ten of the most useful ColdFusion functions.)

Tags are the commands you give the server for interacting with the database, the file system on the server, other servers, or the page. For example, you can use a tag to tell the server to select data from a database, to read a file that resides on the server, or to show the results of processing.

ColdFusion tags are similar to HTML tags. For example, they're enclosed in angle brackets and often have start and end tags. Start tags have the tag name (think of it as a command) in brackets, like this:

```
<TAG>
```

End tags add a slash, like this:

```
</TAG>
```

For the most part, ColdFusion tags share the following features:

- ✔ Most have start tags and end tags
- ✔ Most take attributes, and most attributes have values
- ✔ All start with *CF*

If you can remember these three features, you'll recognize ColdFusion when it makes its appearance throughout this book — and you'll find that reading CFML in the text makes more sense.

Tags demand action

If you were to block out the *CF* in the front of most tags, you'd see that they are just verbs that tell the server what you want to do: insert, update, output, mail, and so on. Chances are, if you can think of what you want the server to do, you can guess what the CFML tag is called.

Tags have attributes

Tag attributes tell the server the details of the action. For example, if you want to insert data into a database, you might guess (correctly) that the tag is called CFINSERT. But if you thought about it longer, you'd realize that the server also needs to know some specifics about the database, such as the database name and the name of the table in the database where the data should be inserted.

Here's another example of how you might guess the CFML name of a tag. Suppose you want to include a segment of frequently used code in your page, and you've stored this code in a separate file (so that all your pages could access it). What do you suppose the tag to include the code is called? CFINCLUDE? Yes. What might the server need to know? The name of the file holding the code you want to include.

Here's an example of CFML that includes the contents of another file in the page on which it's run:

```
<CFINCLUDE template="onload.cfm">
```

The `template` attribute gives the name of the file to be included.

Functions Act on Data

When you want the server to process the data you've received from the visitor but not necessarily interact with the database, you need not a tag, but a function. A function *does something* to data. What can functions do? Functions can find which position in a text string contains a certain character, perform math, format a date, allow conditional processing, and lots more. In Chapter 9, we describe functions in detail.

Functions perform on values

Usually, a function is performed on a value — and a value can include the value of a variable. For example, check out the following two functions:

```
#Len('disestablishmentarianism')#
#Len(memo_field1)#
```

and

```
#Trim(memo_field1)#
```

The Len( ) function calculates either the length of a string — if the value in parentheses is enclosed in quotes (as in the first line) — or the length of the value of a variable that contains text.

The Trim( ) function operates on a variable and trims any stray spaces from the right side of a string. For example, suppose a visitor enters data that we store in the memo_field1 variable. We use the Trim( ) function to make sure any stray spaces after the visitor's entry are deleted before we write the entry to the database.

Functions take parentheses

You probably noticed that the three examples of functions you just saw all have a set of parentheses following them to hold a variable or a value. In fact, all functions have parentheses, regardless of whether or not they act on data. Consider the following functions:

```
#Now( )#
#Rand( )#
```

With either of these, if you try to put anything inside the parentheses, you'll get an error.

Now( ) returns the date and time in a format you can't use. However, ColdFusion provides a plethora of functions that operate on Now( ) to format the date or time or parse part of the date or time (such as the month or the hour). See Chapter 17 for more on the Now( ) function.

Rand( ) returns a random number between 0 and 1. If you're assigning passwords or playing a game of chance, this function can come in handy.

Functions can be nested

Nesting functions in ColdFusion is when the fun begins! Functions can generate data as well as act on data. When you need to perform calculations on data that you've generated, you must *nest* functions (put one inside another).

Consider the two following examples:

```
#Round(Rand()*10)#
```

and

```
#DateFormat(Now(), "mm/dd/yyyy")#
```

In the first example, we generate a random integer between 0 and 10 by using the Rand( ) function to return a decimal between 0 and 1 and then multiplying that decimal by 10 (yes, you can do math in a function). Finally, to make sure that we get an integer, rather than a decimal value such as 7.125, we use the Round( ) function to round off the number.

In the second example, we're formatting today's date, which we generate using the Now( ) function, in standard mm/dd/yyyy format. The *mask* (the characters you use to tell ColdFusion how to format the date and time) for formatting dates is intuitive.

Functions and pound signs

You've probably noticed that pound signs (#) bracket functions. These are generally needed only when the result of the function (or variable) will be shown on the page. Pound signs tell the server to evaluate what's within the pound signs and display the value.

Anything within pound signs is delivered to your visitor's desktop as a *result*. Therefore, what you see on your page as you develop it won't match what the visitor sees.

What you see on the page isn't what will be displayed for *processing*, but that's true also for *output*. Because the server delivers a result, you need to be careful when formatting your page not to leave as much space for the results as you do for the ColdFusion that produces the results.

Preview the page often to be sure you've left the correct amount of space for the results, which might be much shorter or much longer than the function that produces the results.

Variables Hold Data

Variables enable you to store data either within a page or between pages. Some of the types of data you might want to store include the following:

- ✔ Form data you collect from a visitor
- ✔ Data you have on your server, such as the version of server software that's running
- ✔ Results of calculations you perform, such as the number of records returned when you perform a query on the data

When you request data from your database — either all data or specific data based on criteria you define — it's called a *query*. Two example queries are

Select all books

Select all books written by Dr. Seuss

Chapter 10 discusses the many types of variables, and how you use, reference, and pass them.

Creating variables on-the-fly

One nice feature of ColdFusion is that you can create variables when you need them. You don't need to spell out in advance and all in one place the variables you want to use. For example, suppose you want to display the names of members as first name, last initial (such as Alexis G.). You can use the Left( ) function to extract only the left *n* characters (where *n* is a number) from a value. However, you need to store the results of the Left( ) function somewhere, so you create a variable called `last-initial` to hold the first character of the last name, as follows:

```
<CFSET last-initial = Left(getnames.last_name, 1)>
```

In this example, we create the `last-initial` variable out of thin air. We simply use the CFSET tag and supply a unique variable name, and ColdFusion knows to create a new variable. All the variable names on the right side of the equal sign have to exist already for the processing to work. The `last_name` variable on the right came from the database through a query called `getnames`.

Referencing existing variables

After you create a variable, how do you use it on your page? Simple. You can work with the value of a variable by surrounding it with pound signs (#), just as you do with functions. The pound signs signal the server that you want the value of the variable. You don't use pound signs around a variable when it's being populated — filled with data — or created (when it's on the left side of the equation).

You don't need pound signs all the time when referring to variables and functions. We offer details of when you do and do not need pound signs throughout the book.

You can work with many types of variables. A *form variable* comes into your page from a form on the preceding page. A *url variable* comes into your page from the URL. You also have client variables, server variables, application variables, and more. In addition, *tag-specific variables* are populated only when a certain tag is processed.

Because you can use the same name with variables of more than one type, ColdFusion relies on scope referencing. In *scope referencing,* you preface the variable's name with the scope when you refer to the variable. For example:

```
#url.search#
#form.last_name#
#cffile.filesize#
#variables.domain#
#cgi.remote_addr#
```

Here's what's happening in this code:

- ✔ The `search` variable is passed in through the URL.
- ✔ The `last_name` variable is received from a form on the preceding page.
- ✔ When the CFFILE tag is processed, it returns the file size, which is automatically stored in the `filesize` variable.
- ✔ You can use the CFSET tag to create local variables; we used it to create the `domain` variable. You can preface local variables with `variables` to differentiate them from other types of variables with the same names.

✔ We find out the remote address of the visitor using the `remote_addr` CGI (common gateway interface) environment variable. A number of CGI environment variables are available. CGI environment variables are there whether you use them or not.

Passing variables between pages

What do you do if you want to pass a variable from one page to another? For example, suppose you collected the visitor's logon ID on one page and want to send the ID to the next page so that you can take some action on it. You have four easy ways to make sure data gets from one page to another:

✔ Hidden form field

✔ Cookie

✔ Application framework

✔ URL

Next, we take a look at each of these approaches.

Hidden form field method

If the page from which you are passing data contains a form, the best way to send a variable's data to the next page is through the use of a hidden field on the form.

When you process a form, the variable-value pairs represented by elements on the form are sent to the server and are invisible to the visitor. As long as you're sending all form fields to the next page, you might as well pass along your own variables and values. Just include your variables and values as hidden fields. The hidden fields are sent along with the form fields to the page indicated by the value of the `action` attribute.

Following is the code for the form, though we've left out the fields that the visitor would see and the buttons to submit the form:

```
<FORM action="process-form.cfm" method="post">
fields the visitor would see
<CFOUTPUT>
<INPUT type="hidden" name="referring_id"
       value="#referring_id#">
</CFOUTPUT>
buttons to submit the form
</FORM>
```

Let's walk through this code snippet:

✔ The first line holds the FORM tag with its two required attributes: `action` and `method`. We tell the server to use the `post` method to send the results of this form to the `process-form.cfm` page.

✔ The fourth line is the familiar INPUT tag. The type is set to `hidden` so that this form field will not appear on the screen for visitors to see.

✔ A hidden field won't appear on the page on which the form is displayed, but will be visible to anyone who views the source of the page. Therefore, don't put any information in a hidden field that you don't want a visitor to have.

✔ Also on the fourth line, the name associated with the hidden input field (`referring_id`) is the variable name you'll use to refer to this field on the forms processing page (`process-form.cfm`). The data is available for viewing by anyone who wants to view the source, however, so don't store passwords in hidden fields and think they're really hidden.

✔ Note that we tell the server to assign the *value of the variable* called `referring_id` on this page. If we had used

```
<INPUT type="hidden" name="referring_id"
       value="referring_id">
```

instead, the word *referring_id* would be passed to the processing page as the value of the `referring_id` variable . By placing the variable name `referring_id` within pound signs (#), the server is alerted to insert the value of the variable for the name of the `referring_id` variable.

✔ Note that the hidden input field is nestled in a CFOUTPUT tag. What's that about? The server needs to reach a CFOUTPUT tag (or one of a handful of other tags) to know that it might need to provide results. If the server had encountered a pound sign (#) before coming across the CFOUTPUT tag, it would have sent the pound sign, which in the preceding code means that the variable `referring_id` on the `process-form.cfm` page would have contained #referring_id# rather than the value of the variable.

Cookie method

Another way to pass variables is with cookies. To be accurate, cookies don't pass variables; they hold them on the visitor's computer for another page to access. When you create a cookie, nothing visible happens on your visitor's computer — unless the visitor's security is configured so that the browser displays a warning box when a cookie is set.

If visitors have cookies turned off, you can't use them to pass variables. Your program receives no warning or indication that the visitors are not accepting cookies. The values are simply not set on their browser as you expected.

The following code creates a cookie:

```
<CFCOOKIE
    name="userid"
    value="#userid#"
    expires="1">
```

Here's what you need to know about the CFCOOKIE tag:

- ✔ The `name` attribute should be the name of the variable you want to use on this and subsequent pages.
- ✔ The `value` attribute should contain either the hardcoded value or the variable value you want associated with the variable.
- ✔ We set the `expires` attribute to 1, which means one day. That should be enough time for this page and subsequent pages to process the variable. You can specify a variety of values for the `expires` attribute.

Application framework method

The fourth way to pass data between pages is to use the application framework, a nifty feature of ColdFusion. The Web is naturally *stateless*, meaning there's no connection between one page click and another and there's no way to know the path a visitor is traveling through your site. When you use the application framework, you can pass variables through all your pages by describing them as either application, session, or client variables.

In short, the application framework sews all your pages into one big application. When a visitor moves from one page to another in your site, you know at all times that it's the same person. Chapter 11 covers the application framework in detail.

URL method

You can still send data from one page to another, even if you aren't using a form on the first page, by including the data you want to send in the URL as CGI parameters.

Note: CGI parameters are the name-value pairs you often see at the end of a URL, after the question mark. The name CGI comes from the early method of having a Web page communicate with a server or database: common gateway interface. Early CGI used Perl or C++. ColdFusion is a form of CGI in that it permits a Web page to communicate with a server and a database.

Consider the following HTML:

```
<A href="http://www.santa-
    letters.com?merchant_id=CHRO127&item_no=011234&line
    _no=1&qty=4">Personalize Your Letters Now!</a>
```

This is a straightforward anchor tag with the `href` attribute linking to a site called `www.santa-letters.com`. After the URL is ? and then a series of name-value pairs separated by &. You can also send data through the URL if you do have a form by setting the method to `get` instead of `post`.

Disadvantages of the URL method

One disadvantage of sending data through the URL is that the data is visible in the location (or address) window on the browser. Visitors to your site might find it disconcerting to see their names or other recognizable personal information in the URL. The second disadvantage is that, depending on your browser, you are restricted in the amount of data you can send.

Cookie-free zone

If you're concerned about making sure people who have cookies turned off on their browsers can still navigate your site coherently, pass the CFTOKEN (the mechanism for tracking a browser when you're using the applications framework) in the URL. If you do this, however, test thoroughly to make sure that the token is passed from every single link in the site.

The Results of Processing: Output

Output is what's left after the server has finished processing. Output usually has two parts:

- ✔ What the visitor sees
- ✔ What you've stored on the server as a result of processing

ColdFusion provides two main ways to show the visitor data on the page: the CFTABLE and CFOUTPUT tags.

Displaying output in a table

When you show a visitor data from a database, one of the basic actions you'll want to perform is displaying results neatly formatted in a table. ColdFusion was created with the idea that some developers would want to do only basic processing and others would want to do processing so complex you haven't even imagined it yet.

With ColdFusion, displaying output in a table is easy. You can use the CFTABLE tag without being a pro at creating HTML tables. The CFTABLE tag requires another tag, called CFCOL. Each column of data in a table needs its own CFCOL tag.

Figure 1-4 shows a table created with the CFTABLE tag. We used three instances of the CFCOL tag to produce output columns for the name, city, and state. If you want to jump right into displaying data on your page with the CFTABLE tag, turn to Chapter 6.

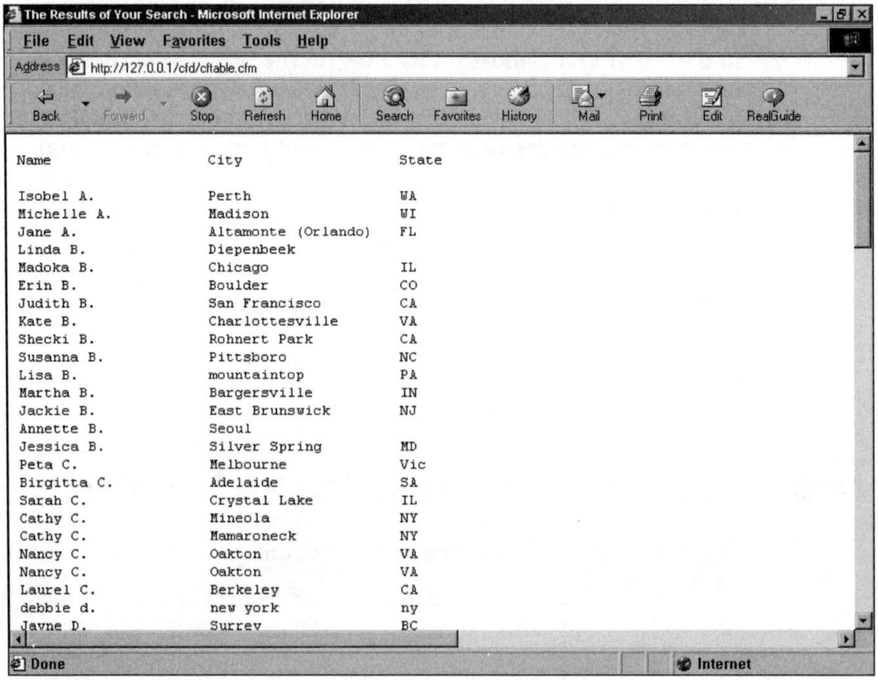

Figure 1-4: Output from a database using the CFTABLE tag.

Displaying output outside the confines of the CFTABLE tag

To format your output in anything other than a table created by CFTABLE, you need to use the CFOUTPUT tag. This tag tells the server to show the results of variables and functions.

You have greater control over formatting when you use a CFOUTPUT tag. For example, you can format a fancy table of the score a visitor received on a quiz, complete with a list of questions answered incorrectly and the correct answers. If you have the data and you can figure out how you want to display it using HTML, the CFOUTPUT tag gives you the power to put the right variables in the right place.

Figure 1-5 is an example of the results of a CFOUTPUT tag. The page shows the table with images; two of the columns also have links to other pages. You simply couldn't format a table this nicely — with a shaded background on most of the cells, borders on the table, and cell padding — using CFTABLE.

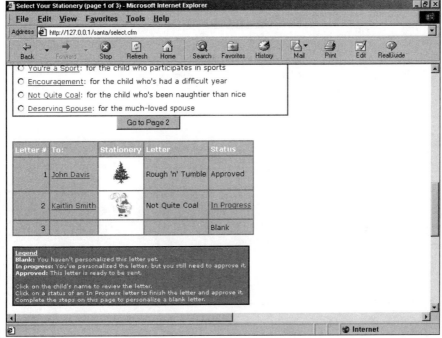

Figure 1-5: Displaying creatively formatted output requires the CFOUTPUT tag.

Chapter 12 discusses extracting data from a database using the CFQUERY tag and presenting it on your page using the CFOUTPUT tag. Additionally, the chapter shows some cool things you can do to display grouped data.

Chapter 2

Configuring a Development Environment

In This Chapter

▶ Creating a development environment

▶ Installing the appropriate Web server

▶ Enabling file-execute permissions

▶ Installing ColdFusion Server

▶ Installing Studio

*W*hen you're ready to get serious about ColdFusion development, you'll want to invest in Studio. At $295, it's reasonably priced for a rapid application development (RAD) tool.

A 30-day evaluation copy of Studio is on the *ColdFusion 4 For Dummies* CD-ROM, so you might as well install it and take a tour to see whether it makes your life easier and your CFML development faster.

Do you want to develop locally, but don't have the budget right now for Studio and don't need many advanced ColdFusion functions? If so, you can create your own local development environment with HomeSite and ColdFusion Express — the free, scaled-down version of ColdFusion Server — for a fraction of the cost. You'll need to use your browser to preview your work (unlike in Studio), but that's only an Alt+Tab away.

One benefit of using Studio over HomeSite (which is also on the CD) is that Studio talks directly to your database. In addition, when you work with Studio, you can see your CFML as plain text and view your page rendered in a browser after it has been processed by ColdFusion Server (if you installed it).

Do you prefer to create your own local development environment, with your own single-user copy of ColdFusion? If so, check out the section in this chapter on installing the Microsoft Personal Web Server (PWS), which you need to use some Studio functions. (PWS is suitable if your desktop computer is running Windows 95 or 98. Other operating systems are also covered.) Then you install the single-user version of ColdFusion Server on your computer. Finally, you install Studio and configure it to take advantage of PWS and ColdFusion Server.

However, you don't need to run your own copy of ColdFusion Server to get a lot out of Studio. It's a powerful HTML — and CFML — editing environment, with many features that can save you lots of development time. Although CFML files can be edited with any text editor, you'd be making a mistake to dismiss Studio as "just another editor."

The Development Environment

You can install Studio by itself and use it as your HTML and CFML development tool. If you want to use Studio as a RAD tool for ColdFusion, however, you need access to the following resources:

- ✔ A Web server
- ✔ ColdFusion Server
- ✔ A database
- ✔ An ODBC entry for the database

These elements constitute the development environment and enable you to work more effectively with Studio. You can install this development environment locally on your own computer or access it remotely on your ISP's or WPP's (Web Presence Provider's) server.

For free

In the summer of 1999, Allaire released ColdFusion Express, a free version of the award-winning ColdFusion Server with limited functionality. If you've hesitated to invest in ColdFusion Server because of the cost, hesitate no longer. ColdFusion Express allows you to do most Web processing, but leaves out tags that permit you to interact wth mail (such as CFMAIL and CFPOP), with files (such as CFFILE), and with other servers (such as CFFTP and CFHTTP), as well as other more advanced features. Most of what we cover in this book can be accomplished with ColdFusion Express.

Accessing a remote development environment

If you'll be doing development on a remote computer — a server you maintain or have access to elsewhere — installing and configuring Studio is straightforward. Simply follow the directions later in this chapter under "Installing ColdFusion Studio."

To use a remote development environment, you must have adequate permissions on the remote server. Specifically, you must have RDS (Remote Development Services) permission to all resources you'll need, including files and ODBC entries. (Although you can also connect to a remote server within Studio using FTP, some of the most useful Studio features are available only if you use RDS.)

Talk to your server administrator and make sure you get the required permissions. Otherwise, you can't preview your work in Studio's internal browser or view remote data sources within Studio's Query Builder. These and other RDS-enabled features are discussed later. If your ISP or WPP doesn't give you RDS access, consider a new WPP.

The next step in the process is installing a Web server. Chapter 4 covers this in detail.

Configuring your development environment

One important feature of Studio that we haven't yet mentioned is the application wizard. The chapters in Part II introduce the basic wizards that Studio offers. If you want to take a look at the choice of wizards, choose File➪New and click the CFML tab.

Studio is very customizable. You can do much of the customization in the Settings dialog box, which is shown in Figure 2-1. As you can see, this dialog box has quite a few tabs.

To be able to preview your work through the Studio internal browser, you need to create development mappings. A *development mapping* is how you tell Studio where your files are stored on the development workstation and how to view them through the browser.

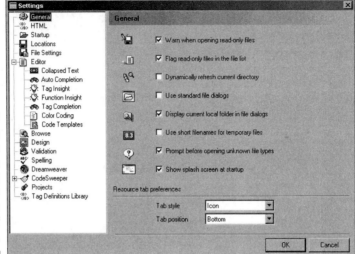

Figure 2-1:
The Settings
dialog box is
where you
configure
many of the
features of
Studio.

To configure development mappings, follow these steps:

1. **Choose Options⇨Settings.**

   The Settings dialog box appears.

2. **Click Browse from the choices on the left side of the dialog box, and then click the Development Mappings button.**

   The Remote Development Settings dialog box appears as shown in Figure 2-2.

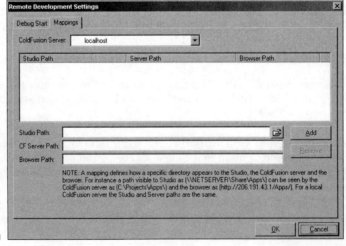

Figure 2-2:
The Remote
Development
Settings
dialog box
is where
you define
development
mappings.

3. **From the server list at the top of the Remote Development Settings dialog box, select the RDS server for which you want to create mappings.**

   For a local development environment, click localhost.

   If your server doesn't appear in the list of servers, click the drop-down list and select Add RDS Server. Then follow the instructions in Step 3 of the next section, "Connecting to your database," to add your RDS server.

4. **Select the folder into which you'll be saving your CFML files.**

   - To search for the folder, click the browse button, which is just to the right of the Studio Path text input box. After you find and select the folder, click OK. All three text input boxes are populated with Studio's best guesses.

   - Alternatively, you may type the address. If you type it, Studio keeps up with you by populating the other two text boxes as you type.

5. **Check to see whether the Studio path, CF Server path, and Browser path are all correct.**

   If you directed Studio to the correct folder in Step 4, Studio should correctly guess the Studio path and the CF Server path. Studio might not guess the Browser path correctly, depending on how you mapped virtual drives on your Web server.

6. **If any of the paths are wrong, make the necessary corrections.**

   Figure 2-3 shows a Web site in the C:\My Documents\My Webs\Santa folder. Studio populated the Studio Path field and the CF Server Path field based on the information we provided. It guessed that the Web server directory was the standard root directory for the localhost: http://127.0.0.1/. In this case, that's wrong.

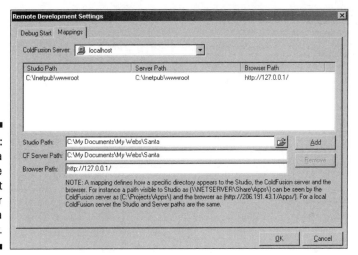

Figure 2-3:
Creating a
remote
development
setting for
the Santa
directory.

We created a virtual directory called Santa in PWS using the Personal Web Manager's Advanced Options. This Santa mapping points to the Santa folder, as shown in Figure 2-4. Consequently, we need to update the Browser Path field in Studio to reflect the fact that the Web site is located at http://127.0.0.1/santa, as shown in Figure 2-5.

7. **When the three paths are correct, click Add.**

   The mapping appears in the list under the name of your ColdFusion server.

8. **Click OK to close the Remote Development Settings dialog box. Then click OK again to close the Settings dialog box.**

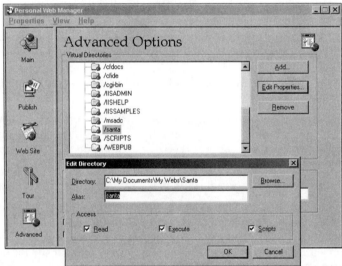

Figure 2-4: Creating a virtual directory in the Personal Web Manager for the Santa Web site.

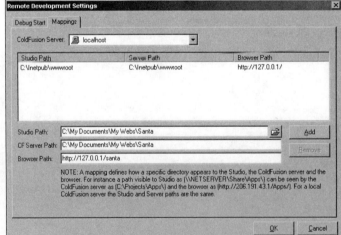

Figure 2-5: The local-host remote development settings now reflect the correct browser path.

Now you'll be able to open files from your development directory and see the processed ColdFusion in the browse view of the editor pane.

Connecting to your database

In the preceding section, you saw a reference to an RDS server. The database must reside on a server to which you can connect using Remote Development Services, or RDS. (Despite its name, you can make an RDS connection to a local server.)

The administrator must configure ColdFusion Server to permit RDS access. Additionally, the administrator must give you the RDS password defined in Administrator.

The username for Studio RDS logon is needed only when you are using the Advanced Security Server Sandbox feature, where access is controlled at the user level. Otherwise, you need only the RDS password for the server.

To connect to an RDS server, take these steps:

1. **Click the Files tab, which is in the resource pane (at the bottom left of the Studio interface).**

2. **In the list of drives in the top half of the resource pane, select Allaire FTP&RDS.**

3. **In the Remote Server pane, right-click Allaire FTP&RDS, and then select Add RDS Server.**

   The dialog box shown in Figure 2-6 appears.

   Type a brief description, provide the host name (the domain name or IP address, without `http://`, of the server to which you want to connect), and leave the port set to 80 unless you have specific instructions to set it to something else. Also provide the RDS password that you received from the administrator.

4. **Make your entries in the dialog box.**

   Even if you are connecting to an RDS Server on your local workstation, you'll still need to fill out these fields. The host name will be 127.0.0.1, and you'll have to provide the password you used when you installed ColdFusion Server.

   If you need to connect with SSL, click to insert a check mark in the Use Secure Sockets Layer (SSL) box. If you share the computer with someone else and want to be prompted for the password every time, rather than having Studio remember the password for you, click to select the Prompt for Password box.

Configure RDS Server

COLDFUSION

Remote Host

Description: Over The Web

Host name: www.overtheweb.com

Port: 80   ☐ Use Secure Sockets Layer (SSL)

ColdFusion RDS Security

User Name: over1234

Password: ********

☐ Prompt for Password

OK   Cancel

Figure 2-6:
Adding an
RDS Server
in Studio.

5. Click OK.

The RDS server you just configured is now listed (with a plus sign to the left of it) in the Server pane of the Remote Files tab.

You should test to see whether this connection is successful. Click the plus sign next to the server to see its available drives. If there is a failure, you'll want to check the connection properties you entered. To do that, right-click the server name and then choose Properties.

After you have an RDS connection, you can view ODBC entries on the RDS server, and view databases, tables, and even field definitions through the Database tab.

Permitting Your Web Server to Execute Files

After you've installed your Web server, you have to make sure that it permits files to be *executed* as well as *read*. Most Web servers have file-execute permissions turned off by default. To enable file-execute permissions, follow the instructions in Chapter 4 that correspond to your Web server.

Installing ColdFusion Server

After you've installed your Web server and configured it to permit file execution, you're ready to install ColdFusion Server. If you have the Enterprise or Professional version of ColdFusion Server, see Chapter 4, which describes the installation process in detail.

The single-user version of ColdFusion Server is included on the Studio CD — and on the *ColdFusion 4 For Dummies* CD. To install this version of ColdFusion Server, follow these steps:

1. **Insert the CD containing ColdFusion Studio into your CD-ROM drive.**

   If your computer is configured not to take action when a CD is inserted, you must initiate the installation process by choosing Start⇨Run, typing **d:\setup.exe** (where *d* is your CD-ROM drive), and then clicking OK.

   If your computer is configured to autorun inserted CDs, you don't need to do anything special.

   The installation begins, and you see a screen urging you to quit all other Windows applications before proceeding.

2. **Quit any other applications you have running and then click Next.**

   The license agreement appears.

3. **Agree to the terms of the license agreement by clicking Yes.**

   User information appears next, as shown in Figure 2-7.

4. **Enter your name, company, and serial number. If you're installing an evaluation copy of the software, you can leave the Serial field blank. Click Next.**

   A screen asks you to select the destination location, as shown in Figure 2-8.

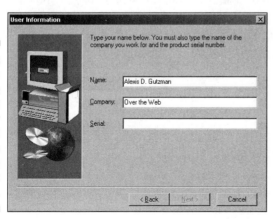

Figure 2-7:
ColdFusion requires that you provide your name and company as part of the installation process.

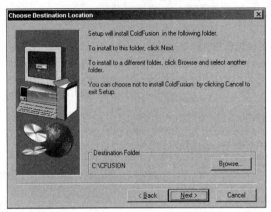

Figure 2-8:
Select the
destination
directory for
ColdFusion
Server. A
word to the
wise: Use
the default
location.

5. **Indicate where you want to install ColdFusion Server.**

   The default is C:\CFUSION. If you feel tempted to install ColdFusion Server in your Program Files directory, resist. ColdFusion Server is picky, so it's best to install it in the default directory.

6. **Click Next.**

   You are warned that the directory does not exist and are then asked whether you want to create the directory.

7. **Click Yes.**

   The setup process guesses which Web server you're using, as shown in Figure 2-9.

8. **If the setup process hasn't guessed correctly, select the correct option.**

9. **Click Next.**

   Setup guesses the location of your home directory, as shown in Figure 2-10.

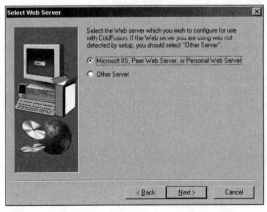

Figure 2-9:
The setup
program
guesses
which Web
server
you're
using.

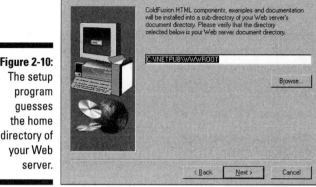

Figure 2-10:
The setup program guesses the home directory of your Web server.

10. **If setup guessed incorrectly, browse and select the correct home directory of your Web server.**

11. **Click Next.**

    You see a list of components that setup can install, as shown in Figure 2-11.

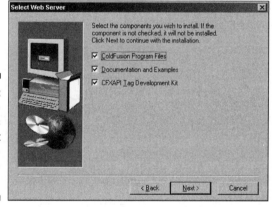

Figure 2-11:
Select the components you want the setup program to install.

12. **Make your selections.**

    You definitely want to install the ColdFusion program files. The documentation and examples are excellent, so select those as well. If you don't plan to do any custom tag development, you can omit the last option.

Allaire has identified a security risk in installing the example program files and online documentation. If the computer on which you're installing ColdFusion (your workstation or a server) is accessible to the Internet, you should *not* install these files. Or at least take extra pre-cautions to prevent their being executable by Web visitors. See the Allaire Security Zone Web site (`http://www.allaire.com/developer/securityzone/`) for more information.

13. **Click Next.**

    The next screen requests that you provide a password for ColdFusion Administrator, as shown in Figure 2-12.

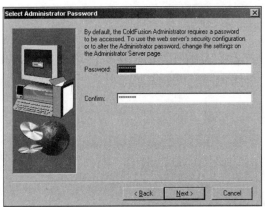

Figure 2-12:
Provide a
password
for
ColdFusion
Adminis-
trator.

You aren't asked for a password if you're upgrading from ColdFusion 4.0 because it's smart enough to use the one you already have.

14. **Use *password* or something equally memorable and then click Next.**

    If you forget your password, you have to reset it by re-installing ColdFusion Server.

    Because you're installing a single-user copy of ColdFusion Administrator, security through a password isn't important — as long as you can secure access to your physical computer and your Web server isn't open to users on the Internet (or users on your intranet). Otherwise, choose a more effective — and hard-to-guess — password.

15. **When asked, provide a password for Studio RDS Users, and then click Next.**

    This is the password users are prompted for when they try to use Studio's RDS feature to access this server. The same caveats apply: If others might have access to your server, choose your password care-fully. If security is not an issue, make life easy on yourself and use the same password you entered for ColdFusion Administrator. (By the way, although you must enter a password when prompted in the installation, you can go into the Basic Security area of Administrator later and remove the check next to these two passwords. Again, do this at your own risk!)

The next screen requests a program folder, as shown in Figure 2-13.

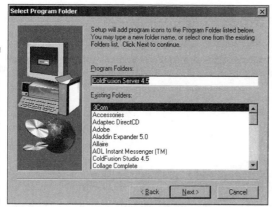

Figure 2-13:
Here's
where you
select the
folder for
launching
and admin-
istering
ColdFusion.

16. **Select the program folder from which you want to be able to launch and administer ColdFusion and then click Next.**

The default is ColdFusion Server 4.0. The next screen verifies the choices you made in the previous screens, as shown in Figure 2-14.

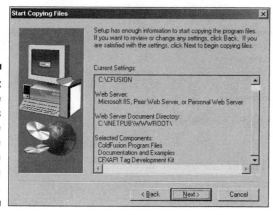

Figure 2-14:
Confirm the
choices
you've made
so that the
installation
can
proceed.

17. **Review your choices, and then click Next.**

    The ColdFusion Server installation process begins.

18. **When the installation is complete, agree to restart your computer.**

    After you restart your computer, check out your taskbar for two additional icons, shown in Figure 2-15.

ColdFusion RDS Service

ColdFusion

Figure 2-15:
Two new
icons are
in your
taskbar.

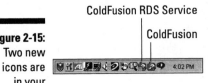

Installing ColdFusion Studio

Regardless of which Web server you've installed, and whether your development environment is local or remote, you'll eventually want to install ColdFusion Studio because it's the most effective development environment for creating CF applications.

To install Studio, follow these steps:

1. **Put the installation CD into your CD-ROM drive or double-click the installation file (cfstudio_450_eval.exe).**

   If your computer isn't configured to autorun files on a CD, choose Start⇨Run, type *d*:**\cfstudio_450_eval.exe** (where *d* is your CD-ROM drive), and then click OK.

   The installation begins, and you see a screen urging you to quit all other Windows applications before proceeding.

2. **Quit any other applications you have running and then click Next.**

   The license agreement appears.

3. **Agree to the terms of the license agreement by clicking Yes.**

   User information appears next, as shown in Figure 2-16.

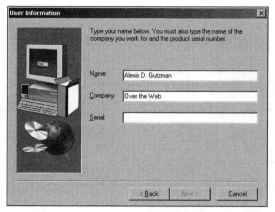

Figure 2-16:
This is where you type your name and other user information.

4. **Enter your name, company, and serial number. If you're installing an evaluation copy of the software, you can leave the Serial field blank. Click Next.**

   A screen asks you to select the destination location, as shown in Figure 2-17.

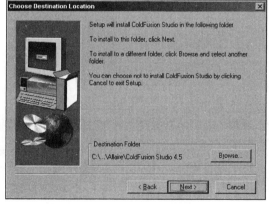

Figure 2-17:
Select the destination directory for ColdFusion Studio.

5. **Indicate where you want to install ColdFusion Studio.**

   The default is C:\Program Files\Allaire\ColdFusion Studio4.5.

6. **Click Next.**

   You are warned that the directory does not exist and are then asked whether you want to create the directory.

7. Click Yes.

A screen asks where you'd like to install TopStyle Lite, the stylesheet editor that Studio uses.

8. Click Next to permit Setup to install TopStyle Lite in the default directory (C:\Program Files\Bradbury\TopStyle1.5).

A list of components that setup can install appears, as shown in Figure 2-18.

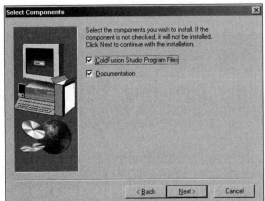

Figure 2-18:
Select the components you want setup to install.

9. Make your selections.

You definitely want to install the ColdFusion Studio program files. The documentation is excellent, so select that option as well, if you have space.

If you chose not to install the documentation when installing ColdFusion Server (due to security risks), it's safe to install these documents here because the location you install them to is not typically accessible by Web visitors. (Unless you take steps to change things, Web visitors can see files only in the webroot. The concept of a webroot is discussed in Chapter 1.)

10. Click Next.

The next screen requests a program folder, as shown in Figure 2-19.

11. Select the program folder from which you want to be able to launch and administer ColdFusion and then click Next.

The default is ColdFusion Studio 4.5. The next screen verifies the choices you made in the previous screens, as shown in Figure 2-20.

Figure 2-19:
Select the
program
folder for
launching
and admin-
istering
ColdFusion.

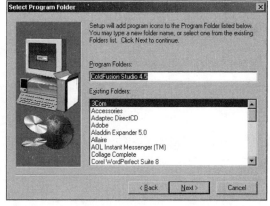

Figure 2-20:
Confirm the
choices
you've made
so that the
installation
can
proceed.

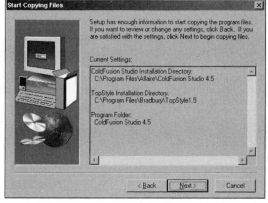

12. **Review your choices, and then click Next.**

    The ColdFusion Studio installation process begins.

13. **When the installation is complete, agree to restart your computer.**

Now that you have your development environment configured, you're ready
to start Studio and take it for a spin. To find out what the many icons in
Studio mean and to see how Studio can make your development more productive, turn to Chapter 4.

Chapter 3

Using ColdFusion Studio

A lot of power is packed into the Studio screen. In this chapter, we take a tour of what's on the screen and how you can modify the environment to give you access to the tools you need most. You also discover the location of the HTML and CFML tools and how to find instant help with tags, functions, and Studio itself.

Getting the Lay of the Land

When you open Studio, you'll notice an almost overwhelming number of places where you can take action, as shown in Figure 3-1. To avoid that feeling of being overwhelmed, you need to know where to look for what. We're here to help.

From a functional perspective, you can divide the screen into four areas:

✔ Main toolbar

✔ Quick Bar

✔ Editor pane

✔ Resource pane

We discuss each of these major pieces of real estate next.

Main toolbar   Quick Bar

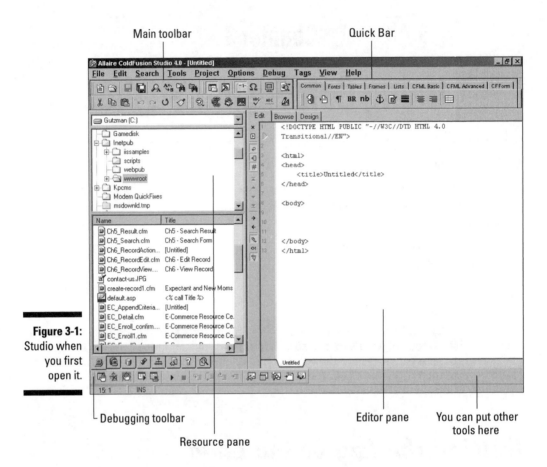

Figure 3-1:
Studio when
you first
open it.

└─ Debugging toolbar

Resource pane

Editor pane   You can put other
tools here

The Main Toolbar

The *main toolbar* (labeled in Figure 3-1), should look familiar. It has the icons you see in most Windows applications: new file, file open, save, cut, paste, and so on. It also has a few you probably haven't seen before.

Upon closer inspection, you'll notice that the main toolbar is actually comprised of four toolbars docked together in the upper-left corner of your screen. These toolbars are the

✔ Standard toolbar

✔ View toolbar

✔ Edit toolbar

✔ Tools toolbar

If you would rather use that space for something else, you can choose not to view these toolbars or simply drag them elsewhere on the screen. If you drag the toolbars to a perimeter of the Studio screen, they dock in place there; otherwise, they float on top of the Studio screen.

To move a toolbar, click the double horizontal bar to the left of the toolbar and drag the toolbar elsewhere. If you move a toolbar all the way to the left or the right side of the screen, the toolbar changes orientation and the icons are stacked vertically instead of horizontally, as shown in Figure 3-2. You can also drag toolbars into the Quick Bar, as we discuss later.

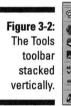

Figure 3-2:
The Tools
toolbar
stacked
vertically.

The standard toolbar

The standard toolbar, shown in Figure 3-3, includes the most basic types of actions you can take on a file:

✔ **New File.** Creates a new file, using a Default template. The file is a standard HTML file, unless you change it (Options⇨Settings⇨Location⇨ Default Template. The template is the same template that appears in the editor pane when you open Studio for the first time. Many other options for creating new files are available under File⇨New.

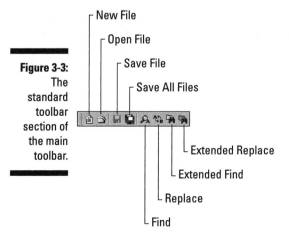

Figure 3-3:
The
standard
toolbar
section of
the main
toolbar.

New File
Open File
Save File
Save All Files
Extended Replace
Extended Find
Replace
Find

✔ **Open File.** Opens a file. Studio assumes that the file you want to open is in the directory selected in the resource pane (discussed later). If you want to change the default directory in which files are opened (and saved), change the directory that's selected in the resource pane. Or simply navigate in the resource pane to the file you want to open, and then double-click it.

✔ **Save File.** Saves the file you're working on in the editor pane. The save file icon is active only if you've made a change to the file. You can tell whether you've made a change to a file in the editor pane by looking at the file name, as shown in the Editor tab at the bottom of the editor pane. The name is blue when you're working on a copy that's different from the saved version and black after you've saved it.

✔ **Save All Files.** Saves all open files. This is a timesaver when you work on more than one open file at a time.

✔ **Find.** Opens a dialog box that enables you to search the active, open file in the editor pane for a text string.

✔ **Replace.** Opens a dialog box that enables you to search the active, open file in the editor pane for a text string and either replace all instances of the string in the file from this point down (or up) or selectively replace each instance, one at a time.

✔ **Extended Find.** Studio has a powerful extended find function. You can search for a text string or a regular expression in the current file, all open files, all files in a directory (and optionally its subdirectories), or all files in a project. Studio opens a new result pane across the bottom of the Studio screen, as shown in Figure 3-4, showing where in each file it found the text string you were seeking. To view a particular instance of the found string, simply double-click the entry in the results list. For more information on how to use the result pane, see its discussion later in the chapter. To close the result pane, click the x in the upper-right corner of the pane.

✔ **Extended Replace.** Studio can replace text across all files in a directory (and optionally its subdirectories), all open files, or all files in a project. You can optionally search for string patterns using regular expressions, and you can choose to have Studio back up files before changing them. When Studio has finished replacing, it prompts you to reload all changed files, and then opens a result pane showing what it did, which can be used the same way as the extended find result pane.

Figure 3-4:
The result
pane that
appears
under the
editor pane
after using
Extended
Find or
Extended
Replace.

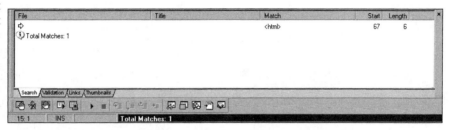

To customize the toolbars or the Quick Bar (discussed later), right-click a toolbar or right-click in the Quick Bar area, and then select or deselect any toolbar from the list that appears. The list shows all toolbars that are displayed (checked) or can be displayed (not checked). If you select a toolbar that's not currently displayed, it's opened as a free-floating one that can be docked as described previously. If you select one that's currently displayed, it's removed.

The view toolbar

The view toolbar, shown in Figure 3-5, enables you to turn on or off (that is, view or not view) several different panes on the screen.

Keyboard shortcuts

Nothing makes working with Studio more efficient and effective than knowing the appropriate keyboard shortcuts for the commands you use most often. Each of the commands in this chapter has a corresponding shortcut, as do nearly all commands in Studio. Fortunately, it's easy to remember what those shortcuts are: Simply look for the command on the menu bar. There, nearly every command shows it's shortcut as well.

The documentation provided with Release 4.5 includes a .pdf file that lists all Studio shortcuts. It's in your Program Files\Allaire\ColdFusion 4.5\Help\Allaire_Support folder, and it's called shortcut_keys.pdf. The usual Windows shortcut keys work (for example, copy is Ctrl+C and paste is Ctrl+V), but the ones listed next are default shortcuts specific to Studio.

(continued)

(continued)

Command	Shortcut key	Command	Shortcut key
Go to previous start tag	Ctrl+[	Open tag inspector	F4
Go to next start tag	Ctrl+]	Toggle special characters	Shift+Ctrl+X
Edit current tag	Ctrl+F4	Toggle tag insight	Shift+F2
Edit⇨Toggle Bookmark	Ctrl+K	Toggle tag tips	F2
Edit⇨Goto Next Bookmark	Shift+Ctrl+K	Show help for current tag (HTML only)	F1
Insert expanded code or open templates list	Ctrl+J	Toggle Quick Bar	Ctrl+H
Edit⇨Indent	Shift+Ctrl+.	Toggle result pane	Shift+Ctrl+L
Edit⇨Unindent	Shift+Ctrl+,	Options⇨Settings	F8
Search⇨Extended Find	Shift+Ctrl+F	Options⇨Customize	Shift+F8
Search⇨Extended Replace	Shift+Ctrl+R	Open Anchor dialog	Shift+Ctrl+A
Find matching tag	Ctrl+M	Insert Bold tag	Ctrl+B
Tools⇨Open Tag Chooser	Ctrl+E	Insert BR tag	Shift+Ctrl+B
Tools⇨Mark Spelling Errors	Ctrl+F7	Insert BR tag and new line	Ctrl+Enter
Tools⇨Validate Document	Shift+F6	Insert align center in DIV tag	Shift+Ctrl+C
Tools⇨Validate Current Tag	F6	Insert Comment tag	Shift+Ctrl+M
View⇨Full Screen	F10	Insert Italic tag	Ctrl+I
View⇨Resources Tab	F9	Insert nonbreaking space	Shift+Ctrl+ Space
Go to previous document	Shift+Ctrl+Tab	Insert Paragraph tag	Shift+Ctrl+P
Go to next document	Ctrl+Tab	Insert Start brackets <>	Ctrl+,
Go to line	Ctrl+G	Insert End bracket </>	Ctrl+.
Find matching tag	Ctrl+M	Repeat last tag	Ctrl+Q
Open current document in external browser	F11	Delete line	Ctrl+Y
Open current document in DreamWeaver	Ctrl+D	Delete string	Ctrl+Del
Toggle browse mode (edit/browse)	F12	Delete previous string	Ctrl+ Backspace
Toggle design mode (edit/design)	Shift+F12	Open IMG dialog box	Shift+Ctrl+I
		Development Mappings	Alt+M
Toggle focus between editor and resource pane	Shift+F9	Open CodeSweeper dialog box	Ctrl+Alt+F

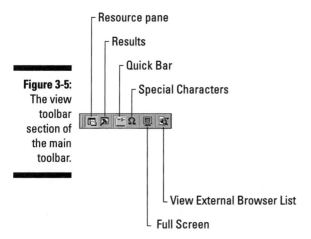

Figure 3-5:
The view
toolbar
section of
the main
toolbar.

Resource pane

Results

Quick Bar

Special Characters

View External Browser List

Full Screen

The view toolbar contains the following icons:

- ✓ **Resource pane.** Removes (or adds) the resource pane to your screen.

- ✓ **Result pane.** Displays the result pane, if there are any results. If you've just performed an extended find, extended replace, or document or link validation (discussed later), it removes the result pane from the screen, but does not erase its contents.

  If you'd like to print the results shown in the result pane — or perhaps e-mail them to someone for review, you can! Just right-click the results and choose browse. The results are rendered in your external browser as an HTML display, which you can then print from your browser or save and e-mail.

- ✓ **Quick Bar.** Removes the Quick Bar from the screen or returns it to the screen if it's missing.

- ✓ **Special Characters.** Displays all the special characters (referred to as *entities* in HTML) across a pane along the bottom of the screen. You can insert the HTML code for special characters into your page by clicking the special characters in the pane.

- ✓ **Full Screen.** Makes the editor pane take over the entire screen, except for the menu at the top of the screen, as shown in Figure 3-6. There's no clue, however, about how you get back to the regular screen. (You choose View and click to remove the check mark from Full Screen.) Full-screen mode is a great way to work when you need to see a lot of your HTML and CFML. Use Ctrl+F12 to toggle between full-screen mode and regular mode.

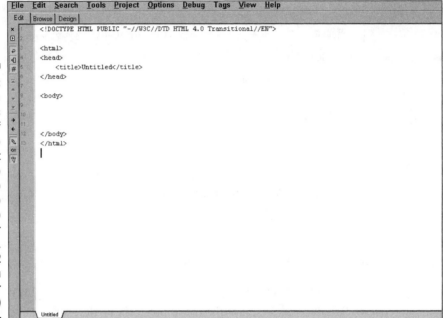

Figure 3-6:
Full-screen
mode gives
you lots of
room to
work but
offers no
clue as to
how to
return to
regular
mode.
(Ctrl+F12
returns you
to regular
mode.)

✔ **View External Browser List.** Displays a list of browsers. Use this list when you want to view your work in an external browser. When you install Studio, it automatically adds to this list any browsers installed on your computer. If you'd like to add a browser later, choose Options⇨Configure External Browsers.

The edit toolbar

The edit toolbar, shown in Figure 3-7, contains many familiar icons and a few that are probably new to you.

The two icons that won't necessarily be obvious to you are

✔ **Repeat Last Tag.** Repeats the last tag that Studio helped you create. If you click the bold icon in the fonts toolbar, for example, and then click Repeat Last Tag, you get two BOLD tags. If you type a <BR> tag, however, and then click Repeat Last Tag, Studio won't create another BOLD tag (because you typed it yourself). Instead, it will repeat whatever tag it last helped you build.

✔ **CodeSweeper.** Cleans up your HTML and CFML by making formatting changes. The drop-down icon gives you a choice of five formatting profiles. A warning appears telling you that formatting changes you make through CodeSweeper are not reversible. If you select Configure CodeSweeper, the dialog box shown in Figure 3-8 appears. In this dialog box, you can change the capitalization of HTML and CFML tags, the capitalization of attributes, and the indentation of new lines. Use CodeSweeper to make your source code more readable.

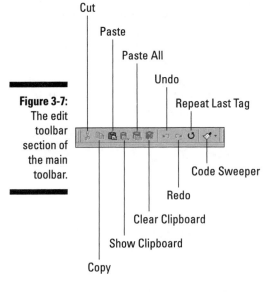

Figure 3-7:
The edit
toolbar
section of
the main
toolbar.

Cut
Paste
Paste All
Undo
Repeat Last Tag
Code Sweeper
Redo
Clear Clipboard
Show Clipboard
Copy

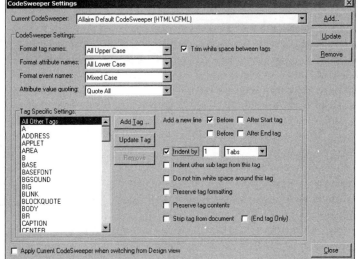

Figure 3-8:
The
Code-
Sweeper
Settings
dialog box
lets you
select how
you want to
clean up the
formatting
of your
HTML and
CFML.

The tools toolbar

The tools toolbar, shown in Figure 3-9, has icons for HTML editing commands that you might find useful:

- ✔ **Color Palette.** Opens an active color palette, from which you can select a color while seeing its hexadecimal representation. This is an ideal tool when you are using an attribute that takes color, such as the bgcolor attribute of the BODY tag or the color attribute of the FONT tag. Just position your cursor where you want the color code (in hex) to be (for example, after color="), click the color you want from the color palette — and don't forget to close your double quotes. The palette shown by default is the color-safe palette, which in browser terms means colors that should be safely rendered as displayed in most browsers.

- ✔ **Verify Links.** Displays a list of links in your open document in the result pane, as shown in Figure 3-10. Any relative URLs are resolved so that you see the actual directory and file names of the links.

Color Palette

Validate Current Document

Spellcheck

Figure 3-9:
The tools toolbar section of the main toolbar.

Stylesheet Editor

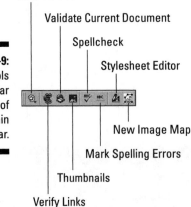

New Image Map

Mark Spelling Errors

Thumbnails

Verify Links

To test the links, click the Start Link Verification icon in the result pane. You can use the result pane to find the problem code by double-clicking one of the listed errors. Note also that you can sort the list by clicking any of the displayed columns. Sorting by the status column can be a quick way to locate erroneous links in a large list of links. For even finer control of the verification process, use the icons listed on the left of the result pane (and shown in Figure 3-10). You can set the root URL for relative links if you're not satisfied with the root URL that Studio used. You can set the server timeout, which defaults to 15 seconds, and you can identify the proxy server IP address, if you connect to the Web through a proxy server. After you have your results, you can send a list of broken links to your browser for printing.

Figure 3-10:
Click the
Verify Links
icon to see
the list of
links in the
open docu-
ment in the
result pane.

└─ Start Link Verification

└─ Stop Link Verification

└─ Set Root URL

└─ Set Timeout

└─ Set Proxy

└─ Print Failed Links

✔ **Validate Current Document.** Opens the result pane and shows you the
results of basic HTML and CFML validation. The results show a combination of errors and cautions, warning you about nesting errors, tag
attribute mistakes, and missing end tags where they're both required
and optional.

You can disable the cautions; they serve only to obscure the real errors.
To do so, use Options⇨Settings⇨Validation⇨Validator Settings.

✔ **Thumbnails.** Displays thumbnails of every image in your open directory.
Because it forces all images into a square shape, the thumbnails may
show distorted images, but they don't affect the actual images.
Thumbnails appear in the Thumbnails tab of the result pane.

The result panes you've seen in Figures 3-4 and 3-10 are indeed the same result pane. To switch between results of different actions, click the tabs across the bottom. Again, as with Extended Find results, you can right-click and browse the results for printing or e-mailing. The Web page displayed is a little different than the "print failed links" indicated in Figure 3-10.

- ✔ **Spellcheck**. Checks the spelling of text but not tags in your open document.

- ✔ **Mark Spelling Errors.** Adds a wavy red underline to any incorrectly spelled words in your open document. It checks spelling, marking errors as you type.

- ✔ **Stylesheet Editor.** Opens the stylesheet editor, which is a useful tool for creating cascading style sheets.

- ✔ **New Image Map.** Opens the image-map creation tool. You are prompted to select an image and name your map, after which a standard image-mapping tool appears. You can create hot regions as rectangles, circles, or polygons. After you define a hot region, the tag editor for the AREA tag opens, requesting information about the behavior you want as a result of the actions by the visitor. You can define quite a few qualities about a hot region, including events. When you've completed your image map, select File⇨Save and Exit.

The Quick Bar

The Quick Bar is a handy place to store toolbars. When you open Studio, the Quick Bar contains most of the toolbars related to HTML and CFML.

The Quick Bar is a clever way to use the real estate on the page. By clicking one of its tabs, you can see the related toolbar. If you have too many toolbars open, you lose development space to icons. The Quick Bar is a good compromise; the icons you need are only a click away.

Note, too, that you can move any displayed toolbar from its docked or free-floating location onto the Quick Bar. If you have too many toolbars, Studio offers right and left arrow icons on the right edge of the Quick Bar to help you navigate.

To add any toolbars not currently displayed on the Studio screen (docked, free-floating, or in the Quick Bar), you can right-click the Quick Bar and turn an unselected toolbar into a free-floating one.

HTML toolbars

Most toolbars in the Quick Bar facilitate HTML development. The toolbars are

✔ **Common**. Contains icons for creating a shell of a page (called Quick Start), creating the body section of a page, inserting tags for a paragraph, a break, a nonbreaking space, an anchor, an image, a horizontal rule, align center, align right, and DIV (used with style sheets). The common toolbar is shown in Figure 3-11.

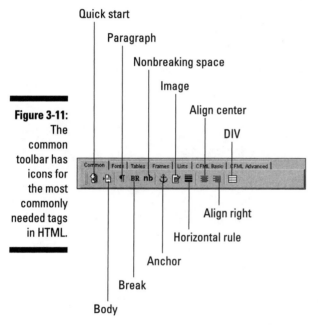

Quick start

Paragraph

Nonbreaking space

Image

Align center

DIV

Figure 3-11: The common toolbar has icons for the most commonly needed tags in HTML.

Align right

Horizontal rule

Anchor

Break

Body

✔ **Fonts.** Contains icons for font color, typeface, color, size, bold, italic, strong, emphasis, preformatted text, headings 1 through 3, subscript, and superscript. Check out Figure 3-12.

✔ **Tables.** Holds icons for creating tables and parts of tables. The first icon is for the Table Wizard, a useful tool for building simple or complex tables. Next are icons that display dialog boxes for creating a table, rows, headings, and data. Following those are icons to insert HTML for a table, row, heading, cell, or caption directly into your page. Finally, you can use the Table Sizer icon to create a simple table of a certain size by highlighting the number of rows and columns you want in your table. The tables toolbar is shown in Figure 3-13.

Font specification (dialog box)

Font size = -1 tag

Italic

Emphasis

Heading level 1

Heading level 3

Superscript

Figure 3-12:
The fonts
toolbar has
icons for
formatting
fonts.

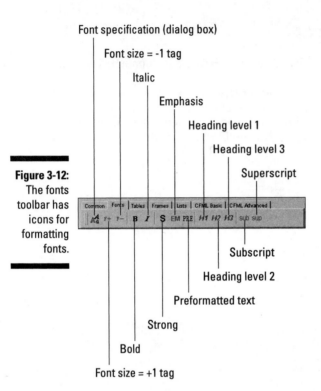

Subscript

Heading level 2

Preformatted text

Strong

Bold

Font size = +1 tag

Insert Table

Insert Table Row

Insert Table Header

Insert Table Data

Table

Table Row

Table Header

Table Data

Caption

Figure 3-13:
The tables
toolbar
helps you
create
tables.

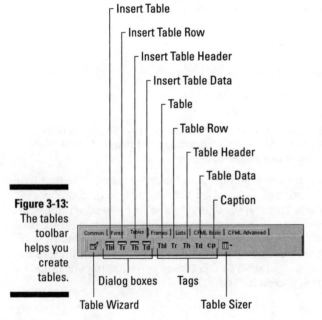

Dialog boxes   Tags

Table Wizard   Table Sizer

✔ **Frames.** Helps you create pages with framesets, pages with target frames, and the NOFRAMES tag of a frames page. The frames toolbar is shown in Figure 3-14.

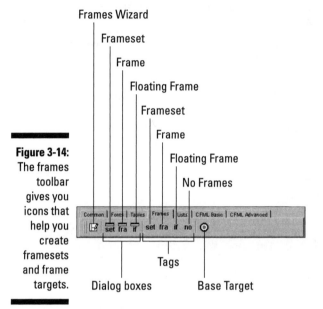

Figure 3-14:
The frames toolbar gives you icons that help you create framesets and frame targets.

✔ **Lists.** Useful for creating ordered (numbered), unordered (bullet), and definition lists. See Figure 3-15.

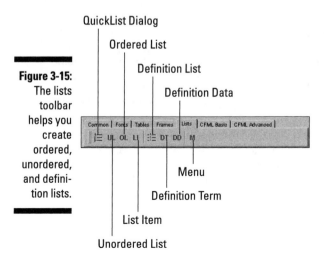

Figure 3-15:
The lists toolbar helps you create ordered, unordered, and definition lists.

✔ **Forms.** Not offered in the Quick Bar when Studio is installed by default, but worth adding as described previously. The forms toolbar, shown in Figure 3-16, is useful for creating forms pages. Each icon opens up a dialog box for the specified form element. All attributes for each tag are in front of you, so it's easy to remember to include all necessary attributes for each form field.

The forms toolbar is so useful, you should add it to your Quick Bar to make it more easily accessible.

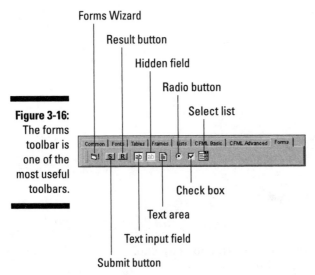

Figure 3-16:
The forms
toolbar is
one of the
most useful
toolbars.

Forms Wizard
Result button
Hidden field
Radio button
Select list
Check box
Text area
Text input field
Submit button

CFML toolbars

The Quick Bar loads with three CFML toolbars that help you with basic CFML, advanced CFML, and CFFORM:

✔ **CFML Basic.** Includes icons for CFQUERY, CFOUTPUT, CFINSERT, CFUPDATE, CFTABLE, CFCOL, CFLOOP, CFINCLUDE, and CFLOCATION. For each of these, a dialog box prompts you for the necessary attributes. The toolbar also includes icons for CFIF, CFELSEIF, CFELSE, CFSET, CFPARAM, and comments, which simply insert the selected tag into your page. The CFML Basic toolbar is shown in Figure 3-17.

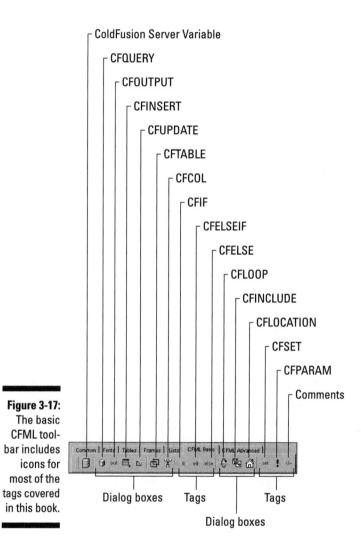

ColdFusion Server Variable
CFQUERY
CFOUTPUT
CFINSERT
CFUPDATE
CFTABLE
CFCOL
CFIF
CFELSEIF
CFELSE
CFLOOP
CFINCLUDE
CFLOCATION
CFSET
CFPARAM
Comments

Figure 3-17:
The basic
CFML tool-
bar includes
icons for
most of the
tags covered
in this book.

Dialog boxes   Tags   Tags

Dialog boxes

✔ **CFML Advanced.** Includes icons for setting cookies and interacting with other services to retrieve pages, send mail, and perform other server processes. If you're using ColdFusion Express, you won't need this toolbar because most of these tags aren't part of Express. See Figure 3-18.

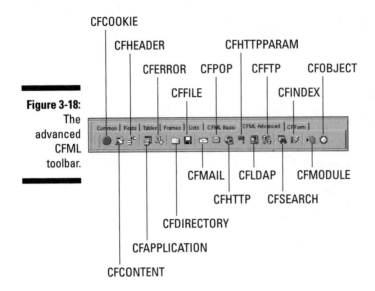

CFCOOKIE
CFHEADER
CFERROR CFPOP CFHTTPPARAM
CFFILE CFFTP CFOBJECT
CFINDEX

Figure 3-18:
The
advanced
CFML
toolbar.

CFMAIL CFLDAP CFMODULE
CFHTTP CFSEARCH
CFDIRECTORY
CFAPPLICATION
CFCONTENT

We discuss the third CFML toolbar, CFFORM, in Chapter 13.

The Editor Pane

The editor pane, shown in Figure 3-19, is where you'll spend most of your time in Studio. One of the first things you notice when you're looking at the Edit tab of the editor pane is that not all the text on your screen is the same color. Studio colors the tags to make editing easier for you.

Comments, for example, appear in gray. It's easy to know if you've forgotten to include the closing comment tag –> or - - -> (for ColdFusion comments) because the remainder of your document appears gray. When you close the comments tag, the rest of the tags in your document are colored properly.

If you want to change the color scheme for your tags, you can do that in the Settings dialog box (F8 or Options⇨Settings), under the Color Coding tab. Select the scheme you want to color, and then click Edit Scheme. You can select the color for each type of tag (anchor tags, style tags, table tags, and so on). When you're satisfied with your selections, click OK, and then click OK again. Color coding does not affect the underlying document; it just changes how you see it in Studio.

Tag validation

Tag completion

Tag insight

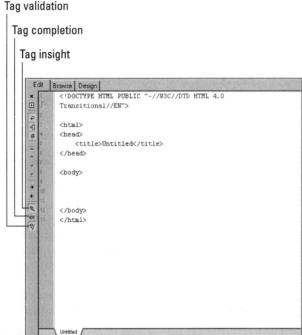

Figure 3-19:
The editor
pane in
Studio is
where you'll
do most of
your work.

Several useful tools are tucked into the left border of the editor pane. Some act as toggles to enable or disable editing features. The following four are worthy of mention:

✔ **Split Current Document.** Permits you to view and edit your document in two places at once. If you've ever wished you could compare code in two places in the same document, your wish has been granted. After your code is longer than a page, you'll find this tool invaluable.

✔ **Tag Insight.** Offers you a list of attributes that go with the tag you're typing, if you type a tag by hand. Figure 3-20 shows what tag insight looks like in action. When you press the spacebar while entering a tag, wait one second, and a list of the appropriate attributes for the current tag are displayed as a drop-down list. Use the keyboard arrow keys to go to the attribute you'd like to include, select it, and then press Enter. Or you can simply continue typing the beginning characters of the attribute, and when the attribute name appears in a pop-up box, press Enter to have the typing finished for you. If an attribute has an available list of possible values, those are presented as well and can be selected in the same way. Tag insight is a particularly useful tool if you can't remember which attributes go with the tag you're typing.

Figure 3-20:
Tag insight
gives you a
list of
attributes for
the tag
you're typing
(the TABLE
tag in this
example).

If the tag insight feature is getting in your way, you can disable it by selecting the icon for it in the edit toolbar (the third icon from the bottom, to the left of the editor pane). Conversely, if you really like it and don't want to have to wait a full second for its pop-up list, you can have Studio present the list more quickly. Use Options⇨Settings⇨Tag Help, and choose the Settings button under Tag Insight. Use the slider bar to choose the amount of delay you want Tag Insight to wait before showing you the pop-up list of alternatives.

✔ **Tag Completion.** This tool is both a service and a hindrance. It automatically includes a closing tag when you type the > at the end of the opening tag. Be sure to turn it off if you're editing an already working page. Otherwise, every time you type > at the end of a tag, tag completion will insert another ending tag! When you're creating a page from scratch, tag completion can save you typing and help you remember to close your tags. It just takes a while to get used to.

✔ **Tag Validation.** If you want to make sure you're not making up tags as you go, consider turning on tag validation. When on, it automatically checks your tags to make sure you're using only valid HTML 4 tags and valid CFML tags. For example, if you try to use a FONT tag, it will tell you that the FONT tag is deprecated in HTML 4 and may become obsolete, which is annoying after the first time you see it. But if you type CFWHEN, thinking it's a valid CFML tag (which it's not), the tag validation feature helps you out by telling you that CFWHEN isn't found in any currently active versions.

Browse view

The editor pane has three views: edit, browse, and design. You can switch between them by clicking the tabs at the top of the pane. Browse view, which is available by clicking the Browse button at the top of the editor pane, lets you see the page you're developing as it would appear in a browser, without leaving the Studio workspace.

The browser used for this internal browse feature is controlled in Options⇨ Settings⇨Browse. A generic, built-in browser is available by default, but you'll probably want to select Internet Explorer, if you have that installed.

If you're running any version of Netscape Navigator less than 5.0, you can't select it as your internal browser in Studio unless you download the NGLayout Engine from Netscape. Any version of Internet Explorer can be set to launch as the internal browser in Studio because IE was developed to be installable as a component within another program — Netscape was not.

The browse view works with any HTML files you may edit, but if you try to use it with a CFML file, you will receive an error message until you make some additional modifications. As the message indicates, you need to create a development mapping, which is simply a way to help Studio execute and display the template. (We describe how to configure development mappings in Chapter 2.) Remember, ColdFusion Server must process a CFML file before it can be browsed.

When you're in browse view, in addition to being able to view and navigate within the displayed template, you also have available several useful tools. Figure 3-21 shows the tools available in browse view.

The two most useful features, which may take you a while to find on your own, because the icons are so small, are

- ✔ **Browser size.** Click the browser size icon, and then change your browser size to either 640 x 480 or 800 x 600. Studio shows you how your page will look at the specified resolution. This tool is ideal for seeing what's "above the fold" on your pages and where you're forcing your visitors to scroll. To set the browser size back to full screen, change the option to Fit to Window.

- ✔ **Open in External Browser.** This useful tool opens the page in an external browser that you defined as the default under Options⇨ Configure External Browsers.

Previous

Next

Stop

Refresh

Browser Size

Open URL

Toggle Rulers

Open in External Browser

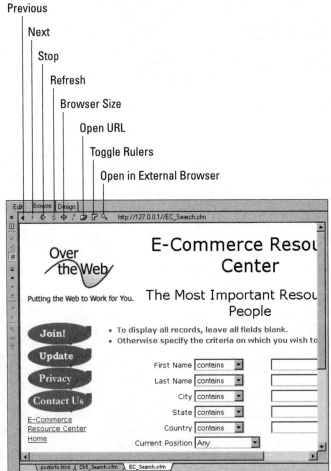

Figure 3-21:
Browse
view and
the icons
that accom-
pany it.

Design view

Design view is the WYSIWYG (what-you-see-is-what-you-get) view of Studio. If you like to create Web pages by dragging and dropping elements into place, and you like to see how a page will look as you work, design view might seem like the view for you!

Design view is meant to be used with HTML or CFML files before you do any substantial CFML development. It's a great way to lay out the HTML-only portion of your page before you add processing. In design view, nothing gets executed, so the CFML and HTML both appear as text.

Before wondering why in the world Allaire would offer such a feature if it doesn't work with CFML, keep in mind that Studio is an extension to HomeSite, which is a pure HTML editor, and design view works wonderfully with that product. In addition, the design view feature is actually a design control from Microsoft, and was not designed to interpret (or ignore) CFML. Macromedia DreamWeaver is an HTML editor that does a better job than design view. It successfully recognizes and ignores CFML tags, so it does a better job of designing than Studio in this one respect. Allaire has even enabled easy integration of DreamWeaver from within Studio.

Design view may still be useful, however, when you're in the early stages of page development and are focusing solely on the HTML presentation of the information. At that phase, the WYSIWYG features could be a real timesaver. Figure 3-22 shows you what's available in design view.

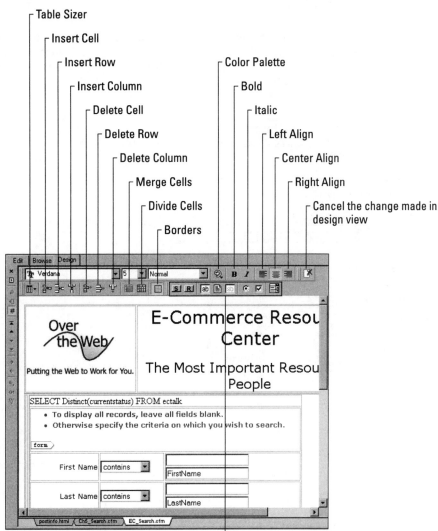

Figure 3-22: Design view is not suitable for editing CFML files.

Table Sizer
Insert Cell
Insert Row
Insert Column
Delete Cell
Delete Row
Delete Column
Merge Cells
Divide Cells
Borders

Color Palette
Bold
Italic
Left Align
Center Align
Right Align
Cancel the change made in design view

Tools toolbar

The Resource Pane

The resource pane, shown in Figure 3-23, is a marvel of clever design. Hidden in the resource pane are the following ways you may want to get at your data:

- Through files on the local computer, a network, on an RDS server, or on an FTP server

- Using a database on the local computer or on an RDS server

- Through projects

- In site view

You can also store frequently used code snippets in the Snippets tab of the resource pane, get help in one of the ten hefty manuals that accompany Studio (including the official HTML 4.0 specification for any tag), and view your code using the nifty tag inspector.

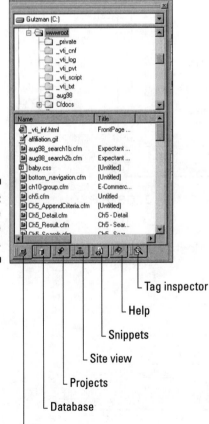

Figure 3-23:
The
resource
pane.

Tag inspector

Help

Snippets

Site view

Projects

Database

Files

Getting at your files

Studio is flexible about where you store the files you work on. Using the tabs in the resource pane, you can get to your files on either your local computer, on a computer on which you have only FTP access, or on a computer on which you have RDS access. The following list explains these options:

✔ **Files.** If your files are located on your local computer or on a network drive mapped on your local computer (such as an F: drive), you can find your files by selecting the drive and then the directory in which they reside. Directories are in the top half of the resource pane. In the bottom half of the resource pane, click the file you want to open.

If your files are located on a remote computer, you can access them by going to the Allaire FTP & RDS "drive" of the Files tab, and adding either an FTP server or an RDS server. To add an RDS server, the computer to which you're connecting must have ColdFusion Server installed. To add a server, right-click the words Remote Server, as shown in Figure 3-24, and select either Add RDS Server or Add FTP Server. Complete the dialog box with the server's name and the logon information. After you set up the remote server, you can view files on that server in the bottom of the resource pane.

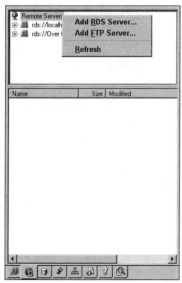

Figure 3-24: You create an RDS or an FTP mapping through the Allaire FTP & RDS drive of the Files tab of the resource pane.

In Windows environments, you can also use the Local Files tab to access files available on networked drives, using the Network Neighborhood feature of Windows. The tab appears in the list of drives at the top of the pane. With this, and the capability to use mapped network drives as mentioned, the local aspect of the Local Files tab is a bit of a misnomer. It also opens access to "remote" files located on your network.

✓ **Database.** To see the tables and fields in your databases, view data in those tables, or generate SQL with a visual query builder, click the Database tab of the resource pane. Your server (either the remote computer or the local computer, if that's where your data source definition resides), must be configured as an RDS server first. Figure 3-25 shows the data sources defined on localhost.

Figure 3-25:
The Database tab of the resource pane shows the data sources on the local computer.

To use the Database tab (query builder) against data sources defined on your computer, you must have a remote file server set up for your localhost (as it's referred to in this context). This may not seem logical, but because the database feature uses RDS (as does the Studio debugger), it's a requirement. Fortunately, it's easy to add your localhost from the Remote Files tab. If you don't have a localhost listed in the Remote Files tab, right-click remote servers at the top of the Remote Files tab. Choose Add RDS Server, and then type **localhost** for both the description and the hostname. If you already have a localhost listed but it's not working, right-click the localhost entry, and then select Properties. In either case, if an RDS password was specified when Studio was installed (as we discuss in Chapter 2) or was added in ColdFusion Administrator, enter the password here; leave the user name blank.

✓ **Projects.** Projects are one way that Studio permits you to group your files. To group your files into projects, click the Projects tab of the resource pane, and then click the New Projects icon at the top of the Projects window.

✓ **Site view.** If you want to see the site hierarchy, click the Site View tab of the resource pane. Studio will create a tree of the site with links between pages.

Code snippets

If you find that you often need to type some text or a set of tags, you can create a code snippet in the Snippets tab of the resource pane. From there, you can then double-click the snippet at any time to add the specified code to your editor window.

The Snippets tab starts out empty. Simply right-click in the white space, and you can create a folder. Then right-click the folder to start creating snippets. Figure 3-26 shows the Snippet dialog box.

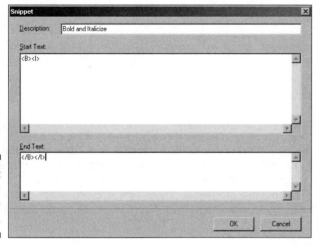

Figure 3-26:
Creating a
new code
snippet.

The option to provide start text and end text enables you to wrap the snippet around an insertion point in your editor. If you highlight some text before applying the snippet, the snippet is wrapped around it. If you don't select text, after you apply the snippet, the cursor is left between the start and end text ready for you to type.

After you've created a code snippet, you can insert it into your document or apply it to a selected area by double-clicking the snippet's name in the Snippets tab of the resource pane.

Getting help

Help is accessible either from an index of topics or by searching for keywords through the Help tab of the resource pane, shown in Figure 3-27. You can even bookmark topics for fast access the next time. The topics covered include HTML, CFML, ColdFusion application development, SMIL, and cascading style sheets.

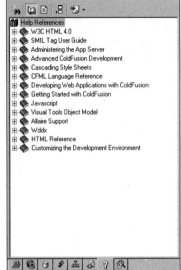

The help system works as follows. When you open a topic for display, the topic is shown in the browse window of the Studio editor pane. The display is a fully functional HTML display, so hyperlinks in the displayed document are active and links in the pages often offer a way to browse forward or backward, as well as up a level in the document's structure. When you have finished viewing the help, click the Edit tab at the top of the editor pane to return to the file you were editing before calling up help.

Tag inspector

Although the tag insight and tag editor features provide a way to view and modify all the attributes of a given HTML or CFML tag, there's yet another way: the tag inspector. This two-way editing feature (changes made here are reflected in the document and vice-versa) is also useful for a less obvious purpose. The tag inspector enables you to traverse a complex document; when you select a tag in the inspector, the document window is changed to the location of that tag in the document and vice versa.

You can use the tag inspector also to view a document's structure in a hierarchical representation of tags within tags (shown in the top window of the inspector).

In Figure 3-28, you can see all the attributes and style sheet properties that may be defined for the TABLE tag.

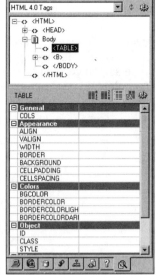

Figure 3-28:
Everything
you ever
wanted to
know about
the TABLE
tag, but
were afraid
to ask.

Tag editors

Tag editors are one of Studio's hidden gems. By right-clicking a tag (HTML or CFML) and choosing Edit Tag (if offered), or by placing the cursor on a tag and pressing Ctrl+F4, a dialog box appears showing the tag's attributes in logical groupings. Often, the most important attributes are presented up front, while less frequently used attributes are offered behind available tabs.

Note also that a small pair of icons appears in the lower-right corner of these tag editors. These very useful icons call up help for the tag! You can choose between showing the help embedded in the bottom of the tag editor window or in a separate window entirely. The help offered here is virtually the same as that offered through the Help option in the resource pane, making this a useful alternative that won't require navigating in the resource pane and opening the Help windows.

Despite the richness of the tag inspector, the tag editors may present the most effective way of viewing and editing a tag's attributes. Why? Because they're presented in a more usable order and because, again, you can call up the tag editor directly in the editor pane rather than navigate the resource pane.

Debugging

Studio has quite a few built-in debugging tools; for starters, there's the debug toolbar. You can use Studio's debugging features to walk through your code one line at a time, watching variables change as you go, to figure out why your page isn't behaving properly. For a complete discussion of debugging in Studio, refer to Chapter 14.

Chapter 4

A Big Serving of ColdFusion

In This Chapter

▶ Installing Microsoft Internet Information Server

▶ Setting up some directories

▶ Installing ColdFusion Server

▶ Configuring ColdFusion Server

▶ Registering data sources

▶ Finding ColdFusion Web site hosting

*I*f you're like many Web developers, you've spent most of your Web design career blissfully unaware of things such as servers and system administration — and you probably hope to keep it that way! Perhaps a dedicated cadre of in-house computer professionals handles the dirty work. Or maybe you've contracted your worries out to an Internet Service Provider (ISP) or Web Presence Provider (WPP).

Most of this book is about building ColdFusion templates and applications, but this chapter is about the ColdFusion Server software that processes all the templates you build in other chapters. Several versions of ColdFusion Server are available, as explained in the upcoming sidebar. This chapter focuses solely on the Windows version of ColdFusion Server.

You probably won't be personally responsible for managing the computer running your ColdFusion applications, but you should understand what's involved in the process so that you can effectively communicate with the mystical beings who *do* run your server. And if you'll be responsible for managing ColdFusion Server, this chapter points you in the right direction.

If you're using ColdFusion Studio (see Chapters 2 and 3), you have the option to install a Personal Edition of ColdFusion Enterprise Server. Install it! You can then build and test your ColdFusion applications on a machine other than your production server, which is always a good idea. You also gain complete control over ColdFusion Server settings, which makes it easier to troubleshoot your application (see Chapter 14). This chapter walks you through the entire installation process for getting ColdFusion Server up and running on your machine.

Variations on a Theme: Versions of ColdFusion Server

ColdFusion comes in three versions and runs on a number of server platforms. The biggest differences between versions are in their support of sophisticated Web server capabilities and in the databases you can use with ColdFusion. Currently, the following three distinct versions of ColdFusion Server are available:

✔ **ColdFusion, Professional Edition** is the standard version and provides all the functionality discussed in this book. It's available only for Windows NT, 95, and 98.

✔ **ColdFusion, Enterprise Edition** offers everything that the Professional Edition does along with more sophisticated features for mission-critical and large-scale implementations. These features include load balancing, fail-over redundancy, clustering, and other high-end Web server functionality that's *way* beyond the scope of this book. The Enterprise version also includes native database drivers for some high-end databases (Oracle, Sybase, DB2) and support for

CORBA objects. It's available on Windows NT as well as several UNIX platforms (Solaris and HP-UX), with Linux support expected by the time this book is published.

✔ **ColdFusion Express** is the newest member of the ColdFusion family. It offers a limited set of ColdFusion tags (including all the basic database tags) and works with only desktop databases (Access, FoxPro, and dBASE), Microsoft Excel spreadsheets, and text files. The biggest advantage of this version of ColdFusion is that it's free! It's currently available only for Windows NT, 95, and 98.

The version of ColdFusion Server that comes with ColdFusion Studio is ColdFusion Enterprise Edition. It's a complete copy, but it's limited to a single Web user so that it can't be used for anything other than development. The *ColdFusion 4 For Dummies* CD includes an evaluation version of ColdFusion Enterprise Edition.

Serving Up Information

Before we get into the details of installing ColdFusion, you need to make sure that a Web server is running on your machine. If one is installed and running, great. If not, keep reading. This section takes you through the steps for installing Microsoft Internet Information Server (IIS) for Windows NT as well as Microsoft Personal Web Server (PWS) for Windows 95 and 98. (To get a better understanding of the inner workings of ColdFusion Server, check out Chapter 11.)

Note: A *Web server* is a software application that enables your computer to deliver, or serve, Web pages. Default Windows installations do not typically include the Web server application. Later in this chapter, we tell you how to check whether a Web server *is* installed on your machine and how to install it if it isn't!

ColdFusion Server can function with just about any Web server, but it's designed for sophisticated Web servers with a Web server application programming interface (API). In addition to Microsoft Internet Information Server (IIS), the family of servers from Netscape and O'Reilly fit the bill, so feel free to use one of those instead. Avoid using other Web servers for ColdFusion — they have fewer features and performance will plummet.

ColdFusion works with your Web server to deliver dynamic Web pages, as shown in Figure 4-1. The Web server receives a request from a Web browser and sends the request to ColdFusion Server for processing. ColdFusion sends the resulting Web page back to the Web server for delivery to the Web browser. In a nutshell, that's the only thing ColdFusion does. Of course, as this book shows, the processing ColdFusion does can be pretty amazing!

A Web server is a crucial component in delivering ColdFusion applications. We take the simplest, easiest, and cheapest approach by using Microsoft's free Web server. It might be a little confusing at first because this Web server has a different name under different operating systems — Table 4-1 lists the Microsoft operating systems and the corresponding name of the Web server.

Table 4-1   Microsoft Web Servers for Each Operating System

Operating System	Name of Web Server
Windows 98	Personal Web Server (PWS)
Windows 95	Personal Web Server (PWS)
Windows NT 4.0 Workstation	Peer Web Services
Windows NT 4.0 Server	Internet Information Server (IIS)

Figure 4-1:
The relationship between ColdFusion Server and a Web server.

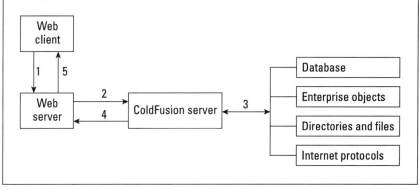

The many flavors of IIS

IIS comes in many flavors, versions, and secret identities, so don't be surprised if your installation process isn't 100 percent like ours. We used Windows NT Workstation 4.0 with Service Pack 3 to install IIS 3.0, which is a typical configuration. Some other possibilities follow:

✓ **Windows NT 4.0 standard distribution.** You can use the Network icon in the Control Panel to install Peer Web Services, otherwise known as IIS 2.0. You might need the original Windows NT installation CD to do this. Think about upgrading to a more recent service pack if possible.

✓ **Windows NT 4.0 with Option Pack 4.** This package upgrades IIS 3.0 to IIS 4.0, which is

a fine product but more complicated to manage.

✓ **Windows 95/98.** The Personal Web Server is the equivalent of IIS. It's not quite as sophisticated, but it works fine for running a test site.

A number of other alternatives are available, such as the Web server that comes with Microsoft FrontPage (which is a variation of Personal Web Server). It doesn't matter which of these you use, especially for getting started, as long as you get one installed. For more help, check out *Microsoft Internet Information Server 4 For Dummies* by David Angell (published by IDG Books Worldwide, Inc.).

All operating systems listed in Table 4-1 include the free Web server, though it's generally not part of the default installation. You need to install and properly configure it, so get out your installation disks and let's get started!

Note: We'll typically use the abbreviation IIS (Internet Information Server) to refer to all of these Microsoft Web servers because they're equivalent as far as ColdFusion is concerned. The exception is when we talk about configuring or manipulating the server software itself, a discussion that is limited to this chapter.

We tell you how to install a Web server on each of the key Microsoft platforms. For help with installing on UNIX, consult the appropriate documentation.

Building an information pipeline on Windows NT

If you're using Windows NT, installing IIS is a snap. The following steps start the installation:

1. **Click the Start⇨Settings⇨Control Panel.**

2. **Double-click the Network icon.**

   The Network dialog box appears with the Identification tab on top, as shown in Figure 4-2.

TIP

You can get to the Network dialog box directly by right-clicking the Network Neighborhood icon on the NT desktop.

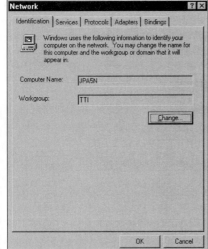

Figure 4-2:
The
Identification
tab of the
Network
dialog box in
Windows
NT.

3. Click the Services tab.

The Services tab is shown in Figure 4-3. Your machine might display a slightly different list of network services, which is fine because we're not interested in anything that's already installed.

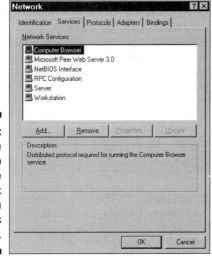

Figure 4-3:
The
Services tab
of the
Network
dialog box in
Windows
NT.

4. **Click the Add button**.

   The list of services in Figure 4-4, like Figure 4-3, might differ slightly on your machine. That's fine.

   Note: If Peer Web Services (on NT 4.0 Workstation) or Internet Information Services (on NT 4.0 Server) is in the list of services, the Web server is already installed. You can skip to the next section of the chapter, "You're Virtually Finished."

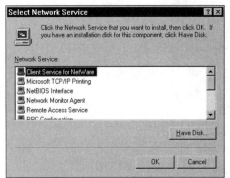

Figure 4-4:
The Select
Network
Service
dialog box in
Windows
NT.

5. **Choose Microsoft Internet Information Server (NT Server 4.0) or Microsoft Peer Web Services (NT Workstation 4.0) and then click OK.**

   The installation program for Internet Information Server (or Peer Web Services) begins.

6. **During the installation of the Web server, choose the defaults.**

   There's no reason to change the defaults, so simply click OK at each choice to proceed through the installation process.

You'll probably have to reboot your computer after the installation process is complete. Take that time to skip ahead a section to discover how to configure your Web server for ColdFusion.

Building an information pipeline on Windows 98

Installing Personal Web Server (PWS) under Windows 98 is no different than installing any other program — simply run the setup program. The hard part is finding the setup program for PWS. You might need the Windows 98 installation CD, so take a minute and find it. We'll be waiting here when you get back!

Note: If a Personal Web Server icon is in your Control Panel, PWS is already installed and you can skip to the next section of the chapter, "You're Virtually Finished." To get to the Control Panel, click Start➪Control Panel.

After you have the CD, just follow these steps:

1. **Click Start➪Run.**
2. **In the Open dialog box, type:**

   x:\add-ons\pws\setup.exe

   where x is the letter of your CD-ROM drive.
3. **When the installation program begins, click OK to get started.**
4. **Choose the defaults during installation of the Web server.**

   There's no reason to change the defaults, so simply click OK at each choice to proceed through the installation process.

That's all there is to it!

You'll probably have to reboot your computer after the installation process is complete. Take that time to skip ahead a section to discover how to configure your Web server for ColdFusion.

Building an information pipeline on Windows 95

Installing Personal Web Server (PWS) on Windows 95 can be a little tricky because several different distributions of the Windows 95 CD are available. In most situations, however, the process is similar to the one for Windows NT:

Note: If a Personal Web Server icon is in your Control Panel, PWS is already installed and you can skip to the next section of the chapter, "You're Virtually Finished." To get to the Control Panel, click Start➪Control Panel.

When you've found the CD, follow these steps:

1. **Click Start➪Settings➪Control Panel.**
2. **Double-click the Network icon.**

   The Network dialog box appears. If the Configuration tab isn't on top, click the tab to move it to the top, as shown in Figure 4-5.

   You can get to the Network dialog box directly by right-clicking the Network Neighborhood icon on the NT desktop.

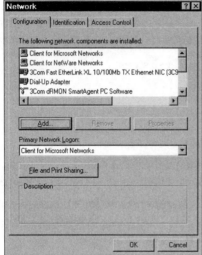

Figure 4-5:
The
Configura-
tion tab of
the Network
dialog box in
Windows
95.

3. **Click the Add button.**

   You see a list of different types of network components (Figure 4-6) that you can add to your system.

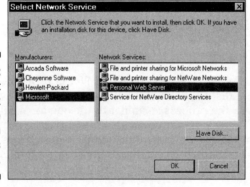

Figure 4-6:
The Select
Network
Service
dialog box in
Windows
95.

4. **Select the Personal Web Server icon and then click Add.**

5. **Choose Microsoft Personal Web Server and then click OK.**

   The installation program for Personal Web Server begins.

6. **During the installation of the Web server, choose the defaults.**

   There's no reason to change the defaults, so simply click OK at each choice to proceed through the installation process.

After the installation program is complete, you'll probably have to reboot your machine.

You're Virtually Finished

Now that you've installed a Web server, the last step is to set up some directories configured for the ColdFusion work you'll be doing. That may require setting up one or more virtual directories and changing some directory permissions. Don't worry — it's not as scary as it sounds.

By default, your Web server holds Web content in a specific directory, often called the *root web directory,* or *webroot.* If your Web server has the Web address www.mycomputer.net, typing the following in a browser window displays the index.html file located in the webroot directory:

```
http://www.mycomputer.net/index.html
```

The default webroot directories for Windows Web servers are C:\ webshare\wwwroot on Windows 95 and C:\inetpub\wwwroot on Windows NT and 98. The index.html file would be located at c:\webshare\wwwroot\ index.html and C:\inetpub\wwwroot\index.html, respectively.

Files in any subdirectories of the webroot directory are also accessible. The proper URL for any file in a subdirectory of the webroot Web directory is as follows:

```
http://www.mycomputer.net/subdirectory/filename
```

To reach files that are not subdirectories of the webroot directory, you must set up a nickname, or *virtual* directory, for the other directory. The next section shows you how.

What's a virtual directory?

A *virtual directory* is a nickname for a directory (or subdirectory) on the Web server. For example, if you have a Web address that looks like the following:

```
http://www.mycomputer.com/users/myname/myfiles/coolfile.html
```

you could create a virtual directory that points directly to the myfiles directory. Suppose you want to call the directory coolstuff. After you set up the virtual directory, the Web address becomes

```
http://www.mycomputer.com/coolstuff/coolfile.html
```

This technique bypasses all the extra typing for the URL. It also makes it possible to use different Web settings (permissions, for example) on that particular subdirectory.

Setting up virtual directories

In this section, we set up a virtual directory for ColdFusion testing and development. We start by going to the administrator interface for the Web server.

If you're using Windows 95 or 98, you can reach the PWS administration pages through the Control Panel. Choose Start➪Programs➪Control Panel and then click the Personal Web Server icon. Or right-click the PWS icon in the system tray and select Properties. Either way, you're ready to continue.

If you're using Windows NT, you can get to the IIS administration pages by clicking Start➪Programs. Select Internet Information Server/Peer Web Services (Common), and then select Administration. You're ready to continue.

Newer installations of Windows 98 and NT might include the 4.0 version of PWS or IIS, which have different installation instructions. Both of those applications work perfectly well with ColdFusion, but are harder to configure and manage than the 3.0 versions discussed here. For more information on configuring IIS or PWS 4.0, check out *Microsoft Internet Information Server 4 For Dummies* by David Angell (published by IDG Books Worldwide, Inc.).

We'll create a virtual directory for ColdFusion development and testing called cftest. To make life easier, we'll use the cftest virtual directory as a nickname for a real directory named c:\cftest on the hard disk. Remember, we can't just refer to the files in that directory in our browser because the Web server looks at files in its webroot by default.

You can choose any names you want for the real and virtual directories, and the names don't have to be the same. Just make sure you remember what you name them!

1. **From the Web server administration page, click the Directories tab.**

   A screen similar to Figure 4-7 appears.

2. **At the bottom of the list of virtual directories, click the Add button to add a new virtual directory.**

   The Directory Properties dialog box appears, as shown in Figure 4-8.

3. **In the Directory box, type the directory where you want to create ColdFusion files.**

   The directory can be an existing directory or a new one. For the example, we entered a directory name of c:\cftest.

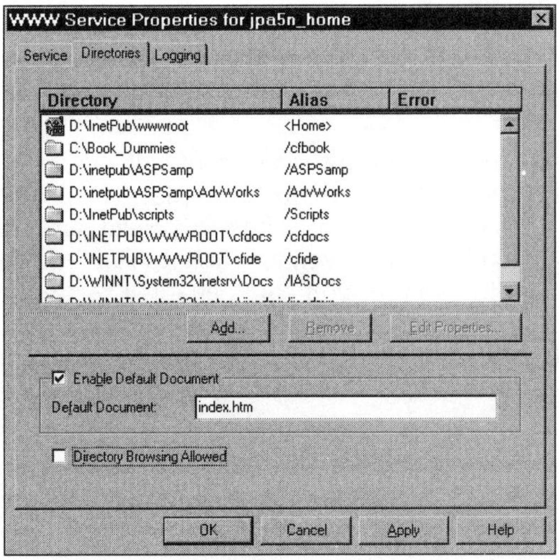

Figure 4-7:
The
Directories
dialog box.

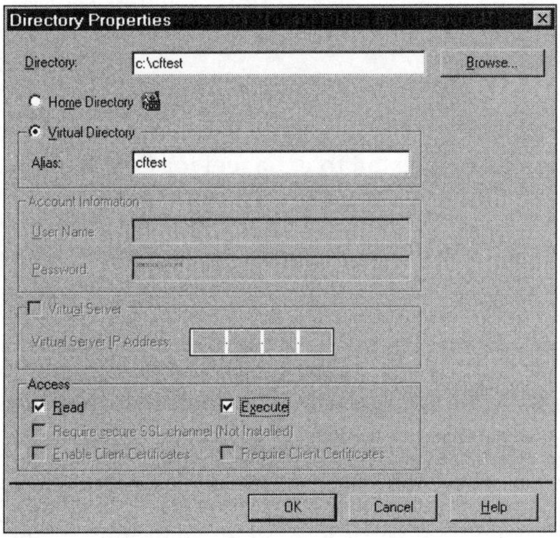

Figure 4-8:
Adding a
new virtual
directory.

4. **If the Virtual Directory option isn't selected already, click to select it.**

5. **In the Alias box, type a nickname for the directory.**

   You can use any alias, or nickname, you want as long as you can remember it! We use cftest throughout the book.

6. **In the Access area, click to select the Read and Execute options.**

   ColdFusion templates, like other server-side scripts, need special permission to run. Read access allows the Web server to display files in the directory, but not to execute programs. Running a script (such as a ColdFusion template) requires Execute permission as well.

7. Click OK.

You just set up a mapping from `http://your.machine.net/cftest` to the `C:\cftest` directory.

You could simply use a subdirectory of the webroot called cftest (`C:\Webshare\wwwroot\cftest` in PWS, for example). The problem with this approach, however, is that the webroot has only Read permission by default, so your ColdFusion templates won't be able to run. You could set the permissions for this one directory, or you could enable Execute permission for the entire webroot directory tree, but that latter approach can cause security risks. You might be able to get away with this arrangement on a development machine, but we suggest that you avoid it if possible.

The Main Dish, Served Cold

After you install your Web server, getting ColdFusion Server on your machine is a piece of cake. For most people, the default installation values work fine, but we walk you through the process just to be sure. Put the CD in your drive and we'll get started.

The *ColdFusion 4 For Dummies* CD contains an evaluation copy of ColdFusion Enterprise Server that you can install to get a feel for ColdFusion. It's located in the cfserver directory on the CD.

You'll encounter few surprises when installing ColdFusion Server. Here's a brief overview:

1. From the CFSERVER directory, run the Setup.exe program.

2. Fill out your name (and organization) in the blanks provided.

3. In the serial number box, leave the word *Evaluation*.

If you're installing a real copy, such as the Personal Edition of ColdFusion Server that comes with ColdFusion Studio or the full-fledged Professional or Enterprise version of ColdFusion Server, your serial number is on the registration card.

4. Choose an installation directory.

The installation directory for ColdFusion Server defaults to C:\cfusion. If your Web server is installed (and by now it should be), it and its root directory are automatically detected.

5. It's okay to put the documentation in the default directory, so accept the default.

6. After choosing the ColdFusion components you want to install, click Continue.

You can uncheck the CFX API and documentation boxes if you need to save room.

You need the ColdFusion program files. The examples are helpful while you're learning ColdFusion and the documentation is handy all the time. The CFXAPI development kit is for creating your own ColdFusion tags using C++, so feel free to uncheck this box if you need to save disk space. Advanced security services provide sophisticated ways to manage application security.

Although the example applications and documentation are useful, you should *not* install them on a machine that will be connected to the Internet due to security risks (the documentation includes executable examples). See the Allaire Security Zone (http://www.allaire.com/security) for more information.

7. When asked, enter a ColdFusion Administrator password.

The password is required to secure the application that manages ColdFusion Server settings, which are discussed in the next section. As long as you remember your password, you can easily change it later.

Make sure you choose a password you can remember. If you forget your password, you have to reinstall ColdFusion Server to reset it.

8. When asked, enter a ColdFusion Studio password.

This password is required to restrict access to your server when it is accessed using ColdFusion Studio. Studio can give a developer virtually free access to any file or data source on the server, so it is essential to protect your server with a password.

9. Select a folder for the ColdFusion icons.

The default is fine. The installation choices you made are displayed in a dialog box for your approval.

10. Click Next.

The installation begins.

11. When instructed, reboot your computer.

When your computer finishes rebooting, ColdFusion Server is running. And your 30-day timer is running if you're using the evaluation copy.

That's all there is to it!

You can verify that everything is working normally by pointing your Web browser to http://your.machine/cfdocs and choosing Test your ColdFusion Installation.

Service with a Smile: Configuring ColdFusion

After you install a Web server and ColdFusion, you can jump in and start building ColdFusion applications. However, you should probably configure a few settings in ColdFusion Server first for optimal performance and to enable certain features. This section introduces ColdFusion Administrator, a Web-based interface for configuring ColdFusion Server.

During installation, the ColdFusion Server 4.5 folder was created and placed on the Start menu. To start ColdFusion Administrator:

1. **Click Start➪Programs➪ColdFusion Server➪ColdFusion Administrator.**

   You are prompted for a password.

2. **Enter the password you created in Step 7 in the preceding section.**

   You are shown the first page of Administrator.

You can set a *lot* of parameters for ColdFusion Server, but we focus on the few that are crucial for getting effective results. The initial ColdFusion Administrator home page is shown in Figure 4-9.

Figure 4-9:
The
ColdFusion
Adminis-
trator is a
ColdFusion
Web
application.

ColdFusion security

The ColdFusion Server software keeps your data and applications as safe as it can. This is true both when anonymous users are accessing ColdFusion Server through the Web and when developers are working on a server with ColdFusion Studio.

IIS manages Web server security in general. You, however, can manage the Administration password and the ColdFusion Studio password using the Basic Security page (Figure 4-10) of ColdFusion Administrator. Make sure that both passwords are enabled by clicking to insert a check mark in the two boxes under Basic Server Security.

To reduce some of the hassle of using passwords on a development machine, you might be tempted to turn off ColdFusion Administration and ColdFusion Studio passwords. If you do this, however, be careful: After you start singing the praises of ColdFusion, someone in your office might begin using ColdFusion Studio too and accidentally delete files or data that are no longer protected. Worse, if your server is connected to the Internet, anyone on the Internet can either access Administrator or use their copy of Studio to access any file on your system!

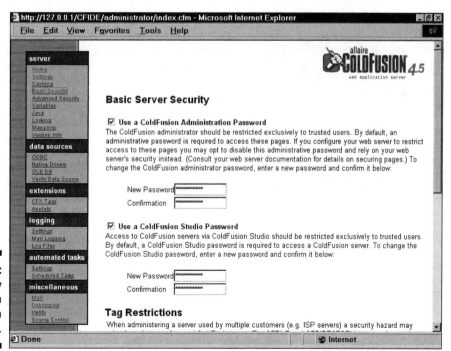

Figure 4-10: Basic security settings in ColdFusion Administrator.

The postcomputer always beeps twice

One neat feature of ColdFusion is how easily it generates and sends e-mail. In Chapter 8, you find out how to use the CFMAIL tag to create templates for generating e-mail. But unless you want to specify a mail server on each use of the CFMAIL tag, make sure that ColdFusion Server knows what mail server to use to send the mail, as follows:

1. **In the ColdFusion Administrator interface, click the Mail option.**

   The Mail option is under the Miscellaneous heading on the menu to the left of the screen. The screen shown in Figure 4-11 appears.

Figure 4-11: Mail settings in ColdFusion Administrator.

2. **In the Mail Server box, enter the address of your SMTP mail server.**

   See the administrator of your mail server for the address. Note that this is *not* an e-mail address, nor is it the mail server where you receive your mail. This should be the IP address or domain name of the outgoing mail (SMTP) server you use. Check with your system administrator or ISP if you're not sure what this setting should be.

3. **Accept the defaults for Server Port and Connection Timeout unless you know you need different settings.**

   You're ready to start using the CFMAIL tag.

Swatting bugs

One of the most important parts of developing applications is getting rid of the bugs. We talk about this process a lot more in Chapter 14, but for now you should enable a few features of ColdFusion Server to make the debugging process easier.

Figure 4-12 shows the debugging page of ColdFusion Administrator. Make sure that all parameters except Enable performance monitoring are checked. By checking the other options, you tell ColdFusion Server to add information to each Web page it processes. This information is invaluable if you need to track down why your application doesn't work as expected.

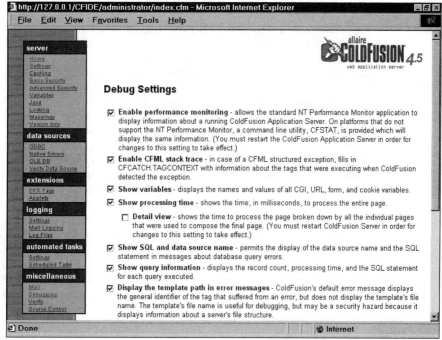

Figure 4-12: Debug settings in ColdFusion Administrator.

If you're on a production machine, make sure that debug information is sent only to the IP addresses of development machines. Otherwise, every visitor to your hot new ColdFusion shopping cart will have a lot of confusing text at the bottom of each ColdFusion page they receive from your server. To limit the IP addresses that receive the debugging info, the Debug page offers a green box in which you can enter addresses. If no addresses are added to the list, all users of the server see debugging info. If even one address is added, only those on that list will see the info.

A Side Order of Data Sources

The final configuration step you need to take care of before getting down to business is introducing ColdFusion to the data files it will be serving. In ColdFusion lingo, database files are *data sources* that need to be *registered* so that ColdFusion Server knows about them. Basically, each data file gets a nickname so that it's easier for you to refer to the data source from ColdFusion.

Data sources are typically database files, but they don't have to be. Any file with a recognized driver can be a data source. Drivers are available for different kinds of spreadsheets, text files, and other types of structured data. (We use *data file* and *database* interchangeably.) A *driver* is a file that provides a way to access a data file through a common protocol.

Windows operating systems are preconfigured with drivers for several common data-oriented applications, including Microsoft Access, dBASE, FoxPro, and Excel. Also, drivers are added when you add new database software to your server or install the Enterprise version of ColdFusion.

The nickname given to each data source points to the essential information an application needs to access the data — file name and location, settings particular to that file, and the driver needed to communicate with the file. The driver handles all communication between requests sent to the data source and the data file, so you don't have to be exposed to the messy details. It's sort of like sending a Christmas list to Santa Claus and getting the presents on Christmas morning — you don't need to know how the list got to him or how he gets the presents to you, you just get the presents!

ColdFusion can understand three types of data sources when provided with the right data source drivers:

- **ODBC data sources** are by far the most common type you'll use. ODBC (Open Database Connectivity) drivers are available for almost all desktop data file formats, including Microsoft Access, FoxPro, Excel, and dBASE. Drivers are available also for most popular enterprise databases, such as Oracle and Microsoft SQL Server. See the sidebar for more information on ODBC.

- **OLE DB data sources** are a newer and in many ways more sophisticated form of driver heavily promoted by Microsoft. These drivers are available mainly for enterprise databases such as Oracle and Ingres. If the driver is well designed, data access through OLE DB is much faster than through ODBC drivers.

- **Native data sources** are drivers that effectively connect ColdFusion directly into the database, which drastically increases performance. The Enterprise version of ColdFusion has native drivers for IBM DB2, Oracle, and Sybase databases.

Can't we all just get along?

The major database vendors jointly developed Open Database Connectivity in the late 1980s and early 1990s in response to repeated pleas for common access to their competing database products. In 1992, ODBC became an international standard for database access. Databases that are accessible in this manner are often called *ODBC compliant.*

ODBC provides an *abstraction layer* between the client application (ColdFusion in our case) and the database that helps hide the quirks of each different product. It provides a large measure of vendor independence for database developers because any ODBC-compliant database can be easily replaced with another.

Although this sounds great and works fine for many projects, vendors have added to their databases proprietary extensions that are not necessarily accessible through ODBC. Therefore, the ODBC standard is more of a lowest common denominator than a universal language.

We focus on ODBC data sources, particularly Microsoft Access. The beauty of data source driver architecture is that after you've prototyped or developed your application using one data source (a Microsoft Access database and its corresponding data source driver), you can easily port the database to a more sophisticated system (such as Microsoft SQL Server or Oracle). You simply convert the database file into the new database format and reconfigure the data source to use a corresponding driver.

An example of creating a data source might help. Suppose you're working on an auction system for your Web site that sells vintage toasters. Because only a few folks are interested in vintage toasters, you know that your database of toasters and customers will be small.

Microsoft Access is inexpensive and easy to work with (and has ODBC drivers available), so you can use it to build a catalog of your toasters. You then create a data source called ToasterAuction from that Access database file and build your interactive e-commerce site using ColdFusion and the ToasterAuction data source.

After a few months of holding auctions, you decide to use your newfound toaster wealth to expand into selling Beanie Babies. Because you'll be immediately swamped with thousands of orders, you need bigger guns than Access, so you upgrade to Microsoft SQL Server. You convert the database file from Access to SQL Server and use ColdFusion Administrator to change the configuration details of the ToasterAuction data source to use the SQL Server driver instead of Access.

That's it. ColdFusion keeps chugging along, oblivious to which database is on the other side of the ODBC wall. Your code still works like a charm because nothing ties it specifically to Access or any other database.

Registering ODBC data sources

ColdFusion Administrator provides the easiest way to create (or *register*) ODBC data sources.

In the following example, you register the database for the toaster auction site discussed in the last section:

1. **Start ColdFusion Administrator from the Windows Start menu.**

   The ColdFusion Administrator home page appears.

2. **In the menu on the far left of the screen, click the ODBC link under data sources.**

3. **In the box under Data Source Name, type a name for the data source (see Figure 4-13).**

   The name must be unique on the machine; duplicate data source names are not allowed. Avoid names such as database, dbfile, and the like. For projects hosted by an ISP, you might want to use the name of the site for the data source name (www.webdatabase.org, for example) or possibly your username on that machine (jsmith, for example). In this example, we use ToasterAuction.

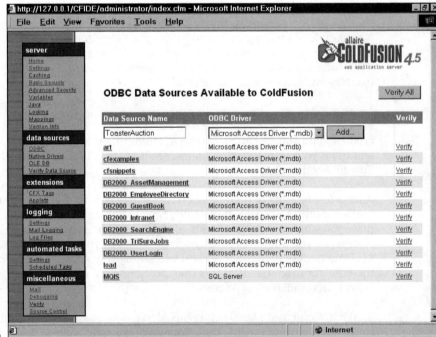

Figure 4-13:
The ColdFusion Administrator screen for adding a data source.

4. **Under ODBC Driver, select the appropriate ODBC driver from the drop-down list.**

   Make sure you select the correct format and version for the database you're using. Otherwise, the driver won't be able to communicate with the data file. We selected Microsoft Access from the list.

5. **Click the Add button.**

   A screen appears with the information needed by the driver you chose in Step 2, as shown in Figure 4-14. We used the fictional Access database name toaster.mdb as an example.

6. **Enter the information requested by the driver.**

   For the Access driver, you need to fill in only the Database File box to get going. Although the driver page varies for each ODBC driver, the broad details are the same. The most important information is the name and location of the database file.

   If you click the Browse Server button for the Database File box and browse to find the database file name and location, you're less likely to make a mistake.

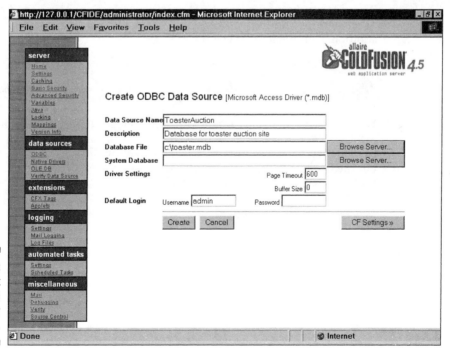

Figure 4-14:
Microsoft
Access
ODBC driver
information.

Note: Do not fill out the System Database box.

If you protected the database with a username or a password or both, you need to enter that information in the Default Login boxes for Username and Password. Otherwise, you must remember to specify these values for any tag in your application that accesses this data source.

Type some text in the Description box, if you want. Leave everything else as is.

7. Click the Create button.

Your data sources appear as in the list in Figure 4-13, but now the word *Verified* is in the rightmost column. If instead the word *Failed* is in the rightmost column, something is wrong with the settings; typically the file name is the problem.

Quick, simple, and easy. If only everything about computers was like this!

You can register ColdFusion ODBC data sources also by using the ODBC icon in the Windows NT Control Panel. (In Windows 95 and 98, it's called 32-bit ODBC Administrator.) You create ColdFusion data sources in the System DSNs (data source names) tab of the ODBC dialog box. Using the ColdFusion Administrator interface, however, is quicker and easier and gives access to additional, optional ColdFusion settings.

Registering other types of data sources

You can use ColdFusion Administrator to configure ODBC data sources for any ODBC driver installed on the server. More advanced users will probably use Microsoft SQL Server fairly frequently, but we'll focus on Access throughout the book because it is easier for new users to deal with and perfect for prototyping ColdFusion applications.

You can use ColdFusion Administrator also to register OLE DB and native driver data sources. This process follows a procedure similar to the one shown in the preceding section. For your first attempts at developing applications with ColdFusion, however, steer towards the ODBC data sources unless you have to choose something else.

Finding Someone to Clean Up

If you're like most people, you'd rather have someone else take care of the server so that you can focus on developing Web database applications. We heartily agree with you! One option is finding someone to host your ColdFusion applications for you.

Dozens, perhaps hundreds, of companies offer ColdFusion hosting services, but finding them is tougher than finding companies that have plain-vanilla Web hosting. Your typical ISP, such as AT&T, Mindspring, Erols, or AOL, might not offer ColdFusion. Those that focus on Web hosting (check the advertisements in trade journals and Web magazines), however, often list ColdFusion support as a standard feature or option.

Allaire provides a database (surprise!) on their Web site that can help you find an ISP that provides ColdFusion hosting. The address for Allaire is

```
http://www.allaire.com/
```

In this section, we discuss pricing, platforms, and everything else you need to know to make wise decisions about hosting ColdFusion applications with an external service provider.

Pricing

For most people looking for a commercial Web hosting company, the bottom line is cost. Because developing databases and developing e-commerce applications are virtually synonymous, few basic Web hosting packages include ColdFusion — it's normally part of the higher-priced business or commerce packages. Monthly costs range from $20 to well over $100.

But the monthly cost isn't the only consideration. Plenty of gotchas can drive the cost up significantly. Here's a rundown of common practices among Web hosting providers:

- ✔ **Data sources.** You normally get one data source with the package. Additional data sources cost more, often on a monthly basis. Setup charges for new data sources can easily be $50 — though you now know that this is hardly justified for the work involved!

- ✔ **Databases.** Maintaining a sophisticated database, such as SQL Server, is more difficult for the ISP and therefore more expensive. Start out with the base-level database (normally Access), but make sure your ISP provides a more advanced database in case you need it later.

- ✔ **Traffic.** Sites with databases can quickly generate more traffic than sites without. For example, if you replace a single page of your toaster auction site with a sophisticated search and order processing system, you might find that your users burn a lot of bandwidth searching your database repeatedly. The time spent developing your Web database application also increases the amount of traffic through your site — another great reason to run your own development server! If your ISP charges for bandwidth, make sure you're ready for the additional cost.

Reporting on traffic

After you have your site up, you'll want to be able to see what kind of traffic you're getting. WebTrends is the industry standard tool for this purpose. It reads the log file that your Web server automatically creates. It gives you comprehensive reports about traffic, most popular and least popular pages, and traffic over an interval of time. You can download a trial version of WebTrends from `www.webtrends.com`.

For most projects, starting with a low-end commerce package with one Access data source is plenty. You can find a host for such a site in the $20 to $95 per month range. Because traditional Web hosting costs $15 to $50 per month for plain HTML, the additional costs are relatively low. More sophisticated packages with multiple data sources and more powerful servers are still in the price range of a few hundred dollars a month, which should be small potatoes compared to the money you're planning on raking in!

Consider, too, that you've avoided the costs of a full-time, high-speed Internet connection, as well as the costs of hiring one or more full-time administrators to deal with the network, the physical server, the Web server, the ColdFusion Server software, and the database server, not to mention the costs of buying all these!

Platforms

Almost all commercial ISPs who offer ColdFusion hosting use Windows NT machines. A few use Solaris. And as versions of ColdFusion come out for Linux and other operating systems traditionally used by ISPs, a wider set of choices will become available.

Unfortunately, you can't use Access or SQL Server databases on any server platform other than Windows NT because no ODBC or native drivers are available for these databases on other platforms.

Note: If you're developing on a UNIX box with a Sybase or an Oracle database, everything in this book still applies to you!

Everything else

You need to be concerned with a few other issues when someone else hosts ColdFusion. These concerns range from the simple-but-annoying to serious obstacles. For example, you probably should check with your ISP about naming conventions for data sources early in the project so you don't have to revise your code if (or more likely, when) the ISP makes you choose a new data source name.

In addition, some tags are powerful enough to compromise security. For that reason, an ISP might decide to disable them. ColdFusion tags of this type are listed in Table 4-2. Make sure your ISP allows the features you need.

Table 4-2	ColdFusion Tags Your ISP Might Disable
Tag	*What It Does*
CFCONTENT	Defines the file name and MIME content type of file to be downloaded to the client
CFDIRECTORY	Manipulates directories
CFFILE	Manipulates files
CFOBJECT	Registers COM and CORBA objects
CFREGISTRY	Creates entries in the server registry

You also need to work with the provider if your code requires third-party ColdFusion tags. Developers have created ColdFusion tags to do neat tasks such as handle cybercash payments and act as complete shopping carts. (In Chapter 16, we tell you about ten of the best third-party tags).

If you plan on using one or more third-party tags, make sure your ISP is amenable to installing them. If they refuse to install the tags for you, you can still install them in the local directory where your code is stored. This can pose a challenge, however, if you plan to share such custom tags among templates in several directories. See the Allaire documentation on CFMODULE for more information.

Part II
Making ColdFusion Do Simple Stuff

The 5th Wave   By Rich Tennant

"I don't care what your E-Mail friends in Europe say, you're not having a glass of Chianti with your bologna sandwich."

In this part . . .

Have you ever wanted to accept data from a form into a database? How about letting a visitor enter search criteria to search your database? Or sending mail to a visitor either in response to a request for a password or as part of a bulk mailing?

In this part, you see how easy it is to use ColdFusion to insert data you've collected into an HTML form in a database. You also find out how simple it is to query the database with criteria the visitor provides and show search results on a page. Then, you discover how effortless it is to create a page that permits a visitor to update the database. Finally, you find out how elementary it is to send mail based on actions taken on a Web page.

This part of this book answers most of your questions about ColdFusion. If this is the good part, you may ask, why three more parts after this one? Good question. This part also raises a lot of questions — questions that we answer later in the book.

The best part about the next four chapters is that you don't need to be a programmer to do any of it. We show you how to perform these four basic tasks — insert, query, update, and send mail — by having you type the code yourself and then by using the wizards in Studio.

Chapter 5

Adding Records to a Database

● ●

In This Chapter

▶ Collecting data for your database

▶ Writing HTML for the form

▶ Sending data to the database

▶ Building the confirmation page

▶ Making record time creating your application using Studio

▶ Viewing the completed example

● ●

*W*hen the Web was young, all Web pages were static. If Web developers wanted to show a list of members, they would post a form that would send them mail whenever a visitor completed the form. Then they'd go back into the members page and add the newest member to the list. Ugh!

Nowadays, collecting information from visitors to your site is much easier. You simply put a few key elements in place, and ColdFusion does all the hard stuff. In this chapter, you see how to design a database, build a form, and hand data off to the ColdFusion server so that the database is updated in real time. We wrote the chapter around a real example, so you can follow along on your keyboard, if you want.

The section near the end of the chapter is dedicated to creating the sample application the fast way with Studio. If you plan on using Studio for your projects, it's still worthwhile to follow the example from the beginning of the chapter rather than simply skipping to the end. That way, you'll get an understanding of the CFML code that Studio generates for you.

Collecting Data

Suppose you need to create a form to collect data from site visitors. Perhaps your form will have some text fields, a few radio buttons, and a select list asking where the visitor heard about your site. Will your form pose an open-ended question? If so, a text-area field gives visitors all the space they need to write their answers.

Planning

"Measure twice, cut once," declares the carpenter's creed. If only Web developers were patient enough to keep their hands off the keyboard long enough to *think* about what they want to see before they begin putting fields or words on the screen.

Before you start clicking those form-field creating buttons in Studio or typing the HTML for fields, stop and think about what type of data you need. Do you really need the visitor's fax number, for example? People are nervous about giving away personal data — so nervous, in fact, that an entire industry has grown around the issue of privacy on the Web. If you don't have plans for using particular data, don't ask for it.

Ask your visitors for only what you need, tell them exactly how you will use the information you collect, and use it only as you say you will.

Setting the record straight

For the example in this chapter, we look at a site that boasts an online column entitled *Setting the Record Straight (STRS)*, which resides on a site of the same name. This site would like to get the following information from its visitors:

- ✔ Age
- ✔ Sex
- ✔ Zip code
- ✔ Political self-identification
- ✔ Voting pattern
- ✔ Hobbies and interests
- ✔ Suggestions for future topics

By collecting the visitor's age, sex, and zip code, the site can market itself to advertisers.

Zip code data is remarkably accurate in providing income estimates — far more accurate than asking people to tell you how much they make. (They tend to round up by a long shot.)

The visitor's political self-identification and voting pattern help the site understand what type of reader is visiting. Finally, by asking visitors about hobbies and interests as well as topic suggestions, we can deliver columns of interest to the current site visitor. Now that we've identified all the required data, it's time to look at the database.

Privacy, please!

Should there be a law against asking for personal information on the Web? Should minors have to get their parents' permission before completing an online form? The Federal government (also known as Uncle Sam) is concerned about all the data that's being collected and how it's being used. A survey of 1,400 commercial Web sites in 1998 revealed that only 14 percent had stated privacy policies.

It's difficult to say to what extent the Federal government will get involved in determining the types of information you can request and how you can use it, but it's a near certainty that the Feds will take some action at least with respect to Web sites that cater to children, requiring that the sites instruct minors to get parental permission before disclosing personal data. Al Gore is lobbying for a system under which all sites for

kids will have a link to a site where parents can learn more about keeping their children safe online. Legitimate Web-based businesses have already heeded the warnings and have clear, easy-to-find privacy policies on their sites.

A few organizations on the Web are capitalizing on the hysteria that surrounds the privacy issue. Two of the biggies are TrustE and BBBOnLine, which you can find at www.truste.org and www.bbbonline.org, respectively. With both these organizations, if you pay a fee, submit your published privacy proposal to them for review, and agree to undergo unannounced data audits by them, you can post their membership seal on your site. They monitor members to ensure that members comply with their own stated privacy policies.

Designing and creating a database

How are you storing the data you collect? Before you can even tell ColdFusion to store data somewhere, you need to have your database ready to accept data. This isn't the place for a lengthy discussion of relational database theory (we saw that yawn), so we'll keep it brief. You need at least one table and at least as many fields (columns) in your table as you have questions on your page.

Your database might have more fields than you have questions on your page because some of your questions might have more than one answer. In the STRS example, the hobbies and interests question permits visitors to indicate more than one value.

You need to decide how to tell the visitor about completing the form and whether you want each value (answer) to correspond with its own question or many values to correspond with a single question.

We recommend that you start by thinking about how you want to report your data. Whether you want to report data on a Web page (as in Chapter 6), on paper for your manager, or electronically to your customer-profile database, a clear idea about how the data will be used goes a long way toward getting the page — and the database — right the first time. And getting it right the first time goes a long way toward making you look smart to your boss or client.

In the STRS example, we want to report some data to the Web site in the form of survey results. Specifically, we'll report some of the demographic data (age and sex), the political self-identification information, and voting behavior. Because we know that readers of this site are politically involved, showing new visitors the demographics of regular visitors will help newcomers feel like they're part of the gang.

Tracking and reporting that level of personal detail is a double-edged sword: Some visitors might be put off by it.

We aggregate the zip code and hobbies and interests data. Suggestions, which are provided in a suggestions box, are printed or e-mailed to the people who publish the STRS site. We use an Access database created by choosing New Table in design view. Up next, the details of the database fields.

Field-naming rules

Database column names are referenced as *variables* in your ColdFusion code. Therefore, for your database to work seamlessly with ColdFusion, your field names must comply with the following ColdFusion restrictions:

- Field names can't contain spaces or hyphens (-).
- Field names must start with a letter and can contain underscores (_) to separate words. In general, stick to letters, numbers, and underscores.
- Field names can't be the same as any ColdFusion function name, CFML tag name, or other reserved word. For example, don't call your date field by that name; you could call it creation_date instead.

ColdFusion uses form fields that end in _date or _required, for example, to imply data validation. (You find out more in the "Rudimentary field validation" section later in this chapter.) Although this might not be so bad, fields with the _date validation are also converted to an ODBC Datetime format automatically, which you might not expect. Worst of all, the CFINSERT and CFUPDATE tags (also discussed later in this chapter) are designed to not process fields that use those suffixes. Therefore, when a field with one of these suffixes appears on a form, the data entered is not inserted or updated in the database. It's wise to avoid using those suffixes when creating column names, perhaps using date_created instead. See Chapter 13 for more on data validation.

Relational database design

If you've ever worked with relational databases, you've probably thrown down this book in disgust already! The example in this chapter doesn't comply with good database design, and we know it. This book is about ColdFusion. If you don't know database design, we encourage you to read a book dedicated to that purpose, such as *Database Design for Mere Mortals* by Michael J. Hernandez (published by Addison Wesley Developer's Press).

If you want to make the example in this chapter follow good database design principals (and we encourage you to do so after you do it the simple way), read on.

Two fields in our database, the `self_id` field and the field for hobbies and interests, lend themselves to restructuring. They each introduce different ways we could streamline things using multiple tables.

For `self_id`, you would probably want to store all the possible self-identification values in a separate table (called `Self_ID`) and then use the key for each value as the value of the `self_id` field in the survey table. That makes the self_id key the *foreign key* of the survey table. With our five or six possible `self_id` fields, it's not too taxing to remember which value is associated with which type of self-iden-

tification, but it will be much easier to remember and to report from the database if another table translates the `self_id` values into English.

In the database in this example, 12 fields are dedicated to hobbies and interests. That's not good design because if we want to add a thirteenth, or a thirtieth, we have to change the table. A better design is to create two new tables. The first is a simple table with a key value and the name of the hobby or interest. The second is a table that simply ties the `survey` table to the hobbies and interests table. That table might be called `survey2hobby`. It would have one column for the key field in the `survey` table and one column for the key field in the `hobby` table. You could have many entries in the `survey2hobby` table for each survey because a respondent probably has more than one interest or hobby.

So, then, why didn't we do it the right way? This chapter is about CFINSERT. To implement this example with four tables using proper relational database design rather than just the one table we used, we couldn't use CFINSERT.

After you find out more about CFQUERY (in Chapter 12), you might want to return to this chapter and redo the example.

✔ Use descriptive names, but don't be too terse or too verbose. Calling a field x saves you a few keystrokes now but will give you trouble in six months, when you're trying to remember what you meant by x. On the other hand, calling a field `profession` probably isn't any more descriptive than calling it `prof`.

Planning our fields

In the following list, we describe the data types for the fields in our STRS site:

- ✔ `age` is a byte-sized (0–255) numeric text-entry field.

- ✔ `sex` is a one-character field (`F` is female; `M` is male).

- ✔ `zip` is a text-entry field that can contain up to ten numbers (and a hyphen).

- ✔ `self_id` is a byte-sized numeric field with each value in our select list (Monarchist, Conservative, Republican, and so on) associated with a number in our table (0, 1, 2, and so on, respectively). We'll create another table in the database so that we can tie the numbers to the values we use on our page.

- ✔ `voter` is a simple yes-or-no question: Do you vote regularly? It is a Boolean (votes regularly is `TRUE`, or 1, for our purposes).

- ✔ **Hobbies and interests** is more than one field. We'll provide a checklist of hobbies and interests, as follows: `Politics`, `History`, `War`, `Current_Events`, `Foreign_Policy`, `Foreign_Affairs`, `Travel`, `Judiciary`, `Sports`, `Regulation`, and `Environment`. We then ask whether the visitor has this hobby or interest, and we store the answer for each hobby or interest in a Boolean field (where "this is a hobby or interest" is `TRUE`).

The design of the previous set of fields is not optimal. Ideally, we'd store the actual words for the hobbies and interests in a separate table and then use only the key values of those words in our primary table. However, in the interest of staying focused on ColdFusion and not getting lost in database design, we've elected to sacrifice good database design for a simpler example.

- ✔ `Suggestions` is a memo field, and it holds whatever the visitor types.

Additionally, you might want some standard database fields, such as the following:

- ✔ **A primary key**. The key uniquely identifies this record within this table. Typically, the database assigns the key (using an autonumber, an identity field, or a sequence, depending on the database), so you don't need to worry about making sure that it's unique. Normally, you won't need to use the key outside the database. If you choose for a record some key other than the one that the database assigns, such as last name, you run the risk of having more than one record with the same value. The example in this chapter doesn't have a primary key because we have no need to get at any individual record later to make updates.

✔ Creation **date**. You might want to be able to report how many people completed the survey on a given day (perhaps as a result of advertising). You can either send date and time data with the rest of the data for ColdFusion to insert into the database or let your database insert the data when it creates a new record. In the example in this chapter, we told Access to add a datestamp and timestamp whenever a record is added.

If your database doesn't allow you to datestamp or timestamp fields, you can let ColdFusion timestamp a record on insertion. When using CFINSERT or CFUPDATE (in 4.01 or higher), you can define a form field with the name of a table column that will hold a date or time, and you can store a special value for the field on the form: currentdate() or currentdatetime(). Note that you do *not* wrap the tags in pound signs in the form. The tags are special string values interpreted during CFINSERT or CFUPDATE on the action page. And more importantly, the values are computed at the time of the insert or update, which is usually what you want. This is documented in only the 4.0.1 documentation update page (not in the CFML reference for the tags). Also, the doc doesn't mention the existence of currentdatetime(), but testing showed that it worked as expected.

✔ Deleted. We don't need a deleted field in the example, but if we were collecting membership data, we'd have to give our members a way to remove themselves from our membership roles. By having a *deleted flag* in the database, we could keep their data for historical, tracking, or logging reasons, but avoid counting them and reporting on them as members. If we were going to have a deleted flag in the database, we'd also want a *date and time deleted* field so that we'd know when they had signed off.

To follow along with the example in the chapter, you can create a table in Access with the fields shown in Table 5-1.

Table 5-1	Field Definitions for the Survey Table in the STRS Database		
Field name	**Field type**	**Length (If Applicable)**	**Notes (If Applicable)**
age	Numeric	Byte	
sex	Text	1	M/F
zip	Text	10	
self_id	Number	Byte	0 to 5 based on response to Select list

(continued)

Table 5-1 *(continued)*

Field name	Field type	Length (If Applicable)	Notes (If applicable)
voter	Boolean		Y/N
Politics	Boolean		Y/N
History	Boolean		Y/N
War	Boolean		Y/N
Current_Events	Boolean		Y/N
Foreign_Policy	Boolean		Y/N
Foreign_Affairs	Boolean		Y/N
Travel	Boolean		Y/N
Judiciary	Boolean		Y/N
Sports	Boolean		Y/N
Regulation	Boolean		Y/N
Environment	Boolean		Y/N
Suggestions	Memo		
Creation	Date/time		Automatically populated by Access

Creating a form to collect data

Finally, with all our planning out of the way (phew!), we can determine how we want to request information from site visitors. We'll create the following types of fields:

- **Text,** to accept text answers such as age and zip
- **Select list,** to give the visitor a choice of answers such as self-id
- **Check box,** to ask yes-or-no questions such as "Do you vote regularly?"
- **Radio buttons,** to ask questions with mutually exclusive answers, such as "Sex: male or female?"
- **Text area,** to accept long answers such as suggestions

Rudimentary field validation

Many times, you'll want *required fields* on your form. For example, you might require an account ID if you're creating an account for a visitor. HTML provides no way to ensure that data is entered in a given form field, but this is an area where ColdFusion shines. It's easy to create a required field or to validate data to ensure, for example, that visitors enter numbers into a numeric field.

ColdFusion can perform five types of server-side data validation:

- **Required**. Verify that some data is entered into a field.
- **Integer**. Verify that the data supplied is an integer.
- **Float**. Verify that the data supplied is a number that may contain a decimal point.
- **Range**. Verify that the data supplied is within a certain range.
- **Date and Time.** Verify that the data supplied is a valid date, or time, or both.

ColdFusion validates any fields for which you requested validation after the visitor clicks the submit button. If any fields fail validation, the visitor sees an error page with error messages for all fields that failed.

You can create custom error messages for each field. Providing good error messages will help visitors complete the form correctly.

You indicate to ColdFusion that you want field validation by including hidden fields in your form. The following creates a form field called `age` that's both required and required to be between 1 and 112:

```
<FORM action="process.cfm" method="post">
<INPUT type="text" name="age" size="5">
<INPUT type="hidden" name="age_required" value="Please enter
        your age.">
<INPUT type="hidden" name="age_range" value="Min=1 Max=112">
<INPUT atype="submit">
</FORM>
```

When used in an INPUT tag in this sort of hidden field validation, the `value` attribute, with one exception, holds a friendly error message that ColdFusion displays to the visitor if the value entered is invalid. The exception is range validation, in which case the `value` attribute is `Min=x Max=y`, where `x` and `y` are the limits of the range. See Chapter 13 for more information on validating form data.

Although you can control the message displayed for a given field's validation, you can't modify the page on which validation errors are displayed to list a help desk number, for instance, or use some standard site color or background. But you can create your own template to hold that sort of modified error page using the CFERROR tag. See the Allaire documentation for more information.

Producing the HTML for the Form

Creating forms isn't trivial, so we'll run through the HTML for the form and each form field. The FORM tag is necessary, and directs the results from this page to the page indicated in the `action` attribute for processing.

```
<FORM action="process-query.cfm" method="POST">
...enter fields here...
</FORM>
```

The various form-control fields must go between the FORM tag and the end-FORM tag. Notice the use of `method="post"` in the FORM tag. This is required to properly submit the form data fields for processing and is discussed further in "Handing Data to the Database," later in this chapter.

Input text boxes

To collect the visitor's age, use the INPUT tag:

```
<INPUT type="Text" name="age">
```

The `type` must be set to `Text` so that we see a standard data-entry field on the screen. Note that the value of the `name` attribute is `age`. The value of the `name` attribute must match the name of the field in our database; otherwise, we have to do a lot more work to get the data into the database on the processing page.

To collect the sex, we use two radio buttons. Here goes:

```
<INPUT type="Radio" name="sex" value="M">
<INPUT type="Radio" name="sex" value="F">
```

Here's what these lines of code do:

- The `type` is set to `Radio` in both buttons. This gives us two radio buttons right next to each other. We could add HTML formatting to get them to appear on top of each other instead.

✔ The `name` is set to `sex` for both radio buttons. If you want the radio buttons to be a set (that is, you want them to provide alternate values for a single field), make sure the names are the same in all radio buttons. The values of the attributes are not case sensitive.

✔ The `value` is set to M for the first radio button and to F for the second. We've already decided for the database that M is male and F is female. If we sent the words *male* and *female,* the database would choke because we told it to make `sex` a one-character field.

Unless you provide labels for your input fields, only the fields will appear on the page, without any indication to visitors as to what type of data you'd like them to enter. Be sure to provide a label for each field. The label can be any sort of text, in any format. The complete set of code for this example is at the end of the chapter, with the HTML you need to label the fields and create some nice formatting.

The `zip` field is similar to the `age` field — but it's less likely to have understated values! It's a text-input field:

```
<INPUT type="Text" name="Zip">
```

In this code, note the following:

✔ The `type` is Text because we want to permit visitors to enter their own zip code.

✔ The field name is `zip` to match the field name in the database.

Drop-down select lists

For the `self_id` field, we let the visitor select from a list. A select list has two parts: the SELECT tag, and the OPTION tags:

```
<SELECT name="self_id">
    <OPTION value="0">Monarchist
    <OPTION value="1">Conservative
    <OPTION value="2">Republican
    <OPTION value="3">Moderate
    <OPTION value="4">Independent
    <OPTION value="5">Liberal
    <OPTION value="6">Democrat
</SELECT>
```

Note the following about this SELECT tag:

✔ The name on the SELECT tag must match the field name in the database. Notice that the field name contains an underscore.

Underscores (_) are okay; hyphens (-) aren't.

✔ The OPTION tags correspond directly to what appears in the select list. In the case of this select list, seven items are in the list.

✔ The `value` attribute is optional. It's necessary only if you want a different value to be stored in the database from the value on the screen or if the value listed on the screen has a space.

In our example, we could have left out the `value` attribute, giving us the following:

```
<OPTION>Monarchist
<OPTION>Conservative
<OPTION>Republican
<OPTION>Moderate
<OPTION>Independent
<OPTION>Liberal
<OPTION>Democrat
```

Because we wanted to pass to the database a number instead of a text string, we provide the `value` attribute with the correct number for each text string.

You must put quotation marks around the value of the `value` attribute. If you don't and the value contains a space, you'll get unexpected results — and unexpected results are never good.

We might also want to get this list of option names and values from a lookup table in our database. That's something we could do with CFOUTPUT or even more easily with CFSELECT, which is discussed in Chapter 13.

Check boxes

For the "votes regularly" question, we want to ask a yes-or-no question: Do you vote regularly? The easiest way to ask a yes-or-no question is with a check box:

```
<INPUT type="Checkbox" name="voter">
```

The following items are worth noting about this INPUT tag:

✔ The type is Checkbox because we want a check box on the screen.

✔ The name is voter to match the Boolean field in the database.

> ✔ Because we don't want the voter box to be checked when the page loads, we don't need a `checked` attribute.

> ✔ We don't have to set the `value` attribute because the browser automatically sends on for a checked check box, which equates to `TRUE`, or 1.

The next group of fields contains a list of interests and hobbies, each of which is basically a yes-or-no question ("Are you interested in ...?"). We make a check box for each, as follows:

```
<INPUT type="Checkbox" name="politics"> Politics<br>
<INPUT type="Checkbox" name="history"> History<br>
<INPUT type="Checkbox" name="war"> War<br>
<INPUT type="Checkbox" name="current_events"> Current
        Events<br>
<INPUT type="Checkbox" name="foreign_policy"> Foreign
        Policy<br>
<INPUT type="Checkbox" name="foreign_affairs"> Foreign
        Affairs<br>
<INPUT type="Checkbox" name="travel"> Travel<br>
<INPUT type="Checkbox" name="judiciary"> Judiciary<br>
<INPUT type="Checkbox" name="sports"> Sports<br>
<INPUT type="Checkbox" name="regulation"> Regulation<br>
<INPUT type="Checkbox" name="environment"> Environment<br>
```

The only point to note here is that the check box names match the field names in our database. Again, if a given choice is checked, it will pass an on value that is stored as 1 for the table column of the same name.

Text-area fields

The suggestions box has to be a text-area field:

```
<TEXTAREA name="suggestions" cols="60" rows="4"
        wrap="VIRTUAL">Enter your suggestion here.
</TEXTAREA>
```

Note the following about the TEXTAREA tag:

> ✔ The `name` matches our database field name; case doesn't matter.

> ✔ The `cols` attribute indicates the number of columns on the screen that you want for the suggestions box. A column is measured in characters, so a `cols` value of 60 means the column fits 60 characters across.

> ✔ The `rows` attribute tells the browser how many rows of text should be visible at once; we chose to show 4.

More relational database design issues

If you were to use the relational database design suggestions mentioned in the previous sidebar in this chapter, you'd be able to use a simple ColdFusion query to extract the list of check boxes that we've hardcoded. If you named your table hobby, as we suggested, and made it two columns wide — the first column for the key (called hobby_ID) and the second column for the text name of the hobby or interest (called hobby_name) — the following would produce the check box list on your page:

```
<CFQUERY name="gethobbies"
    datasource="STRS">
    Select * from hobby
</CFQUERY>
<CFOUTPUT query="gethobbies">
<INPUT type="checkbox"
    name="hobby_name"
    value="hobby_ID">
    #hobby_name#<BR>
</cfoutput>
```

One advantage of this approach is that you have less to type. Another advantage is that if the list of hobbies changes, you need to change only the data in the hobby table, not the code on the page or the database structure.

When you assign multiple check boxes to the same variable name, a comma-delimited string of values is sent to the processing page. You need to parse the values from the string, which might look like this (depending on what hobbies the visitor checked):

```
Hobby=travel,sports
```

Again, if you use this now to collect the data, you're not going to be able to use the CFINSERT tag that this chapter discusses, but your application will be more scalable. We recommend that you follow the simple application for now, knowing that the database design is not optimal. Then, when you've mastered CFQUERY and SQL, come back and do it the better way.

✔ The wrap attribute tells the browser to take care of line wrapping for visitors so that their typing doesn't scroll off the right side of the page. Setting wrap to virtual is good because the browser won't insert any line feeds or carriage returns at the end of each line. If we had set the wrap attribute to physical, the browser would insert both a carriage return and a line feed at the end of each line of text, which we'd have to remove when we processed the text.

✔ The text we provided, "Enter your suggestion here," gives on-screen instructions to the visitor. To enter text, the visitor must first delete the text we provided. Also, if the visitor doesn't enter anything, "Enter your suggestion here" is written to the database, which wastes space. For those reasons, some people don't like to put text in the text-area fields.

Be careful to specify the wrap=virtual option if you want that behavior. Internet Explorer works as if you included the option, whether you really did or not. If you don't include wrap=virtual in Netscape, however, the program works as if you specified wrap=off.

Finally, the following text appears in the suggestions box when visitors load the page:

```
Enter your suggestion here.
```

Visitors can then type over the text with their suggestions.

Submit and reset buttons

To make the form do anything, you must at the very least include a submit button. Most forms also include a reset button. We include both:

```
<INPUT type="Submit" value="submit">
<INPUT type="Reset" value="Clear the Form">
```

Note the following about the submit and reset buttons just defined:

- ✔ The `type` is set to either `Submit` or `Reset`. `Submit` sends the data from the form to the server (based on the `action` attribute of the form field). `Reset` clears the fields in the form on the page, without submitting the form.

- ✔ In the `value` attribute, you set what you want to appear on the button. The defaults are Submit Query and Reset, which the user would find unclear. We named the first button *submit* and the second one *Clear the Form*. Although you can do fancier stuff, such as using graphics for buttons, remember that most visitors know what to do when they see standard buttons and might be confused with something new.

Handing Data to the Database

Now that we've defined our data requirements, created a database to hold our data, created a form to accept the data on the page, and created an ODBC data source, we're ready to hand over the data we've collected to the database.

When the form is submitted, the form's action page is processed. The action page is typically specified to be a different page than the one into which the visitor enters data. Figure 5-1 shows the processing cycle, including data validation.

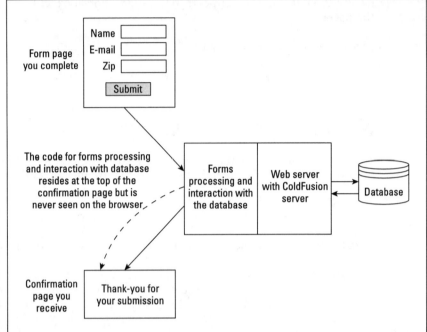

Figure 5-1:
How data is
processed
through
your
pages in
ColdFusion.

Creating the form

For your forms page to find your processing page, the `action` statement on your FORM tag must be correct. The FORM tag includes the information that tells the server *where* to send the data it collects. It also tells the server *how* to send it. For our example survey form, the FORM tag reads as follows:

```
<FORM action="process-survey.cfm" method="post">
```

Where you send your data is the first attribute you set in your FORM tag. The page to which you send your form for processing is typically a ColdFusion page (.cfm) elsewhere on your site. In our example, that page is called `process-survey.cfm`.

The other attribute that's required in the FORM tag is `method`. Using `post` as the `method` for sending the results of your form page to the processing page is standard. The disadvantage of `get`, the other `method`, is that the form data is sent as a query string that appears to the user in the browser's location window, which can reveal more information than you care to share. There is also a limit to how much data you pass that way. The `post` method overcomes these problems.

Processing the form

The action against the database, in this case the insertion of a record into the database, occurs when the processing page loads. By the time the user sees the results of the processing page, ColdFusion Server has already performed its magic.

The simplest way to tell the server to insert data is with the following statement:

```
<CFINSERT datasource="strs"
     tablename="survey">
```

In our example, the data source is STRS. We don't have to tell ColdFusion anything more about the database, such as what the underlying application is or where to find the file, because our server has an ODBC entry for STRS. In the second line, we have to tell ColdFusion which table to take action against because a database can have more than one table.

Notice that we don't need to list the form fields (from the previous page) holding data to be entered into the database. CFINSERT's magic is that it automatically enters all the fields in the form, as long as each form field name matches a column name in the named table.

CFINSERT

We can give the database additional information about our data using attributes of the CFINSERT tag. The CFINSERT tag takes many attributes, but under normal circumstances, the `tablename` and `datasource` attributes are the only two you need. If you need to insert into your database only a subset of the fields for which you collect data on your form page, include the `formfields` attribute.

Up next is the complete CFINSERT tag definition:

```
<CFINSERT
datasource="datasource_name"
tablename="table_name"
formfields="field1, field2, ...">
username="username"
password="password"
tableowner="owner"
tablequalifier="table_qualifier"
dbtype="type"
dbserver="server_name"
dbname="database_name"
provider="text"
providerdsn="datasource_name">
```

datasource	**Required.** The data source name for the database on which you are performing your query. (See Chapter 4 for more on data sources.)
tablename	**Required.** The name of the table into which you are inserting data.
formfields	**Optional.** The list of form fields from the form page that should be used for the insertion. If you're collecting any other data, have named your buttons (shown later), or are sending any hidden fields that are not in the table, you need to specify which fields to insert. The values used are those in the form fields of the same name. If you don't include the formfields attribute, ColdFusion assumes that every form field equates to the name of a column in the named table and should be inserted. If you list the specific fields you want inserted, the key for the table must be in the list.
username	**Optional.** If your database is password protected, you must provide the username and password, either here or in the datasource definition. (You have to go out of your way to password-protect a database un Access, and the process is beyond the scope of this book to explain.)
password	**Optional.** Goes with username, if your database is password protected.
tableowner	**Optional.** The owner of the table.
table-qualifier	**Optional.** The qualifier of the table.
dbtype	**Optional.** Unless you're using a native driver for your database, don't use this one. You can set it to ODBC (the default) if you're not, but if your ColdFusion Server (or the one at your ISP or WPP) is not ColdFusion 4, the tag will fail. If you're using a native driver, you'll find that using the appropriate dbtype will give you faster queries than using an ODBC connection.
dbserver	**Optional.** If you defined the dbtype to be a native driver, you can use this to override the server specified in the datasource definition.
dbname	**Optional.** The database name when dbtype=sybase11 or oledb, overriding that specified in datasource.

> *provider*   **Optional.** The COM provider (for OLE-DB only).
>
> *provider-dsn* Optional. The data source name for the COM provider (for OLE-DB only).

Specifying fields with CFINSERT

Someday, you might want to pass a number of form fields into the processing page, and then take one of a number of different paths through the processing page based on the value of one or more variables. Consider the logic in Figure 5-2.

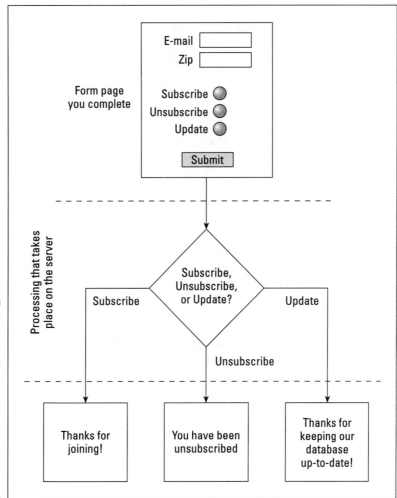

Figure 5-2: The logic behind a page that requires one of three types of processing, based on how the form is completed.

Based on the value returned by the set of radio buttons shown in Figure 5-2, one of three actions is taken against the database:

- ✓ **New record inserted.** If the visitor clicks the radio button for subscribing to the list, all the fields are inserted into the database.

- ✓ **Existing record marked as unsubscribed.** If the visitor clicks the radio button for unsubscribing to the list, different statements are processed: (1) to identify that the person is, indeed, already subscribed; (2) to ensure that the person has provided enough information to confirm his or her identify; and (3) to ensure that the unsubscribed flag is updated to TRUE.

- ✓ **Existing record updated with new data.** If the visitor clicks the radio button for updating data, a different statement is processed to ensure that the person is as identified and that the data in the database is updated with the data provided.

Using the branched logic described in the preceding list, the CFINSERT tag as used for the STRS example would fail. Why? It would fail because one of the fields being passed, the `action` field, is not a field in the database. To get the CFINSERT tag to work, we must add an additional attribute, as shown in the following code:

```
<CFINSERT datasource="membership"
    table="members"
    formfields="age, sex, zip, self_id, voter, politics,
        self_id, voter, politics, history, war,
        current_events, foreign_policy, foreign_affairs,
        travel, judiciary, sports, regulation, environment,
        suggestions">
```

CFINSERT is the easy way ColdFusion gives you to update a database without having to know SQL. To see how to insert data into the database with CFQUERY, check out Chapter 12.

Creating the Confirmation Page

After the form fields are processed, the page containing the processing CFML is displayed. What will your visitors see?

You can handle what is commonly referred to as the *confirmation page* in two ways. One is to display a thank-you message on a page (didn't your mother tell you to always send a thank-you note when someone gave you something?) and require that the visitor click something to return to the part of the site from whence he or she came.

The other way to handle the confirmation page is to put ColdFusion on a processing page that is never seen, and then route visitors to either the page from which they came when they entered the survey page or the confirmation page you'd like them to see now. (Perhaps the visitor just registered to use your site and you want to take him or her to the members-only home page.) Figure 5-3 shows the processing alternatives for the confirmation page.

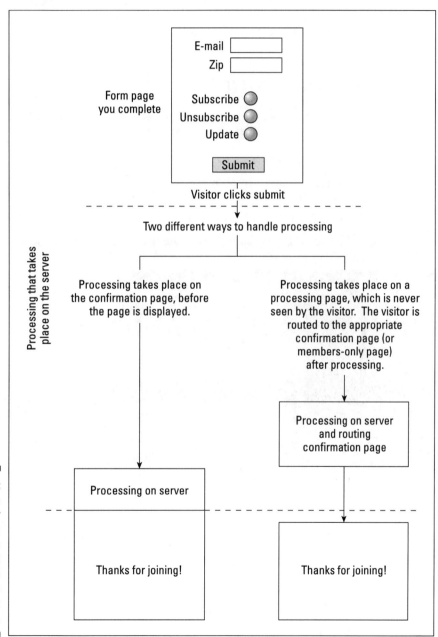

Figure 5-3: Some options for handling form processing and displaying a confirmation page.

Special Section: Studio

With Studio, building a method to show and process a form as in our STRS example is simple. In this section, we show how you can ask Studio to create two pages. The first holds the form fields; the second takes action against the database to insert a new record into the database.

The Data Entry Wizard

Now comes the easy part: creating the data-entry form and action page. It's easy because Studio does all the work for you:

1. **Click File⊃New.**

   Notice the four tabs shown at the top of the dialogue: HTML, DHTML, CFML, and Custom.

2. **From the CFML tab, select Data Entry Wizard and then click OK.**

   You see the first dialog box in the wizard, as shown in Figure 5-4.

Figure 5-4:
In Step 1 of the Data Entry Wizard, you give your form a name and instruct Studio where to save the files it generates.

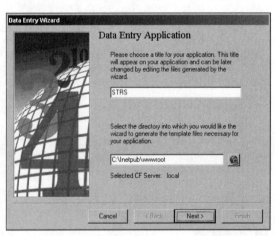

3. **In the first text box, give your form a title. In the second box, type where you want the files saved.**

   The wizard creates files with names beginning with the title you specify, and it creates them in the directory you specify. You should tell the wizard to save the files to the same directory that you configured Studio to use when you set up the development mappings. Please see Chapter 2 for details. Otherwise, be sure to specify a directory in the webroot.

4. Click Next.

You see the second dialog box of the wizard, as shown in Figure 5-5.

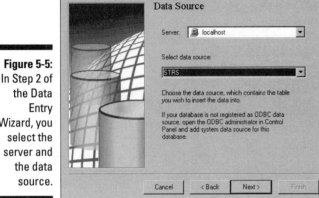

Figure 5-5:
In Step 2 of
the Data
Entry
Wizard, you
select the
server and
the data
source.

5. In the first drop-down list, select your RDS server. In the second drop-down list, select the data source on that server for which you want to create a data-entry form.

6. Click Next.

You see the third dialog box of the wizard, as shown in Figure 5-6.

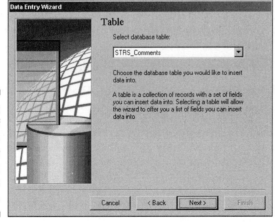

Figure 5-6:
In Step 3 of
the Data
Entry
Wizard, you
select the
table.

7. In the drop-down list, select the table for which you want ColdFusion Server to build the data-entry application.

8. Click Next.

The last dialog box of any importance in the wizard appears, as shown in Figure 5-7.

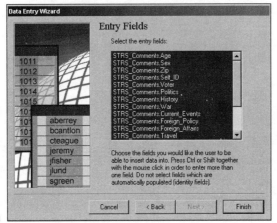

Figure 5-7:
In Step 4 of
the Data
Entry
Wizard, you
select fields.

9. Select all the fields that you'd like included in the form.

Chances are that if you have a primary key field, you don't want that in the form. You also might not want to include a deleted flag or a deleted date field if you have those. If you have a creation date field, it's best to populate that yourself, so leave that field off the list as well.

To select more than one field, hold down the Ctrl key and click each field individually. Or you can hold down the Shift key and click the first and last fields you want included, and then use Ctrl+click to deselect any fields you don't want included.

10. When you're satisfied with the list, click Finish.

The Wizard output summary screen appears, as shown in Figure 5-8.

11. Read the summary.

Because the wizard is creating only two screens, which is what you were expecting, you won't find anything earth-shattering here. The first file has the form. The second file does the processing. Take note of the file names.

12. Click Close.

That's the end of the magic. Take a look at your form page in browse view of the editor pane. The bare-bones form for STRS is in Figure 5-9.

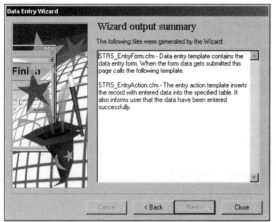

Figure 5-8:
This screen
tells you
what files
you can
expect to
see in your
directory
and what
they do.

Figure 5-9:
The form
that Studio
produced
for the STRS
example.

You or any of your visitors can view the results in any browser by entering the URL of your site and the appropriate directory and file name for the form file created by the wizard.

You still have to modify the HTML so that the page matches the rest of your site. In addition, you probably want to change the caption for each field because Studio defaults to the field name, which doesn't always give the visitor enough information. Studio also sets the `size` attribute of any text-input field to the width of its corresponding column in the database, which means some of those fields might be longer than you want.

To view the processing/acknowledgment page, you must complete the form in browse view of the editor pane and then click the submit button. As you can see in Figure 5-10, the wizard gives you useful results for debugging, but visitors probably don't need to see the values they just typed in. A thank-you message or directions as to what else they might find interesting in your site would be more appropriate.

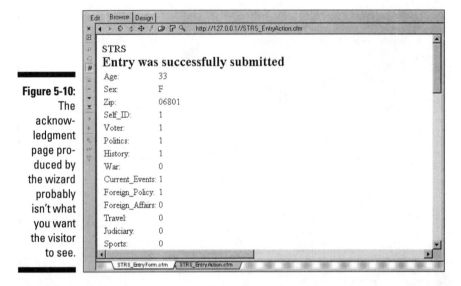

Figure 5-10: The acknowledgment page produced by the wizard probably isn't what you want the visitor to see.

Take a look now at the entry-action page's code in the Editor tab of the editor pane. The CFML Studio generated to act on the database is at the very top. It's exactly what we wrote on our own previously in the chapter. Most of what Studio has given you is a lot of HTML as well as interaction with the database — Studio is copying the field names directly from the database using the ODBC connection — so you know your field names are spelled correctly in the form.

The Completed Example

Here's the completed code for the STRS example. Formatting HTML has been added, as have field names to indicate to visitors which question each check box answers.

The form

Note that the check boxes are wrapped into a table, to allow proper alignment of three check boxes in each row:

```
<!DOCTYPE HTML PUBLIC "-//W3C//DTD HTML 4.0
          Transitional//EN">
<HTML>
<HEAD>
<TITLE>STRS Survey</TITLE>
</HEAD>
<BODY>
<H1>STRS Survey</H1>
Please take a moment to complete our survey. Data will be
          used in aggregate form only.<P>
<FORM action="process-query.cfm" method="POST">
Your age: <INPUT type="Text" name="age"><P>
Your sex:<br>
<INPUT type="Radio" name="sex" value="1" checked="Yes"> Male
          <br>
<INPUT type="Radio" name="Sex" value="0"> Female<P>
Zip code: <INPUT type="Text" name="Zip"><P>
With which group do you most closely identify yourself? <BR>
<SELECT name="self_id">
    <OPTION value="0">Monarchist
    <OPTION value="1">Conservative
    <OPTION value="2">Republican
    <OPTION value="3">Moderate
    <OPTION value="4">Independent
    <OPTION value="5">Liberal
    <OPTION value="6">Democrat
</SELECT><P>
Please check box if you vote regularly:
<INPUT type="Checkbox" name="voter"><P>
<HR>
Please indicate your hobbies and interests:
<TABLE>
<TR><TD><INPUT type="Checkbox" name="politics"> Politics</TD>
<TD><INPUT type="Checkbox" name="history"> History</TD>
<TD><INPUT type="Checkbox" name="war"> War</TD></TR>
<TR><TD><INPUT type="Checkbox" name="current_events"> Current
          Events</TD>
<TD><INPUT type="Checkbox" name="foreign_policy"> Foreign
          Policy</TD>
<TD><INPUT type="Checkbox" name="foreign_affairs"> Foreign
          Affairs</TD></TR>
<TR><TD><INPUT type="Checkbox" name="travel"> Travel</TD>
<TD><INPUT type="Checkbox" name="judiciary"> Judiciary</TD>
<TD><INPUT type="Checkbox" name="sports"> Sports</TD></TR>
```

(continued)

```
<TR><TD><INPUT type="Checkbox" name="regulation">
        Regulation</td>
<TD><INPUT type="Checkbox" name="environment">
        Environment</TD></TR>
</TABLE>
<TEXTAREA name="suggestions" cols="60" rows="4"
        wrap="VIRTUAL">
</TEXTAREA><P>
<INPUT type="Submit" value="Submit"><P>
<INPUT type="Reset"><P>
</FORM>
</BODY>
</HTML>
```

The processing and confirmation page

For the processing and confirmation page, you really couldn't ask for less!
You, however, don't have to be quite this brief:

```
<!DOCTYPE HTML PUBLIC "-//W3C//DTD HTML 4.0
        Transitional//EN">
<CFINSERT datasource="STRS"
tablename="survey"
dbtype="ODBC">
<HTML>
<HEAD>
<TITLE>Thank you!</TITLE>
</HEAD>
<BODY>
<H1>Thanks for completing our Survey!</H1>
<A href="home.html">Click here to return to our home
        page.</a>
</BODY>
</HTML>
```

Although Studio saves you a lot of typing and debugging, giving you a working application in a short time, it's still worthwhile to understand the CFML
so that you can make changes to the pages that Studio provides.

Chapter 6

Displaying Information

● ●

● ●

Suppose you have a database of books. Visitors will want to see not all the data but only a subset of the data, such as books about John C. Calhoun. In this chapter, you find out how to use ColdFusion to selectively extract data from a database.

As with all the chapters in Part II, first we show you how to display data in the database by hand, without the aid of spiffy Studio, and then we show you how to perform the same tasks in Studio. In the do-it-yourself example, you create two Web pages. On the first page, you publish a form and collect data from the visitor. On the second page, you use that data to query a database for a subset of its data. In the Studio example, you create three Web pages; the additional page shows the details of one of the records listed on the second page.

We don't have you code the three-page example by hand because doing so would involve too many other elements that just aren't important in this chapter. Here, we concentrate on the CFTABLE tag. In other parts of the book, however, we cover just about everything that the Studio example produces. In Chapter 12, for example, we cover the CFOUTPUT tag in detail.

ColdFusion makes displaying data from a database very easy, but it doesn't know anything about your data. It's smart, but not *that* smart! That's where you come in. Your job, should you accept it, is to create the SQL to query the database. Don't worry, we show you how.

Selecting the Criteria for Displaying a Record

You have data and your visitor wants to see it. If this was a face-to-face encounter, and your visitor came to you because he or she knew you had data about books, you might start the conversation by saying: "What do you want to know?" And then your visitor might respond, "What's a good book about HTML that includes the entire HTML 4 specification?" Perhaps you'd answer, "I suggest *The HTML 4 Bible*, by Bryan Pfaffenberger and Alexis D. Gutzman."

This type of interaction is possible because you understand all the words and can answer the visitor's question, or query. Because computers aren't as good as pulling the content from sentences, you need to consider how to get useful data from visitors.

Consider how much more useful data you'd collect if you asked a visitor the following questions: What is the topic of the book? Would any keywords narrow the search? These two questions would probably yield fewer words and more specific information than one open-ended question on which to base your query of the database.

The expectant moms' database

Rather than use a book database for the example, we use a site maintained by one of the authors. In support of private pregnancy-related and childbirth-related mailing lists sponsored by a partner site, this site hosts a database where members of the various mailing lists can sign in and look up information about other members, such as the name they've chosen for their baby, their birth plans, and their birth stories. Visitors need a few ways to select data and a few ways to order the data.

Turn to Chapter 11 for information about security.

Figure 6-1 shows one of the data collection screens for this site. As you can see, the members are asked to provide a lot of data, but because they're providing information for their online friends and they know it's secure, they don't mind sharing it.

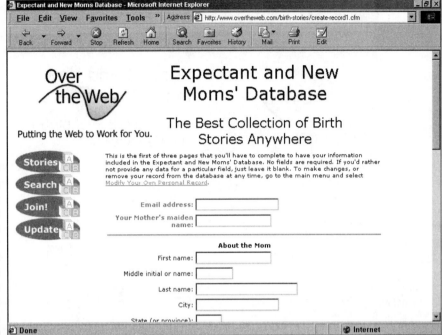

Figure 6-1:
One of the
forms that
members
of our
pregnancy
site use to
provide
personal
data.

The fields for narrowing the search

Visitors can narrow their search and exclude records that don't match some of the search criteria. We permit searching based on city, state, and country.

To make searching easier and prevent typos by the visitor, we provide select lists with the cities, states, and countries for which there are records.

Visitors can also sort by due date, by the mother's first name, by city, by state, and by country. There's even a secondary sort criterion, so visitors can sort by country and then by city, for example, to get all the records sorted by city within the country. Figure 6-2 shows the form page that visitors use to provide search and sort criteria.

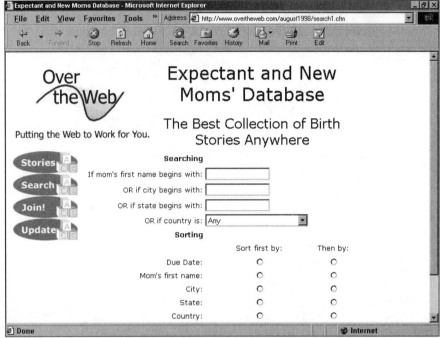

Figure 6-2:
Requesting search and sort criteria from the visitor.

Asking the Database for Information

When you ask the database for information, or run a *query* against the database, you need to know certain rules. In fact, queries have their own language, called *SQL* (standard query language). SQL predates the popular Microsoft SQL Server product and has become the industry-standard language for querying most database management systems. In this book, when we refer to SQL, we mean the language, unless we specifically refer to SQL Server.

SQL short course

You can use SQL to get data from a database, add data to a database, delete or update records in a database, change fields in multiple records, add columns to tables, and add and delete tables. In this chapter, you only get data from the database, so you don't need to read about all the types of data processing and manipulation that SQL can do.

CFINSERT (see Chapter 5) is ideal when you need to insert only the fields from the form in the database. If you want to insert some fields (such as constants) into the database as part of a record, however, you need to use the SQL Insert command.

The only SQL command you need to know to get data from the database is the SELECT command. Here's an example of the simplest SELECT command:

```
SELECT *
FROM Mom
```

This SELECT command gets all records and fields in the table called Mom. We don't indicate the name of the database containing the Mom table; the database name and any security information associated with the database are communicated in the CFQUERY tag itself.

SELECT and FROM are *reserved words* and can't be used for field names. The asterisk (*) tells the database to select all fields. Because we didn't list any criteria, all data in the table called Mom is included in the results set.

When we discuss databases, fields are like columns in a spreadsheet and records are like rows in a spreadsheet. We use the terms *field* and *column* and the terms *record* and *row* interchangeably in this book.

Indicating the fields you want to display

When you use the SELECT * statement, every field is returned. Sometimes, though, you don't want every field in a table to be returned to your page. If you want to extract only the fields you will display, list the field names after SELECT, as in the following example:

```
SELECT first_name, city, state
FROM Mom
```

It's a good idea to select only those columns you need when building a query. Using SELECT *, although simpler, can be an expensive operation as a table grows larger, in terms of both getting the data out of the database and storing the query data that's returned.

For a successful query, you need an exact match between the names of the fields in the SELECT statement and the names of the fields in the database.

Selecting records

As mentioned, visitors to your site often don't want to see every record in your database. Instead, they'll provide search criteria so that you can show them only relevant records. In the following example, we list some criteria:

```
SELECT first_name, city, state
FROM Mom
WHERE city = 'Charlottesville' or (state = 'CT' and city =
          'Bethel')
```

The WHERE clause tells the database the criteria that the record has to meet to be selected. In this example, only records in which the city is Charlottesville or both the city is Bethel and the state is CT will meet the criteria and be selected.

Sorting records

As long as you're requesting data from the database, you might as well let the database sort it for you. If you're returning a list of names, for example, it might make sense to sort the list alphabetically. If you're returning data with prices, you might want to sort by price.

Think about what the visitor really wants to see. Then provide the data in a logical order.

Because we know that mothers might want to sort by location to find others who live close by, we sort by state and then by city within state:

```
SELECT first_name, city, state
FROM Mom
WHERE city = 'Charlottesville' or (state = 'CT' and city =
         'Bethel')
ORDER BY state, city
```

With the ORDER BY clause, you can dictate the order in which the data is returned. If you sort the data by more than one field, ORDER BY sorts by the first field first, and then by the second field when records share the same value for the first field, and so on.

The entire statement is called the SELECT statement and consists of multiple clauses, with each clause preceded by a keyword. Consequently, the SELECT statement is required to have a SELECT clause and a FROM clause, and may or may not have WHERE and ORDER BY clauses, as well.

SQL functions in database queries

SQL, like ColdFusion, uses functions. And they're as powerful in SQL as they are in ColdFusion. Four of the more common functions that you might want to use are Count( ), Sum( ), Max( ), and Distinct( ). All do pretty much what you expect.

The Count( ) function

The Count( ) function counts the number of records that the query is returning for each group.

The Sum ( ) function

The Sum( ) function sums the value in a given field. The field must be numeric for this to work, so we'll switch gears from our example of an expectant woman's Web site to a database that has sales. The following query returns the number of sales using Count( ) and the total sales by state:

```
SELECT state, Count(sales), Sum(sales)
FROM 1999_Sales
GROUP BY state
```

Note that the sales database field is both counted and summed within each state, but it's not listed by itself in the SELECT clause. If it were, the query wouldn't return the results you want.

You put functions only in the SELECT clause, never in the GROUP BY clause.

The Max ( ) function

The Max( ) function is useful if you need to know the last record inserted in the database or the highest value that a given field has in the database. If you're using a unique key on each record and the database assigns that key (using the Autonumber field type in Access, for instance), the last record inserted is the one with the highest key. The following query returns the unique key field (ID) of the last record inserted into the database:

```
SELECT Max(ID) as MaxofID, last_name, created_date
FROM Mom
```

Notice the following:

- ✔ The Max( ) function is operating on the ID field to return the highest ID, where the ID is the name of our key in the table.

- ✔ as is a reserved word. We use it to create a new variable that will hold the returned value of Max(ID). Otherwise, there would be no way to refer back to the result as a CF variable.

- ✔ When the highest key value is returned, it is referenced not by the field name, ID, but by the newly created variable, MaxofID. You could just as easily have called it Fred.

This query returns exactly one record: the one with the highest ID.

The Distinct ( ) function

The Distinct( ) function returns all unique values in a given field. One great use of this function is returning all the states represented in your database for use in a select list. The following query shows Distinct( ) in action:

```
SELECT Distinct(State)
FROM Mom
```

Notice that the Distinct( ) function operates on only one field at a time. If you need multiple distinct fields, perform multiple queries.

SQL with more than one table

All the SQL examples in the preceding section relied on the premise that we'd never want to pull data from more than one table at a time. You'll soon find that you do want to extract data from more than one table at once, especially in tables related to each other. This is an important concept in relational databases.

In our example, we might want to list some basic information about all the mothers, then list information for each mother, and then list the name each mother is planning to use for her child or children for both boys and girls.

The information about the babies is kept in a different table, called child. The mom table has a unique field called ID that identifies each record (the key).

The child table uses the `child_ID` field as its key. To maintain the relationship between mom and child, the child table has the field called ID in each record. The ID field in the child table is called a *foreign key* because it's the key from another table — in our case, the mom table — and because it defines a relationship — in our example, the relationship between mom and child.

Your SQL will change in one simple way when you have multiple tables. If a field has the same name in both tables, you must prepend it with the table name and a period. After we start working with two tables — that is, after we put two tables in the select statement — we must specify in which table the field to which we are referring resides.

It turns out that both the mom and the child tables have a field called `first _name`. We make the reference clear by adding the table names before the field names: `mom.first_name` and `child.first_name`.

Another significant, and more challenging, change in your SQL is the matter of defining the relationship between such related tables. In SQL, this is called a *join,* and you must specify it as another clause in your SQL whenever you select data from multiple tables.

The following code selects the child's name and sex for each mom:

```
SELECT mom.first_name, child.first_name, child.sex
FROM mom INNER JOIN child ON mom.ID = child.ID
ORDER BY mom.first_name
```

In this bit of SQL, we do the following:

- ✔ We ask the database to return the mother's first name, the child's first name, and the child's sex.
- ✔ We tell the database that it will know when a child goes with a mom because the mom_ID field will be the same.
- ✔ Finally, we sort the data by the mom's first name. That way, when we display the data, we can use ColdFusion's grouping functionality to avoid showing the mother's name more than once.

Using SQL with ColdFusion

Now that you've had a short course on SQL, let's mix up SQL with ColdFusion, the way we do it in our pages. For example:

```
SELECT first_name, city, state
FROM Mom
WHERE state = '#state#'
GROUP BY state, city, first_name
ORDER BY state, city
```

That wasn't so bad, was it? Can you find the ColdFusion? The pound signs are a dead giveaway. In this query, only records in which the state is equal to the value of our state variable are returned.

In SQL, you must enclose text fields in quotes. SQL is unforgiving! (Microsoft Access requires the quotes to be single quotes, whereas some other database systems allow double quotes. Use single quotes to be safe.) Numeric and Boolean (yes/no) fields may not be enclosed in quotes. If you find your query is failing, check your quotes first. Many an hour has been wasted looking for a Boolean value that's erroneously in quotes. Boolean fields are often accidentally placed into quotes because people think of them as text (yes or no) rather than numeric (1 or 0), which they really are.

Here's a slightly more complex example:

```
SELECT first_name, city, state
FROM Mom
WHERE state = '#state#'
ORDER BY '#orderby#'
```

In this query, the sort order is determined by the value of the orderby variable. The orderby variable is passed through from the form page, shown in Figure 6-2.

The CFQUERY tag

Now we come to where the rubber meets the road: the CFQUERY tag, ColdFusion's way of extracting data from a database. You put your SQL statement in the CFQUERY tag.

For convenience (yours, that is) we put the entire CFQUERY definition here, but don't let it frighten you. You're unlikely to need more than the first two attributes when you're starting out. When you're ready to use more advanced attributes, flip back to this page to see the entire definition. We list the attributes from most useful to most obscure.

```
<CFQUERY
    name="query_name"
    datasource="datasource_name"
    maxrows="number"
    username="username"
    password="password"
    cachedafter="date"
    cashedwithin="timespan"
    debug="yes/no"
    dbtype="dbtype"
    dbserver="server_name"
    dbname="database_name"
    blockfactor="number"
    timeout="number"
    provider="text"
    providerdsn="datasource_name">
    . . . query here . . .
</CFQUERY>
```

name   **Required.** You can't refer to the results of the query later in your program unless you know the name of the query. The query name should be intuitive. Don't use *results* as the query name; it won't mean anything to you in three months. Query names should follow the same rules as variables in ColdFusion and can include letters, numbers, and underscores but not hyphens. Query names must begin with a letter.

datasource   **Required.** The data source name for the database on which you are performing your query. (See Chapter 4 for more on data sources.)

maxrows   **Optional.** If you want to limit the number of rows returned from the database, specify the number here.

username   **Optional.** If your database is password protected, you need to provide the `username` and `password`, either here or in the `datasource` definition. (You have to go out of your way to password protect a database in Access, and the process is beyond the scope of this book to explain.)

password   **Optional.** Goes with `username`, if your database is password protected.

cachedafter   **Optional.** Use this attribute to take advantage of cached queries. You must have query caching enabled in your server administrator for this to work. ColdFusion will get data from the cache if the query has already been run since the date specified here. The `cachedafter` attribute takes a date in mm/dd/yy format.

cachedwithin   **Optional.** Use this attribute to take advantage of cached queries if query caching is enabled in your server administrator. ColdFusion will get data from the cache if the query has already been run within the specified interval — defined with the CreateTimeSpan( ) function.

debug   **Optional.** This is a great attribute. If you set this attribute to yes, information displayed at the bottom of the page's output shows the query that actually gets run (with variable names converted to their values), the query execution time, and the number of records returned. This is a fabulous debugging tool if you're unable to see the debugging information enabled in ColdFusion Administrator, as we discuss in Chapter 14.

dbtype   **Optional.** Unless you're using a native driver for your database, don't use this one. You can set it to ODBC (the default) if you're not, but if your ColdFusion Server (or the one at your ISP or WPP) is not ColdFusion 4, the tag will fail. If you're using a native driver, you'll find that using the appropriate `dbtype` will give you faster queries than using an ODBC connection.

dbserver   **Optional.** If you defined the `dbtype` to be a native driver, you can use this to override the server specified in the `datasource` definition.

dbname   ***Optional.*** The database name when `dbtype=sybase11` or oledb, overriding that specified in `datasource`.

blockfactor	**Optional.** The number of rows to fetch at one time from the server. For use with only native Oracle drivers and ODBC drivers.
timeout	**Optional.** Only for SQL Server 6.*x* and above. If you're running a particularly thorny query or your server is particularly slow, the query could timeout before processing is completed, leaving you or your visitors with an error message. Rather than take that chance, set a longer timeout. Timeout is measured in milliseconds.
provider	**Optional.** The COM provider (OLE-DB only).
providerdsn	**Optional.** The data source name for the COM provider (OLE-DB only).

Although the CFQUERY tag takes a number of attributes, most of the time you'll need only the `name` and `query` attributes.

The `From` clause specifies the name of the *table* in your database that holds the data you're requesting. The `datasource` attribute of the CFQUERY tag specifies the name of the *database*.

Populating select lists from queries

Let's get back to our application! We want to prompt the user for search criteria. Before we show how to use queries to perform the search, we'll show another important use: using them to build drop-down lists from database data.

You'll notice from Figure 6-2 that we have a drop-down box for the countries. We have a list of countries stored in our database — it's the list of country values that users have entered when registering themselves. We really want to show a list of only those countries for which we have registrants, not a list of all the countries of the world (most of those would result in no records found if used in the search).

Building drop-down lists from database data is an important and frequently used approach in building forms with ColdFusion.

There are challenges, however, to our intention to use the data that users have entered for their country. Users can enter all manner of spellings of country names, which can make it hard to present accurate results when trying to get a list of the "valid" countries.

As you can see in Figure 6-3, our database contains some garbage. For example, someone entered "Australia,Australia,Australia" as a single country. We could have prevented this by providing in the data-entry screen a select list of countries from which to choose, perhaps itself created with a query that looked up a table of all possible country names.

But assume you need to know how to solve this problem with data appearing as it does here. Regardless of the quality of the data, it's probably better for the visitor to be able to see a list of countries for which there is data because the list isn't going to be too unwieldy. (There may be a few multiple spellings of a given country, but probably not too many.)

Figure 6-3:
The select list for countries includes anything anyone has ever entered as a country, including some garbage.

To create a select list using the results of a query, first you have to perform the query. For example, we use the following simple query to get the list of countries from the database:

```
<CFQUERY name="countries" datasource="stories">
SELECT Distinct(Country)
FROM Mom
</CFQUERY>
```

Note that we're using the SQL Distinct( ) function, which you read about earlier in the chapter.

After we have the results of the query associated with a query named `countries`, we can use the CFOUTPUT tag to present the results. The following CFML created the select list of all the countries from the database:

```
<SELECT name="country">
<OPTION value="0">Any
<CFOUTPUT query="countries">
<OPTION value="#country#">#Country#
</CFOUTPUT>
</SELECT>
```

Note that we make a point of sending the value #country# in the value attribute, rather than just letting the form pick it up from the OPTION tag. We did that to make sure that the value is sent in quotes. If you try to send a value that has a space in it and you don't enclose the value in quotes, only the first word of the value is sent.

Your form needs a submit button and a FORM tag, as well. Chapter 5 discusses form elements in greater detail.

The query on the result page

On the result page, you need a query to pull the data from the database. To perform the query, we need the results of the form we saw in Figure 6-2. The query we need at the top of the result page is shown in Listing 6-1. Keep in mind, as you look at this, that the city, state, and country values come from drop-down (select) form fields, and they were created to offer an option that passes a value of 0. We use that to mean that the visitor doesn't care which values are found.

Listing 6-1   Requesting all the Moms from the Mom Table Who Match the Search Criteria

```
<CFQUERY name="ListMoms" datasource="stories">
SELECT * from Mom
WHERE
    <CFIF (form.city EQ 0) AND (form.state EQ 0)
        AND(form.country EQ 0)>
        1=1
    <CFELSE>
        1=0
    </CFIF>
    <CFIF Len(form.city) NEQ 0>
        or city = '#city#'
    </CFIF>
    <CFIF Len(form.state) NEQ 0>
        or state = '#state#'
    </CFIF>
    <CFIF Len(form.country) NEQ 0>
        or country = '#country#'
    </CFIF>
```

```
<CFIF IsDefined("form.sort")>
    <CFIF Len(form.sort) GT 0>
        ORDER BY #form.sort#
        <CFIF IsDefined("form.sort2")>
            <CFIF Len(form.sort2) GT 0>
                , #form.sort2#
            </CFIF>
        </CFIF>
    </CFIF>
</CFIF>
</CFQUERY>
```

Note that we test whether the `form.sort` field is defined, and then only if it is do we test whether the user entered a value. We must do this as nested IF statements because ColdFusion, prior to release 4.01, would get an error if you referred to a variable in a test and it didn't exist. This actually has further implications, but in any case, it's a tremendous improvement that as of 4.01 we can now test both conditions in one IF statement, as in

```
<CFIF IsDefined("form.sort") and Len(form.sort) GT 0>
```

If the first condition is FALSE, it doesn't matter what the second condition says, because the whole condition can never be TRUE (they must both be TRUE). This more intelligent condition processing is known as *short-circuit evaluation*. Before you use the single IF statement, however, make sure your ISP or WPP, if you're using one, is running at least version 4.01 of ColdFusion Server.

Sample data for CFQUERY

If any search criteria are provided, we want to limit the display to those records that meet the search criteria. If no search criteria are provided, we want to display all the data.

Don't be intimidated by the apparent complexity of the query in Listing 6-1. Take a look at it using actual data. Consider how the query would look if the form fields had been populated like this:

```
city=bethel
state=CT
country=0
sort=due
sort2=(null)
```

With these values, the following query would be generated:

```
<CFQUERY name="ListMoms" datasource="stories">
SELECT * from Mom
WHERE  1=0
       OR city = '#city#'
       OR state = '#state#'
ORDER BY #form.sort#
</CFQUERY>
```

We've already described why we need all those CFIF statements: to make sure we don't perform processing for form fields in which the user made no selection. Note that the value of country is 0, so it didn't pass the test of being a valid value; that means the query has no OR country clause. Also, because the value of sort2 is null, meaning that none of the radio buttons were checked for that field, that variable and the comma that would have preceded it are omitted from the query.

The WHERE clause

We need to address only one more piece of code: that funky CFIF statement immediately following the WHERE clause. What's up with that?

```
<CFIF (form.city EQ 0) AND (form.state EQ 0) AND
      (form.country EQ 0)>
      1=1
<CFELSE>
1=0
</CFIF>
```

This statement is necessary because we don't know which of the search fields — city, country, state — will be present, if any. If no search fields are present, we want to return all records in the table (WHERE 1=1, which is always TRUE). We wouldn't normally specify that, but if one or more search fields are present, we have to have some criteria at the beginning of the WHERE clause so that we don't end up with a stray AND at the beginning of the criteria. And we can't leave it off, because if no search fields are present, we'd have a stray WHERE clause with no criteria. The 1=1 is a placeholder. (0=0 works the same way, and you may see that elsewhere.)

We could just as easily have written the WHERE clause as follows:

```
<CFIF (Len(form.city) NEQ 0) OR (Len(form.state) NEQ 0) OR
      (Len(form.country) NEQ 0)>
WHERE  1=0
<CFIF Len(form.city) NEQ 0>
       OR city = '#city#'
```

```
</CFIF>
<CFIF Len(form.state) NEQ 0>
      OR state = '#state#'
</CFIF>
<CFIF Len(form.country) NEQ 0>
      OR country = '#country#'
</CFIF>
</cfif>
```

Based on the first CFIF tag, if none of the three search fields is present, there is no WHERE clause, so all records are displayed.

This is a good time to note that there is no one right way to write this code. In fact, the WHERE clause here is probably better than the one in the CFQUERY example in Listing 6-1 because if no search criteria are present, ColdFusion doesn't process the rest of the CFIF statements and doesn't create a WHERE clause against which every record of the database has to be checked. This saves processing on the database.

Displaying Information the Easy Way

ColdFusion's CFTABLE tag makes it easy to display the results of a query. With the CFTABLE tag, you can display the results of your query either in an HTML table (using the font of your choice) or in tabular format using the HTML PRE tag, which gives you Courier font on most browsers.

The CFTABLE tag requires one or more CFCOL tags be specified within it, one for each query result column to be displayed.

The CFTABLE tag

In the CFTABLE tag, you indicate the name of the query whose results you want to display. Also in the CFTABLE tag, you elect to have the results displayed as preformatted (that is, fixed-width) text or using HTML table construction. Figure 6-4 shows the results of a query using CFTABLE and preformatted text. Figure 6-5 shows the results of the same query using CFTABLE with HTML table formatting.

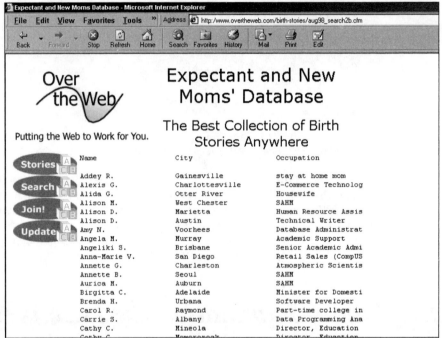

Figure 6-4:
Displaying
output from
a table
using
CFTABLE
with prefor-
matted text.

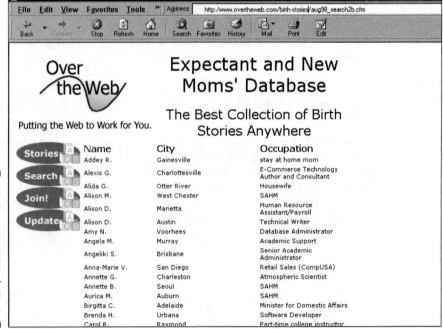

Figure 6-5:
Displaying
output from
a table
using
CFTABLE
with HTML
table
formatting.

The CFTABLE tag, like so many tags in ColdFusion, has many possible attributes. But as always, you'll typically use only a few. In this case, you'll always need to specify a `query` and will likely use `HTMLtable` and `colheaders`. The rest merely add variety to your result.

```
<CFTABLE
    query="query_name"
    HTMLtable="yes/no"
    border
    colspacing="number"
    startrow="number"
    maxrows="number"
    colheaders
    headerlines="number">
    . . . <CFCOL> tags
    </CFTABLE>
```

query   **Required.** The most important attribute is query, which is where you specify the name of the query.

HTMLtable   **Optional.** The `HTMLtable` attribute tells ColdFusion to display the results of the query in an HTML table, rather than in fixed-width font. Unless you're supporting old browsers (that don't recognize the HTML TABLE tag), use `HTMLtable="yes"`.

border   **Optional.** If you've used the `HTMLtable` attribute, you can use `border` to specify a border on your table. However, you have no control over the border width.

colspacing   **Optional.** Useful only when `HTMLtable="yes"` is not specified. The `colspacing` attribute dictates the amount of white space between columns.

startrow   **Optional.** You can pair the `startrow` attribute with the `maxrows` attribute. If you want to show the first 20 items, you need set only the `maxrows` attribute. But if you want to show the second set of 20 items, set `startrow` to 21 and `maxrows` to 20. The default `startrow` is 1.

maxrows   **Optional.** Use the `maxrows` attribute if you want to display not the entire query but only a maximum number of rows. For example, if you were showing computer memory by price, with the best prices first, perhaps you wouldn't want to show more than the top 10 prices.

colheaders   **Optional.** If you use the `header` attribute of the CFCOL tag to assign headers to the table, use the `colheaders` attribute of the CFTABLE tag to show headers at the top of each column. If you don't specify headers in CFCOL, this attribute will simply create a blank header at the top of the table.

> ***headerlines*** **Optional.** Useful only when `HTMLtable="yes"` is not specified. You can use the `headerlines` attribute to indicate how you want the headers you define in the CFCOL tags to appear. The default is to display the header on a single line with a blank line between the header and the data. If you want the header text to take up more than one line, increase the number of `headerlines`.

For our example, the CFTABLE tag looks like this:

```
<CFTABLE query="ListMoms"
    HTMLtable="yes"
    colheaders>
    . . . some CFCOL tags here . . .
</CFTABLE>
```

Note that we use the `HTMLtable="yes"` attribute so that our result is presented in HTML table formatting. We also will be specifying headers in the CFCOL tags for the CFTABLE, so we include the `colheaders` attribute.

The CFCOL tag

For the example of the expectant moms' database, we want to display the following data about the women in our database:

- First name
- First initial of last name (to preserve anonymity)
- Occupation
- City
- Number of other children or none, if there are no other children

CFCOL is used within a CFTABLE to describe the name and order of display in the table of the query result columns.

```
<CFCOL
    text="text"
    header="text"
    width="number"
    align="alignment">
```

> ***text*** **Required.** Whatever you want to appear in the column must go in the `text` attribute. You can include text, URLs, ColdFusion variables or functions, or just about anything else. Be sure to enclose whatever you want displayed in double quotes; that means if you're naming a ColdFusion variable or function, it must be enclosed in pound signs *within* the quotes.

header	**Optional.** If you want a header at the top of the column, specify it here and enclose it in double quotes. If you don't specify one, ColdFusion does not create one for you.
width	**Optional.** When `HTMLtable="no"`, this attribute indicates the maximum width of the column. Values exceeding this width are truncated, and the default is 20. When `HTMLtable="yes"`, you don't need this attribute. HTML uses the widest value in the column to determine the width of the column, and data is never truncated. If you do specify a value, it is passed as the percentage width of the column.
align	**Optional.** This is just like the `align` attribute in most HTML tags; it aligns the column value within the table column. Your choices are left, right, and center.

First name and last name

Normally, a CFCOL tag simply specifies the name of a query column, as we show in the next section. But for our first columns to be displayed here, we do something a little tricky. For aesthetics, we want to show the first name and the last name in the same column.

Remember, CFCOL defines the table columns to be displayed. You can put more than one *query* column in one of the table columns. Yes, this use of columns for two different purposes can be confusing, but it's one of the hazards of bringing together the two worlds of database columns and table columns!

Here's our CFCOL tag for the first name and the first initial of the last name:

```
<CFCOL text="#listmoms.first_name#
      #Left(listmoms.last_name, 1)#" header="Name">
```

The line breaks in this code example look a bit strange, but we're limited in the number of characters that can fit on a single line in this book. On your screen, you could certainly get by with placing this all on one line.

Occupation and city

Writing the CFCOL tags for occupation and city is more straightforward. We simply want to display the query column value as the table column value. That's easy. Each field gets its own column:

```
<CFCOL text="#City#" header="City">
<CFCOL text="#Occupation#" header="Occupation">
```

Number of other children

For the Other Children column, we want to display the number of other children that the woman has. Here's the code:

```
<CFCOL text="#listmoms.count#" header="Other Children">
```

In this tag, the value of the `text` attribute is the value of #count#.

The output

The CFTABLE and CFCOL tags are used to produce the listing on the page. None of the code in Listing 6-2 is new. You've seen it in bits and pieces in the text before this. We list it again here so you can see how it all goes together.

Listing 6-2	Displaying the Results of the Query Using CFTABLE and CFCOL

```
<CFTABLE query="ListMoms"
      colspacing="3"
      HTMLtable
      colheaders>
<!-- the first column has the names -->
    <CFCOL text="#first_name# #last_name#"
      header="Name">
<!-- the second column has the city -->
    <CFCOL text="#City#" header="City">
<!-- the third column has the occupation -->
    <CFCOL text="#Occupation#" header="Occupation">
<!-- and the fourth and final column has the number of other
children the mother has -->
    <CFCOL text="#count#"
      header="Other Children">
</CFTABLE>
```

Using Studio to Display Database Data

The example in this section alone will sell you on using Studio to increase your productivity. Studio does a smooth job of creating a search page and displaying the results on one or more pages — and saves you a ton of coding. The results Studio provides are so nice that they put the pages created by hand earlier in this chapter to shame.

The key to expediting your work with Studio is knowing about Studio's many built-in wizards. Studio has wizards for HTML, DHTML, and CFML. You owe it to yourself to try them all. You never know when one will be just the ticket to solving some tricky (or tedious) problem.

Studio provides a Drill Down Wizard to help you create three pages for a search interface. Most importantly, it creates all the code for you! You merely tell it what tables and columns to use. The three pages are

- ✔ **A form with the search criteria to be provided by the visitor.** The search processing that Studio provides is more complex than anything we show you how to do by hand.

- ✔ **A page listing the results of the search in a table,** with a subset of the result fields (selected by you) displayed with a hyperlink next to each record so that the visitor can choose to see all the details of that record.

- ✔ **A page that shows all the details** (again, fields selected by you) for the record selected by the visitor on the listing page.

Connecting to the database

To use the wizards in Studio, you have to establish an RDS connection to ColdFusion Server, whether your database is on a remote server or your local workstation. Then you have to set up development mappings if you want to view the results of your work in Studio. If you don't create development mappings, you have to upload your work to a Web server (or save it to a directory on your hard drive where your desktop-resident Web server can find it), and then view it in an external browser.

Chapter 2 explains both how to create an RDS connection and how to create development mappings.

Using the Drill Down wizard

The Drill Down wizard creates the three pages that make up the application that displays data from your database based on search criteria. In the wizard, you indicate

- ✔ Which fields are the search fields
- ✔ Which fields you want to provide on the listing page
- ✔ Which fields you want to provide on the detail page

Studio furnishes lists of your fields from which you make your choices.

To begin the Drill Down wizard, follow these steps.

1. **Select File⇨New. Click the CFML tab, and select Drill Down Wizard, as shown in Figure 6-6.**

Figure 6-6:
Select Drill
Down
Wizard from
the New
Document
dialog box.

2. **Complete the first screen of the wizard, shown in Figure 6-7, and then click Next.**

Provide a name for your application. This name will appear at the top of the pages that are generated, but it's used also by the wizard as the prefix to the names of the files that it generates, so keep the name brief but descriptive. In Figure 6-7, we use Ch6.

Figure 6-7:
Name your
application
and indicate
where you
want to
save the
files that are
created.

Watch out if you're running the wizard a second time because you weren't happy with the results of the choices you made the first time. If you use the same application name, Studio tries to replace the old files with the new ones (for good or evil). Although it does prompt you before overwriting the files, it doesn't do so until after you've walked through the entire wizard.

You're also shown an option to specify the directory where you want the generated files saved. You can type a directory path or you can find it by clicking the global browse button to the right of the text-entry field. For a server to appear in the Sever drop-down list, you must have added it as either an RDS or an FTP-connected server in the Remote Files tab in the Resources panel as we describe in Chapter 2.

3. **On the next screen, shown in Figure 6-8, select the server on which the database resides.**

   Again, only servers for which you have created RDS connections appear in the list. *Localhost,* if it's displayed, is your own workstation. Select the server with the database you want to use.

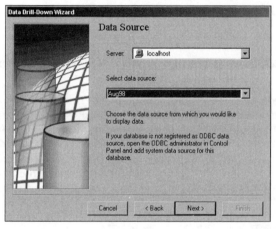

Figure 6-8:
Select the
server
and the
database
with which
you want
to work.

After a moment, all ODBC entries on that server appear in the Select data source drop-down list.

4. **In the Select data source list, select the database with which you want to work, and then click Next.**

5. **Select the tables you want included, as shown in Figure 6-9, and then click Next.**

   To select just one table (like we are doing in this example), click the name of the table.

   To select more than one table, Ctrl-click on each of the tables. If you select more than one table, you'll see an extra screen. For what to do next in that case, check out the next section, "Displaying results from more than one table." Come back here when you're finished. We'll be waiting.

Figure 6-9:
Select the
tables
from the
database.

6. **Indicate which fields you'd like to permit the visitors to search on, as shown in Figure 6-10, and then click Next.**

   If you were coding this by hand, you'd have to think long and hard about how complex you wanted the query to be. It might also make you think twice about how many search fields you want to include because you'd need to build both the form fields and the search criteria on the result page. But because Studio builds the code for you, feel free to choose all the search fields you want. Just be careful not to overwhelm your visitors with too many choices.

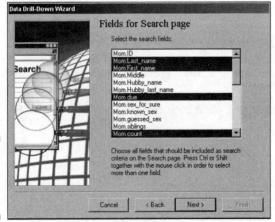

Figure 6-10:
Select the
search
criteria.

7. **Indicate which fields you'd like displayed in the result page, as shown in Figure 6-11, and then click Next.**

To select contiguous fields, Shift-click on the first and last fields. To select noncontiguous fields from the list, use Ctrl-click to select each one.

Use discretion when indicating which fields you'd like to see in the listing. Remember that a detail page appears after this one, so you don't have to show every possible field here. This page should provide enough information so that visitors can decide which single record they'd like to view for more details. Be aware, too, that specifying too many fields could create a result page that's too wide to fit on the screen, forcing the user to scroll right to see the data. Viewers generally don't appreciate that.

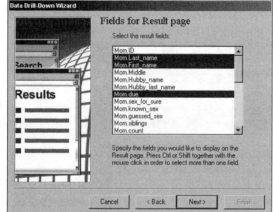

Figure 6-11: Select the fields to be displayed on the result page.

8. **Select the fields you want displayed on the detailed result page, as we're doing in Figure 6-12, and then click Next.**

Figure 6-12: Select the fields for the detail page.

The detailed result page is the one visitors see when they click the detail link that will be offered to them on the search result page. Feel free to select all the fields in the database because Studio arranges them so that visitors have to scroll down, which is instinctive for most Web visitors, as opposed to scrolling across.

9. **Select the key to the table from the list.**

Studio can't generate the detail page without a *key,* the field in the table that uniquely identifies each record. In our example, shown in Figure 6-13, the key field is ID.

Nearly every database table you will encounter will have a key field, even if you don't know of its existence. Microsoft Access makes it difficult for you to create a table without a key. That means if you're using Access, you have a key field in your table — unless you defied Access's dialog box and intentionally created a table without a key.

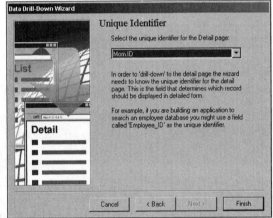

Figure 6-13:
Selecting
the key field.

10. **Click Finish to generate the pages.**

The next screen, shown in Figure 6-14, deserves your attention. It lists the pages that Studio has created and what each one does. Notice that we have three new pages, but four new files. The last file, Ch6_AppendCriteria.cfm, is a custom tag template that's used in the result page to match criteria. Because the same code needs to be used for each field you indicated in the search page, Studio puts the code in its own file and simply calls it from anywhere it's needed.

11. **Click Close to end the wizard.**

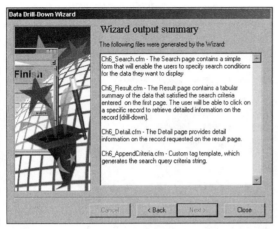

Figure 6-14:
Read this
page
carefully,
so you
know what
files have
been
created!

Now you can take a look at your pages and start making modifications to the design to have them reflect the look and feel of your site.

We talk more about viewing the results in a moment, but first we need to dispose of that business about how to use the wizard when you'll be showing search results from multiple tables.

Displaying results from more than one table

If you need to choose more than one table in the wizard from which to display results (refer to Figure 6-9), you'll see one extra screen. This screen requires that you define the relationships between the tables.

If you've designed your database wisely (and we know you did), you have a relationship between the primary table and one or more secondary tables. In our example, the primary table is called mom. It holds information about the mother. Because a mother can be pregnant with one or more children, we decided to put the data about the child or children she's carrying in a secondary table called child (we have very short memories, so keeping table names intuitive saves us a lot of work).

It's unlikely that we'd ever want to access child data in the absence of mom data, so each child record has the ID of the mom's record. This is how the two tables relate to each other. In SQL language, mom.mom_id = child. mom_id.

In our example, ID is the foreign key and child_ID is the key. A *foreign key* is database lingo for a key that uniquely associates this record with a record in another table.

So, if we intend to show data in the search result page that will come from multiple tables, we need to tell the wizard.

In Figure 6-15, you can see that we selected three tables: child, mom, and sibling. The sibling table holds information about each child's siblings. Again, the sibling table is linked to the mom table by the mom_id field.

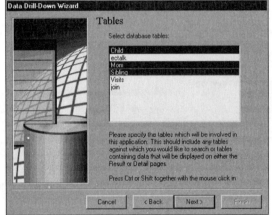

Figure 6-15:
Choosing
three tables
from which
to display
results.

And if we choose more than one table in that dialog box, we need to tell the wizard how these tables are related. Figure 6-16 shows the next prompt to define the relationship.

Figure 6-16:
ColdFusion
makes its
best attempt
at guessing
relationship,
but it's
guessed
wrong in
this case.

ColdFusion tries to help by assuming that common field names between tables are the relationship fields.

Unfortunately, our tables have several fields with the same name. And although they have the same names, they don't represent the primary key and foreign key relationships between the tables. Each of the three tables has an ID field and a first_name field. Two of the tables have a dob (date of birth) field.

In our example, ColdFusion creates relationships between mom.first_name and child.first_name. Because that's not correct, we need to remove the relationships that ColdFusion has created (using the Remove button) and create our own (with the Add button). Figure 6-17 shows the proper relationships.

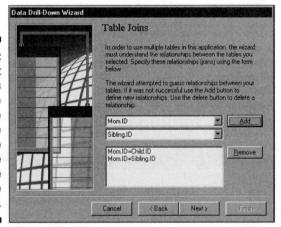

Figure 6-17: The correct relationships between the mom table and the child table and the mom table and the sibling table.

Okay, if you had jumped to this section while working through the description of the wizard interface in the previous section, it's time to go back! (We're waiting for you at the end of Step 5.) Otherwise, proceed to finish up using the wizard by cleaning the generated code. (If only books could have hyperlinks!)

Tweaking the wizard's work

When we're finished with the wizard, it's time to clean up the result page. Figure 6-18 shows the search criteria page. Although it looks usable, Studio's wizard has a serious flaw. Visitors to this site must provide search criteria for *every listed field;* otherwise, they receive an error message referring to missing data.

Be cautious about how many search criteria you provide because you might end up requiring that visitors provide more data than they have.

Check out Figure 6-19. To save space, we remove the word *detail* and associate the hyperlink with the mother's first name instead.

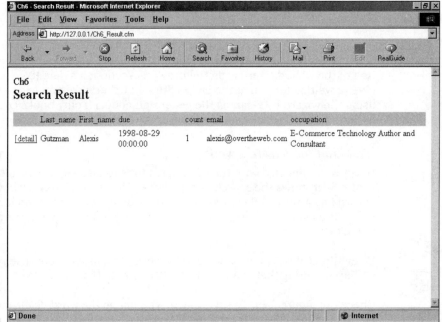

Figure 6-18:
The search page that Studio generates. We provide search criteria to try it out.

Figure 6-19:
The result page generated by Studio. Clearly, we need to pay some attention to the design.

Figure 6-20 is the detail page Studio generates based on the choices we made when we completed the Drill Down wizard.

Next, we have to consider the choices we made in the Drill Down wizard with respect to how many fields would appear on the result page and their effect on the display of that page. The display in Figure 6-19 appears to be acceptable, and when you look at the wizard's search page results for applications you build, you may not see a problem. But perhaps you are working on a screen set to a resolution of 1,024 x 768 or even 1,280 x 1,024. That's a very wide screen, and most users don't use that sort of resolution.

Look at Figures 6-21 and 6-22, which shows the display at two different resolutions. Or, to see the effect on results you create, change your monitor resolution right now to 640 x 480 or 800 x 600.

See? Because real estate is so precious on the screen, you need to be creative about which fields you display on the result page. Otherwise, visitors must scroll to the right to see all the fields, and then scroll back to the left to click the detail link.

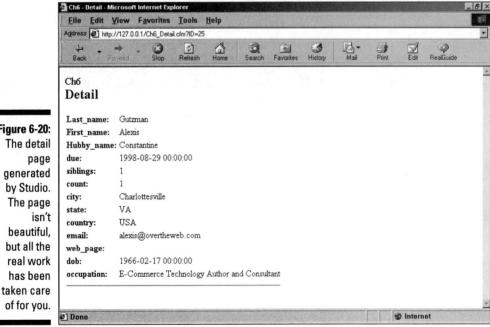

Figure 6-20:
The detail page generated by Studio. The page isn't beautiful, but all the real work has been taken care of for you.

Figure 6-21:
The result
page from
Figure 6-19
at a smaller
resolution.

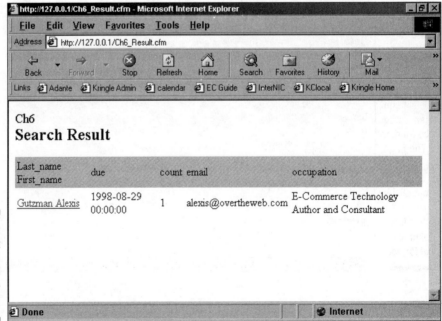

Figure 6-22:
The result
page from
Figure 6-19
at a larger
resolution.

One way to give yourself more screen real estate is to use a smaller font. Experiment with fonts if you find that you can't fit all the fields you need on the listing page.

Most of the changes we want to make to the pages generated by the wizard involve only minor changes to the HTML and a good eye for design. A few key changes, however, require ColdFusion functions.

For example, the entire last name appears on the detail page, but we want to display only the first letter of the last name to protect privacy. The Left( ) function comes in handy here. You can use the Left( ) function to extract only the first character or first *n* characters in a string. The Left( ) function takes two values, as follows: `Left(string, number of characters)`.

Also, in the result listing, the due date is a mess. ColdFusion formatted this date to the longer date/time format when it was validated. (That's a result of using the hidden field _date validation.) How do we want to format it? You might want 8/5/98 or, if you want to appear international, 5/8/98. Or to avoid confusion, perhaps you want 5-Aug-98 or August 5, 1998.

Whichever way you want to format the date, the DateFormat( ) function is there to help. Again, the complete syntax might appear foreboding, but you can use the function in some simple ways. First, the complete syntax:

```
DateFormat(date[, mask])
```

date	**Required.** Use a date variable or value or use a date and time variable or value. If you use a string value, be sure to surround it in double quotes.
mask	**Optional.** Instructions to ColdFusion on how to display the date. You provide these instructions by using letters as placeholders for the actual values, along with optional spaces, hyphens, slashes, or other suitable separators. The mask must be enclosed in double quotes.
d	Day of the month with no leading zero
dd	Day of the month with a leading zero
ddd	Day of the week represented by a three-letter abbreviation
dddd	Day of the week using the complete name of the day
m	Month represented numerically (1—12) with no leading zero
mm	Month represented numerically with a leading zero
mmm	Month represented by a three-letter abbreviation

mmmm	Month name spelled out
y	Last two digits of the year with no leading zero for years when the last two digits are less than 10 (such as 2002)
yy	Last two digits of the year
yyyy	Year represented by four digits

For example, to format the due date (referred to by the due variable) as 8/05/98, use the following:

```
DateFormat(due, "m/dd/yy")
```

To format the due date as 5-Aug-98, use this:

```
DateFormat(due, "d-mmm-yy")
```

If you want to force all days to be displayed with two digits (that is, with a leading 0 if less than 10), use dd rather than d in the preceding example.

The next example formats the due date as August 5, 1998:

```
DateFormat(due, "mmmm d, yyyy")
```

Note, finally, that you can leave the date mask off entirely, and the DateFormat( ) function will simply remove the time portion (if any) and format it as follows:

```
05-Aug-98
```

Studio can take you about eighty percent of the way to a completed application. You, however, still need to tweak the code and make the interface interesting. Even so, Studio is a great timesaver.

Chapter 7

Updating Records

● ●

In This Chapter

▶ Finding the record you want to update

▶ Pulling up the correct record

▶ Displaying data for the visitor to update

▶ Updating the database

▶ Confirming that the update took effect

▶ Building the application in Studio

● ●

*A*fter you let your visitors put data in your database, you may want to let them update their data. This chapter shows you what's involved in creating pages in which your visitors can do just that. Your job is to create the three pages necessary for this task.

On the first page, visitors identify themselves by whatever system you created when they initially provided data (ID and password, e-mail address and password, or some other combination of identifying information). On the second page, you display the visitor's data if you can find it; if you can't find the data, you tell the visitor that his or her sign-in information is invalid. On the third page, you show the visitor a message saying either that the data was successfully updated or — if the visitor chose to be removed from the database — that the visitor has been removed.

As with all three chapters in Part II, Studio can create the pages for you through a wizard. You'll understand ColdFusion better and find it easier to work your way through more advanced chapters, however, if you go through the do-it-yourself project first, before clicking through Studio.

Finding the Data to Update

It's easier to talk about what we need to do specifically rather than describe it in abstract terms, so we jump right into the example project. One of us (guess which one) has an e-commerce resource site at `www.overtheweb.com/e-com/`. On that site, e-commerce pros and wannabes alike can sign into the database, provide personal data, make their credentials available to others, and find others experienced in e-commerce.

The page that members use to provide their data is shown in Figure 7-1. As you can see, the database requests the member's e-mail address and password for logon verification. This site uses fields in red to alert members to required fields.

To permit members to update their own data using the CFUPDATE tag (explained later), our database table must have the following:

- ✔ A field that is the *unique key*
- ✔ A logon ID field
- ✔ A password field

The unique key is the old, reliable `ID` field. We use an autonumber field type in Access to let the database assign a unique key to each record.

Finally, a password is required to prevent other people from having a go at the data. Normally, the `INPUT` type in HTML is set to `password` rather than `text` so that data entered is disguised with asterisks as the visitor types it.

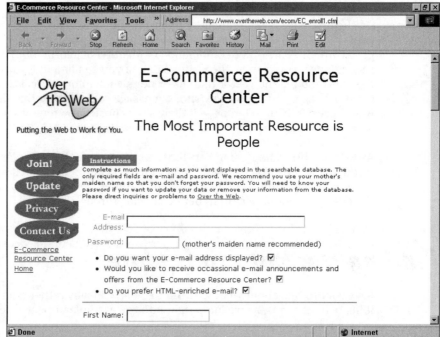

Figure 7-1: Add your listing to the E-commerce Resource Center.

Figure 7-2 shows the first page of this three-page project, where we request the visitor's e-mail address and password. This page contains no ColdFusion; it's a straightforward HTML form page.

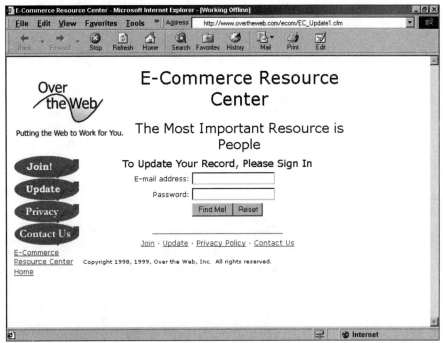

Figure 7-2:
The sign-in page for a member who wants to update data.

Pulling Up the Right Record

After the member has entered his or her information and clicked the Find Me! button, control is passed to an action page that processes the form results.

Extracting the correct record from the database — you'll recall that we want only one record to correspond with this e-mail address and password — requires the CFQUERY tag.

Listing 7-1 is a simple SQL statement that says (in English): "Get all fields from the record of the ecom table in which the e-mail address is equal to the value of the form.email variable, the password is equal to the value of the form.password variable, and the record has not been deleted."

Listing 7-1   Querying the Database for the Record to be Updated Based on E-mail Address and Password

```
<CFQUERY name="getme" datasource="ecom">
SELECT *
FROM ecom
WHERE email = '#form.email#'
      AND password = '#form.password#'
      AND deleted = 0
</CFQUERY>
```

You probably weren't expecting that last AND clause. In this database, when members request that their membership be deleted, it's marked as deleted but not actually deleted. This is a good idea in just about any Web-based database. If you want to know more, see the "Privacy versus an audit trail" sidebar.

Privacy versus an audit trail

Often, to run reports on the success of your system, you must keep some minimal amount of information about anyone who has ever signed into your database. In accounting parlance, keeping visitor data is called an *audit trail*.

E-commerce sites have to be capable of tracking what was shipped where and to whom to prove that they've charged (and paid) state taxes appropriately, even if the member chooses to resign from the site at some later point. As another example, how would you know which ad campaigns worked if you didn't track, at a minimum, the date memberships were created or sales were made? Again, a member's choice to leave would not diminish the value of tracking this information about the visitor.

But should you keep all the information you have about the departing member? Maybe they would not want some of what they've shared with you to be a matter of permanent record in your databases.

To balance the interests of privacy with trust, you can do the following:

- First, create a field in your database (that you populate yourself) with the creation date of the record. You can set Access and most other databases to autopopulate the date when a record is inserted.

- Second, create a deleted date field and a deleted flag, which are populated when members request that their membership be deleted.

- Finally — and this is where many developers get lazy — remove any data about the member that you don't need for auditing. At a minimum, you can overwrite the password, address, phone number, and fax number, unless you need the address and phone number for an audit trail. This depends on whether you keep shipping data with member data or with order data.

Validation

It's a much ignored fact of computer programming — remember when they used to call it that? And only nerdy guys did it? And you made fun of them? Well, we haven't forgotten, either, and now we're cool. They call us Web developers . . . But we digress — that well over half of all programming in most programming languages goes into error handling.

For example, the CFQUERY tag is hunky-dory if every visitor to your site provides a valid e-mail address and password. But what if someone sends you an e-mail address without a password? In that case, the results aren't awful, but they're also not instructive. Figure 7-3 shows what visitors see when they fail to provide either an e-mail address or a password — when you haven't validated whether or not the visitor provided the data you requested.

To make matters worse, if the visitor clicks the "Update my record" button, the screen shown in Figure 7-4 appears.

Be sure to test to make sure your visitors are providing the data you're requesting. Otherwise, they may see screens as awful as these!

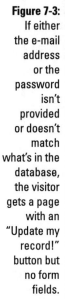

Figure 7-3:
If either the e-mail address or the password isn't provided or doesn't match what's in the database, the visitor gets a page with an "Update my record!" button but no form fields.

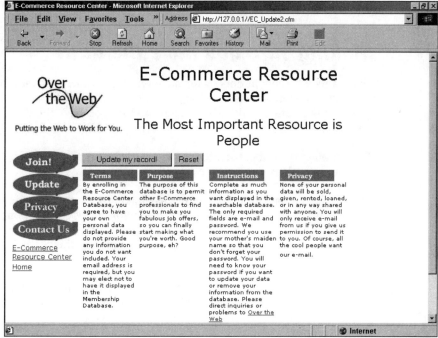

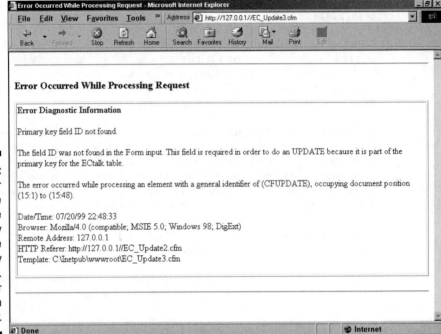

Error Occurred While Processing Request

Error Diagnostic Information

Primary key field ID not found.

The field ID was not found in the Form input. This field is required in order to do an UPDATE because it is part of the primary key for the ECtalk table.

The error occurred while processing an element with a general identifier of (CFUPDATE), occupying document position (15:1) to (15:48).

Date/Time: 07/20/99 22:48:33
Browser: Mozilla/4.0 (compatible; MSIE 5.0; Windows 98; DigExt)
Remote Address: 127.0.0.1
HTTP Referer: http://127.0.0.1//EC_Update2.cfm
Template: C:\Inetpub\wwwroot\EC_Update3.cfm

Figure 7-4:
The error message visitors see when they try to update data they don't have. One error leads to a bigger error.

Making sure you have the data

Merchants who accept checks for payment don't know for a fact that all the checks will clear. Likewise, the biggest part of authentication isn't making sure that the data is valid; it's making sure that you have the data in your possession.

The simplest type of authentication is simply to ask the question: Do I have the data? Simple is good, so we go with that.

We could have performed fancy processing on the e-mail address to be sure it had at least one character and no spaces before the @, at least one character before the dot, and a valid suffix (such as .com, .net, or .uk). But if you want to perform that type of data validation, perform it on the client using JavaScript.

For an invaluable resource, consult the legendary Danny Goodman's *JavaScript Bible* (published by IDG Books Worldwide, Inc.) or *Dynamic HTML: The Definitive Guide*. Don't even think of calling yourself a Web developer without a copy!

In Listing 7-2, we confirm that the visitor has provided both an e-mail address and a password. We test the length of both fields with the Len( ) function. If the length of either field is 0 — meaning no data was provided — we set the notrun flag to TRUE. If both fields have lengths greater than 0, we perform the query and set the notrun flag to FALSE. These types of tests help prevent the display of screens like those in Figures 7-3 and 7-4.

 An even better way to validate form input with ColdFusion is to use either hidden field validation or the CFINPUT tag to enable client-side validation. Each of these approaches is discussed in Chapter 12.

Listing 7-2   Retrieving the Record from the Database only if We have the E-mail Address and Password from the Member

```
<CFIF (Len(form.email) GT 0) AND (Len(form.password) GT 0)>
        <CFQUERY name="getme" datasource="ecom">
        SELECT *
        FROM Ecom
          WHERE email = '#form.email#'
                AND password = '#form.password#'
                AND deleted = 0
        </CFQUERY>
        <CFSET notrun = false>
<CFELSE>
        <CFSET notrun = true>
</CFIF>
```

Notrun?

Where does the notrun flag come from? Out of thin air. We need a way to pass to a later point in the page the information that the query wasn't run because the visitor didn't provide the data. Because we ask the question at this point in the code, we keep note of the answer in the notrun flag. We could just as easily have left off the CFELSE part of the tag and asked the question again later on the page, but that would have been clunkier and less efficient.

The CFSET tag

We slipped another new tag into the mix in the listing. Did you notice? It's called CFSET. We talk about the CFSET tag at greater length in Chapters 9 and 10. Here's the definition:

```
<CFSET variable = value>
```

variable   **Required.** You can use an existing variable or create a new one. By providing a variable name that ColdFusion is unfamiliar with on this page, you create a new variable. You can use

any name you want, as long as the name begins with a letter and doesn't have spaces. You can include underscores in a name, as well. Choose a name you'll remember.

value	**Required.** When you provide a value, you tell ColdFusion what type of variable you're creating (a text field, a numeric field, or a Boolean field) and what you want the value to be. You probably don't realize that you're telling ColdFusion about the field type because you don't do it overtly. ColdFusion determines the type of field you're requesting based on the value you provide.

In Listing 7-2, we create a Boolean variable called notrun. We assign it the value FALSE if the CFIF condition is met or TRUE if the CFIF condition is not met. We use the CFSET tag both to create the variable and to populate the variable with the appropriate value.

If the query doesn't run

If the query doesn't run because either the e-mail address or the password isn't provided, notrun is set to TRUE. Later in the page, a CFIF statement that relies on the value of notrun dictates what's displayed on the page. Here's the relevant code:

```
<CFIF NotRun>
    Your record could not be located. Please return to the
        previous screen and provide both an email address
        and a password.<p>If you have questions, please
        contact <A
        href="mailto:info@overtheweb.com">info@over-
        theweb.com</A> from the email address from which
        you subscribed and your password will be mailed
        to you.
```

The screen that the visitor sees includes helpful instructions. If you don't give visitors clear instructions for completing the screen correctly, they're likely to just keep entering the same data and think that your site is broken. Figure 7-5 shows the screen that appears when the visitor doesn't provide either the e-mail address or the password.

Does seeing the FONT tag in the preceding code bug you? Don't assume that everyone is hip to style sheets and using Internet Explorer 4 or above.

If the query runs

If the query runs, the value of notrun is set to FALSE. (Sure, we could have used a variable called run instead of notrun, and reversed the CFIF statement.)

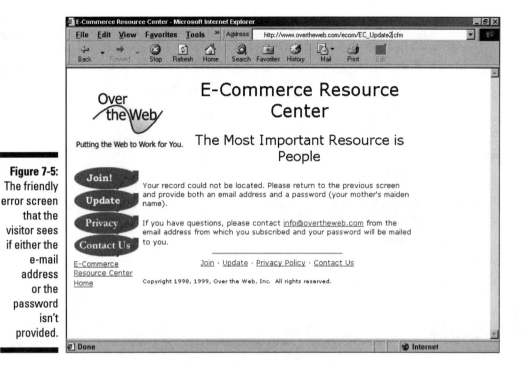

Although the visitor provided values in the e-mail address and password fields, we still don't know whether we'll find a match in the database. We need to perform one more test. If the query returns a record, we display the data for modification. If the query returns no records, we provide a message.

We can test how many records are returned by a query. For every query, ColdFusion creates a special reserved variable called recordcount. The following code contains the check to see whether no records were returned from the query and the message that's displayed:

```
<CFELSEIF getme.recordcount IS 0>
    Your record could not be located. If you have
        questions, please contact <A href="mailto:
        info@overtheweb.com">info@overtheweb.com</A>
        from the email address from which you subscribed
        and your password will be mailed to you.
```

Figure 7-6 shows the helpful error message that's displayed if we find no matching record.

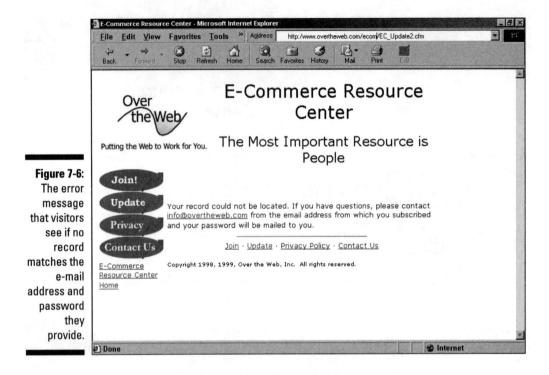

If you find a match

In the best case, the e-mail address and password that the visitor provides
match the e-mail address and password in a record in the database. When
there's a match, the query returns one record. We display each field that the
member can update on the update record page, which is page two of our
three-page project.

Following is the code that displays the fields available for updating:

```
<CFELSE>
    <!-- Entry form -->
    <FORM action="Ecom_Update3.cfm" method="post">
    populated form fields
    </FORM>
</CFIF>
```

Figure 7-7 shows the update page with the fields populated with the data the
member provided originally.

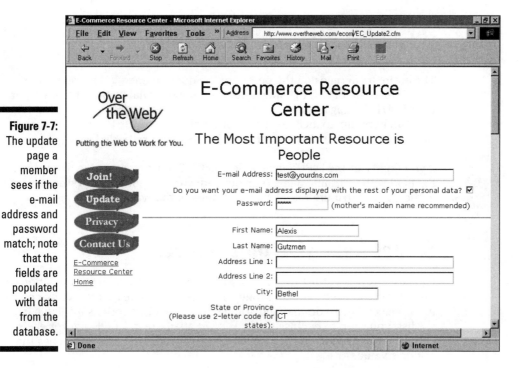

Figure 7-7:
The update
page a
member
sees if the
e-mail
address and
password
match; note
that the
fields are
populated
with data
from the
database.

Displaying the Data for Updating

In the last bit of code, between the FORM tag and the end-FORM tag, is where we would list the populated form fields. To display the values that have been pulled from the database in the form fields, you have to be sure that

- The database is queried for the values
- The form fields are prefilled with query data

In Listing 7-1, you saw the query used to extract from the database the record we want to update.

Text input fields

We want all text-input fields to contain the values from the database that we extracted using the query we performed in Listing 7-1. We need an extra tag — CFOUTPUT — to get the value attributes to display the values of the fields from the query. The following code displays the value of the firstname field from the database in the text-input field by that name:

```
<CFOUTPUT query="getme">
<INPUT type="text" name="firstname" value="#firstname#">
</CFOUTPUT>
```

The entire form relies on the output of the query named getme, so we don't need to use the CFOUTPUT tag around each individual field. Instead, we put the CFOUTPUT tag around the entire form. You can do it either way, but it's less cumbersome to include all the form fields in one big CFOUTPOUT tag than to wrap each individual form field in its own CFOUTPUT tag.

If you don't put the INPUT tag inside a CFOUTPUT tag, the value displayed in the field is the variable name (surrounded with the pound signs) that you put in the value attribute rather than the value of that variable.

Select lists give you choices

Our site has a select list that visitors use to indicate their current position or title. When the page loads, we want to display the value that the visitor chose in the select list. To do that and still have all the other options available in the list, you need to enclose the selected attribute in a CFIF tag. For each OPTION, you need to check whether the value in the database matches the option's value.

In our example, a field called currentstatus holds the value of the member's current position from the select list. The code for the currentstatus field follows:

```
<SELECT name="currentstatus">
<OPTION<CFIF currentstatus is "Web
        Developer">Selected</CFIF>>Web Developer
<OPTION<CFIF currentstatus is "Web
        Designer">Selected</CFIF>>Web Designer
<OPTION <CFIF currentstatus is "Technology
        Manager">Selected</CFIF>>Technology Manager
<OPTION <CFIF currentstatus is "Advertising
        Creative">Selected</CFIF>>Advertising Creative
<OPTION <CFIF currentstatus is "Advertising
        Manager">Selected</CFIF>>Advertising Manager
more options
<OPTION <CFIF currentstatus is "Other">Selected</CFIF>>Other
</SELECT>
```

Check boxes

We have one check box that members use to indicate whether they want their e-mail address displayed on the results page. We call that field displayemail. To make sure the page loads with the check box checked only if the value of displayemail is TRUE in the database, we wrap the checked attribute in the CFIF tag.

Because the displayemail field is Boolean, we don't need an equation in the CFIF tag; instead, we just use the value of the tag. If displayemail is FALSE, the checked attribute won't be present when the page loads; if displayemail is TRUE, the checked attribute is present when the page loads. The code for the displayemail check box follows:

```
<INPUT type="checkbox" name="displayemail" <CFIF
       displayemail>checked</CFIF>>
```

Text areas

We also have a few text areas, where members can provide free-form text about their e-commerce experiences, other experiences, and education. We want these text areas to appear with any text that the member has already typed, so we put the appropriate variable between the TEXTAREA tag and the end-TEXTAREA tag.

In our example, we have a text area field called ecommexp. Here's the code for that field:

```
<TEXTAREA cols="50" name="ecommexp" rows="12"
         wrap="virtual">#ecommexp#</TEXTAREA>
```

Password fields

The password needs to be masked with asterisks (or bullets on a Mac) when the visitor types it in the form. By specifying the input type as password, as shown in the following code, the browser takes care of this for you. There's no point in providing the current password for review, so you can omit the value attribute from this tag.

```
<INPUT type="password" name="password">
```

Hidden fields

This overall section is about displaying data, and hidden fields obviously aren't displayed. But you do need to include a hidden field for the record ID if you want the update on the next page to work. The code for the hidden ID field is

```
<INPUT type="hidden" name="ID" value="#ID#">
```

Updating the Database

ColdFusion makes it easy to update the record in the database by providing the CFUPDATE tag. (Didn't we tell you that you could guess the names of most of the important tags?) All you need to do is make sure you have a unique key on each record in the database. In our example, the ID field is not displayed to members, but does act as the unique key for the record. Each record we create is assigned a number (that's one number higher than the ID of the previously entered number). Some databases enable you to use auto-numbering, in which the database automatically assigns the next number in sequence so that each record has its own key.

The complete definition of the CFUPDATE tag follows. You'll probably never need all the attributes of this tag (at a minimum, you'd need the datasource and tablename), but in the interest of thoroughness, we've listed them.

```
<CFUPDATE
    datasource="datasource"
    tablename="table_name"
    formfields="field_names"
    username="username"
    password="password"
    dbtype="type"
    dbserver="server_name"
    dbname="database_name"
    tableowner="name"
    tablequalifier="qualifier"
    provider="COMprovider"
    providerdsn="datasource">
```

datasource   **Required.** The data source name for the database on which you're performing the update. (See Chapter 4 for more on data sources.)

tablename   **Required.** The name of the table that holds the record you want to update.

formfields   **Optional.** The list of form field names from the form page that should be used for the update. If you're collecting any other data, have named your buttons (shown later), or are sending any hidden fields that are not in the table, you need to specify which fields to update. The values used are those in the form fields of the same name. If you don't include this attribute, ColdFusion assumes that every form field equates to the name of a column in the named table and should be updated. If you list the specific fields you want updated, the key for the table must be in the list.

username	**Optional.** If your database is password protected, you need to provide the username and password, either here or in the datasource definition. (You have to go out of your way to password protect Access, and the process is beyond the scope of this book to explain.)
password	**Optional.** Goes with username, if your database is password protected.
dbtype	**Optional.** Unless you're using a native driver for your database, don't include this. If you're not, you can set it to ODBC (the default), but if your ColdFusion Server (or the one at your ISP or WPP) is not ColdFusion 4, the tag will fail. If you're running a native driver, using the appropriate dbtype will give you faster processing than using an ODBC connection.
dbserver	**Optional.** If you defined the dbtype to be a native driver, you can override the server specified in the datasource definition.
dbname	**Optional.** The database name when dbtype=sybase11 or oledb, overriding that specified in the datasource.
tableowner	**Optional.** The owner of the table.
tablequalifier	**Optional.** The qualifier of the table.
provider	**Optional.** The COM provider (OLE-DB only).
providerdsn	**Optional.** The data source name for the COM provider (OLE-DB only).

Here's the query we use to update the ecom table in the ecom database:

```
<CFUPDATE datasource="ecom" tablename="ecom">
```

If we wanted to limit the fields that go into the database — for example, if we wanted to keep the password field from automatically updating the database — we could list all the fields we want to update using the formfields attribute.

Confirming the Update

After you've updated the database, you need to tell the visitor that the change has taken effect. Figure 7-8 shows the confirmation page that a visitor sees on the E-Commerce Resource Center page.

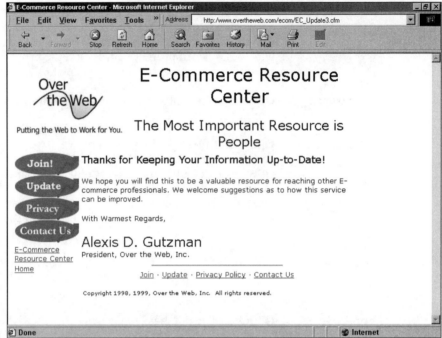

Figure 7-8:
The
confirmation
page a
member
sees after
his or her
record is
updated.

You can customize the confirmation page however you choose. Because it's so obvious that the computer is just spitting back the same data the member provided, showing a confirmation page that repeats everything the member just entered is cheesy.

Studio Speeds Things Up

Studio doesn't provide a wizard that's a perfect match for the project in this chapter; the closest one is the Record Viewer wizard. If you want to use this wizard to create your update pages, you need to do a bit of work to make sure that visitors can update only their own records.

The Record Viewer wizard

The Record Viewer wizard produces three pages for you. The first page permits you to scroll through the data in your site one record at a time. When you find the record you want to change, you can edit it or delete it. You can also add a new record from this page, but that doesn't make sense for our example. The second page allows you to edit the record, and the third page confirms that your changes have been made.

To make this wizard work for our example, we need to use the first page we created by hand (shown way back in Figure 7-2). We also need to add to the top of the second page the code to find the proper record to edit, which is shown in Listing 7-1.

Although you need to do a bit of work on the pages this wizard produces to use it for the example, the wizard still gives you a big leg up on doing it all by hand.

1. **Select File⇨New.**

2. **Select the CFML tab, and then click on Record Viewer Wizard.**

   The dialog box in Figure 7-9 appears.

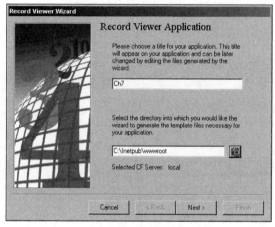

Figure 7-9:
Give your application a name in the Record Viewer wizard and indicate where you want the files saved.

3. **Enter a name for your application.**

   Keep the name brief but descriptive because Studio uses the name as the first part of the file name for each file it creates. This name will also appear at the top of the pages that it creates.

4. **Indicate where you want your files saved.**

   If you're developing locally, you probably want the files to go to your Web server. Click the browse files button to locate the directory where you want your files saved.

5. **Click Next.**

   The dialog box shown in Figure 7-10 appears.

6. **From the drop-down list, select the server and the data source.**

   Which data sources are listed depend on those defined on the server you choose. If you don't see your database listed, make sure you've defined an ODBC entry for one, as we explain in Chapter 4.

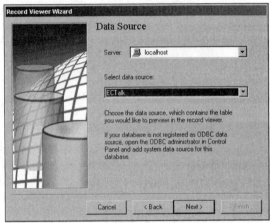

Figure 7-10: Select the server and the data source.

7. **Click Next.**

The dialog box shown in Figure 7-11 makes its appearance.

Figure 7-11: Here you select the table that needs updating.

8. **Select the table you want to update, and then click Next.**

The dialog box shown in Figure 7-12 appears.

9. **Select the fields that you want to appear on the page that allows you to view one record at a time.**

In the case of our example, we've chosen FirstName, LastName, company, State, and country. Be aware, too, that specifying too many fields could create a results page that's too wide to fit on the screen, forcing the user to scroll right to see the data. Viewers generally don't appreciate that.

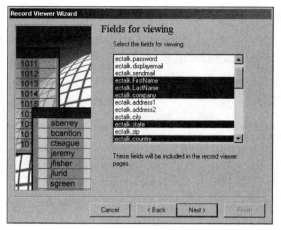

Figure 7-12:
Choose the fields that you want to appear on the page that allows you to select the record for editing.

10. **Click Next.**

   The dialog box in Figure 7-13 shows up.

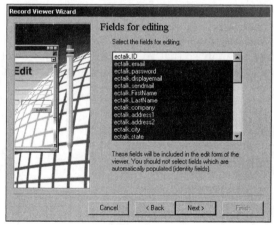

Figure 7-13:
Choose the fields that you want to be editable in the update page.

11. **Click the fields that you want the visitor to be able to edit.**

   If you want to select contiguous fields, click the first one, hold down the Shift key, and click the last one. If you want to select noncontiguous fields, hold down the Ctrl key and click each field you want selected. Chances are you don't want your primary key to be editable.

12. **Click Next.**

   The dialog box in Figure 7-14 appears.

Figure 7-14:
Select the
unique key
for your
table.

13. **Select the unique identifier for your table (the primary key).**

    Studio guesses the primary key to your table. If the program isn't correct, you have to select the key yourself. Our key is ID, which Studio guessed correctly.

14. **Click Finish.**

    Studio creates the files. Figure 7-15 shows the file names and file descriptions. Read them carefully so that you don't accidentally delete one of these files later, when you can't figure out where it came from.

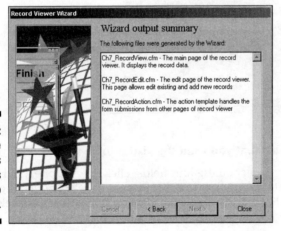

Figure 7-15:
Read the
descriptions
of the files
that Studio
has created.

Modifying the pages created by the Record Viewer wizard

The first page that Studio created in our example, Ch7_RecordView.cfm, needs some adjustments before we can use it to pull up the appropriate record for the visitor to edit. Figure 7-16 shows the page that Studio creates.

This page permits the addition and deletion of records without any verification. These are two good reasons to break open the code and make some changes. A third good reason is that we don't want to permit a visitor to edit someone else's record. At a minimum, the buttons that permit adding and editing need to be removed. The code for all the buttons above the result record appear next:

```
<!-- form buttons -->
<INPUT type="submit" name="btnView_First" value=" << ">
<INPUT type="submit" name="btnView_Previous" value=" <   ">
<INPUT type="submit" name="btnView_Next" value="  >  ">
<INPUT type="submit" name="btnView_Last" value=" >> ">
<INPUT type="submit" name="btnView_Add" value="  Add   ">
<INPUT type="submit" name="btnView_Edit" value="  Edit  ">
<INPUT type="submit" name="btnView_Delete" value="Delete">
```

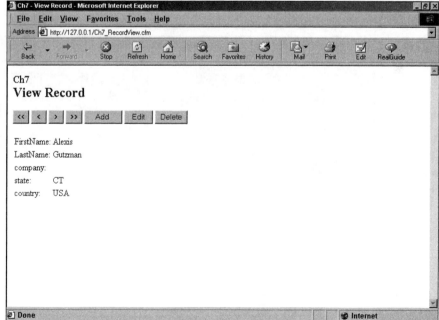

Figure 7-16: The first page of the Record Viewer wizard doesn't work for the E-Commerce Resource Center database example.

Removing the last three buttons will clear up some of the problem. To duplicate the example, however, you'll probably have to create a simple form page to request data that uniquely identifies the record as belonging to the visitor, as shown in Figure 7-2.

The second page needs just a few modifications. Add the code from Listing 7-1 to the top of the page called Ch7_RecordEdit.cfm. Then replace line 3 of that page with the following code:

```
<CFIF getme.recordcount IS 1>
```

Finally, replace lines 7 through 9 of this page with the following one line:

```
WHERE ectalk.ID = #getme.ID#
```

This line of code ensures that the page displays only editable fields if a matching record is found, and that the correct key is used in pulling up the visitor's record.

Figure 7-17 shows the field-editing page that Studio creates.

The third page produced by the Record Viewer wizard is simply a processing page. Nothing is displayed as a result of this page (called Ch7_RecordAction.cfm). The page does the processing and then links back to the first page. You probably want to show a confirmation page that gives the visitor some useful feedback, such as a message confirming that the submitted changes have been accepted.

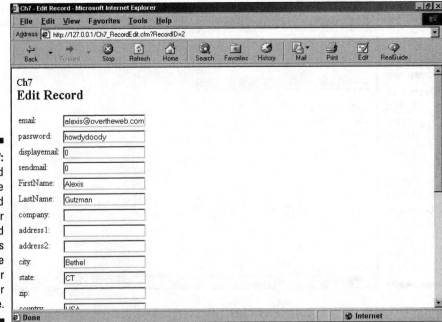

Figure 7-17: The second page of the Record Viewer wizard produces acceptable results for our example.

Chapter 8

Processing Mail

● ●

In This Chapter

▶ Discovering the many uses of the CFMAIL tag

▶ Figuring out which mail server to use

▶ Using variables in your e-mail

▶ Using query results in your e-mail

▶ Sending along mail attachments

● ●

*D*espite the pervasive power and effect of the Web on our lives, many have argued that simple e-mail is the most widely used and most important application on the Internet. Many people use it as the main way to stay in touch both at home and at work, and it's becoming an increasingly important aspect of e-commerce as well.

The capability to create e-mail in your ColdFusion applications can be useful in dozens of ways. Perhaps you want to generate your company newsletter and promotional messages. Or maybe you want to confirm Web site registrations and online purchases. You can use ColdFusion also to assist Web site visitors in communicating with those running the site, by creating a Web form for technical support requests that are then e-mailed to technicians.

Some uses of CFMAIL involve sending a note to one person; others entail sending an e-mail to a related set of people, perhaps using a list of e-mail addresses from a database query. Sometimes the content of the e-mail should be customized for the recipient, such as a registration ID generated from the insertion of a new database record or a status report gathered from a database query.

With ColdFusion, doing all this is easy. In this chapter, we describe the CFMAIL tag and the many ways in which you can use it.

Simple but Varied

On the surface, the CFMAIL tag may seem simple, but you can use it in ways that may not be obvious. The recipients of the message — as well as the contents of the message itself — can be static or dynamic. You can use CFMAIL to

- ✔ Send a simple static message to a single e-mail address
- ✔ Send a simple static message to a list of e-mail addresses obtained from a database query

Beyond that, you can generate the contents dynamically, and the contents can contain any of the following:

- ✔ Any valid ColdFusion variable, function, or other expression, when the contents do not change for each recipient
- ✔ Columns in a query for obtaining the list of e-mail recipients; you use those columns to create a custom message for each user (like a mail merge in a word processor)
- ✔ Column(s) from multiple records in a query, such as when presenting a report within an e-mail. Optionally, this can be grouped so that a set of records is available for each of multiple recipients found in the query.

In addition, the subject and any other attributes of the CFMAIL tag can contain ColdFusion variables, functions, and other expressions.

We show you how to use all these approaches. First, though, look at the syntax of the CFMAIL tag:

```
<CFMAIL
    to="recipient"
    from="sender"
    cc="copy_to"
    subject="msg_subject"
    type="msg_type"
    query="query_name"
    startrow="query_row"
    maxrows="max_msgs"
    group="query_column"
    server="servername"
    port="port_ID"
    mailerid="headerid"
    timeout="seconds"
    mimeattach="path">
```

to   **Required.** The name of the recipient(s) of the e-mail message. This can be either a static address (such as `TO="support@ allaire.com"`), a variable that contains an address (such as `TO="#Form.Email#"`), or the name of a query column that contains address information (such as `TO="#EMail#"`). In the last case, an individual e-mail message is sent for every row returned by the query.

from   **Required.** The sender of the e-mail message. This attribute may be either static (such as `FROM="support@allaire .com"`) or dynamic (such as `FROM="#GetUser .EMailAddress#"`).

cc   **Optional.** Indicates additional addresses to copy the e-mail message to. This attribute may be static or dynamic.

subject   **Required.** The subject of the mail message. This field may be driven dynamically on a message-by-message basis. For example, if you want to update customers on the status of their orders, you might use the following `subject` attribute: `SUBJECT="Status for Order Number #Order_ID#"`.

type   **Optional.** Specifies extended `type` attributes for the message. Currently, the only valid value for this attribute is `"HTML"`. Specifying `TYPE= "HTML"` informs the receiving e-mail client that the message has embedded HTML tags that must be processed. This is useful only when sending messages to mail clients that understand HTML (such as Netscape 2.0 and above e-mail clients).

query   **Optional.** The name of the CFQUERY from which you want to draw data for message(s) you want to send. Specify this attribute to send more than one mail message or to send the results of a query within a single message.

startrow   **Optional.** Specifies the row in the query to start from.

maxrows   **Optional.** Specifies the maximum number of e-mail messages you want to send.

group   **Optional.** Specifies the query column to use when you group sets of records to send as a single e-mail message. For example, if you send a set of billing statements to your customers, you might group on `"Customer_ID"`. The `group` attribute, which is case sensitive, eliminates adjacent duplicates in the case where the data is sorted by the specified field.

server	**Required.** The address of the SMTP server to use for sending messages. The server name specified in ColdFusion Administrator is used if no `server` is specified.
port	The TCP/IP port on which the SMTP server listens for requests. This is almost always 25.
mailerid	**Optional.** Specifies a mailer ID, to be passed in the X-Mailer SMTP header, that identifies the mailer application. The default is Allaire ColdFusion Application Server.
timeout	**Optional.** The number of seconds to wait before timing out the connection to the SMTP server.
mimeattach	**Optional.** Specifies the path of the file to be attached to the e-mail message. The attached file is MIME-encoded.

The CFMAIL tag in 4.5 has two new attributes:

bcc	**Optional.** Indicates additional addresses to copy the e-mail message to without listing them in the message header. The letters *bcc* mean *blind carbon copy*.
groupcasesensitive	**Optional.** A Boolean indicating whether to group with regard to case. The default value is YES; case is considered while grouping. If the `query` attribute specifies a query object generated by a case-insensitive SQL query, set the `groupcasesensitive` attribute to NO to keep the recordset intact.

Sending a Simple E-Mail

Later in the chapter, you see how to use many CFMAIL attributes as well as special features to make more dynamic e-mails based on variables and query results. For now, we start with a simple example: sending an e-mail to someone from within ColdFusion. It's as simple as this:

```
<CFMAIL TO="bobsmith@mainstreet.com"
      FROM="sales@ourcompany.com" SUBJECT="This is a test
      message">
This test message is being sent to Bob Smith. The message
can be as large as you want and can be just simple text
with multiple lines. You do not need to specify HTML
breaks and the like. (HTML formatting is another option.)
</CFMAIL>
```

When executed, this tag sends an e-mail to the named To address. The recipient sees the message as coming from the named From address. The message looks like a regular e-mail message.

Note that the body of the message is simply typed as you want it to be displayed. If you want a line of space between paragraphs, simply press the Insert key. In most HTML and CFML processing, you need to use an HTML <p> (paragraph) tag to represent a space. In this case, however, we're *not* creating HTML, so we don't need to use such devices. We just type as we would in any e-mail program.

Do you want to format your e-mail message as HTML because you're sending it to someone who uses an e-mail program that can process and present HTML-formatted e-mail? If so, see the `type="HTML"` attribute in the preceding section for more information.

When your ColdFusion template executes this code, it doesn't send a response to the user executing the template. In other words, CFMAIL does not create output on-screen. Typically, you would either produce output to relay that the e-mail has been sent (possibly repeating whatever has been sent) or issue a CFLOCATION tag to make the template transfer control to some other page. (For more on CFLOCATION, see Chapter 11.)

Specifying the Mail Server

In the preceding example, we left out an important detail. It's okay for you to leave that detail out as well, as long as you or someone else does some initial administrative setup. In addition, we mentioned that there's no response from issuing the tag, so how do you know whether it succeeded?

Both these issues involve the server processing the e-mail. The server? Isn't ColdFusion sending the e-mail? We don't rely on ColdFusion Server to do that job, just as we don't rely on ColdFusion to act as a Web server. Instead, we need the SMTP, or mail, server.

The SMTP (Simple Mail Transport Protocol) server sends e-mail to the Internet. It's also in charge when there's a problem, such as when a message returns after several days' attempts to be delivered.

Which mail server, then?

We need a way for our CFMAIL tag to know where to pass the mail message for handling. We have two choices. The first is to use the `server` attribute to specify the name of a mail server in our CFMAIL tag. The second choice is to rely on your ColdFusion administrator for specifying a server. Ask your

ColdFusion administrator if he or she has specified a mail server this way. If the administrator has defined a mail server, you don't have to do anything in your CFMAIL tag to specify one. You may use the one they've specified by default — or you may specify one of your own.

It may be in your interest to specify a server in your CFMAIL tag anyway. What if someone mistakenly removes the name of the server from the administrator page? That person will see no effect, but you will when a user executes your template with a CFMAIL tag that fails.

How do I know whether it worked?

We mentioned that the CFMAIL tag doesn't provide feedback for the user to see (or you as a programmer to test). Well, CFMAIL does provide one type of feedback: When the tag has a syntax error, an error occurs as soon as the tag is executed.

The CFMAIL tag only passes the message to the mail server for processing. (Actually, the message is spooled for processing, which can be helpful if you're sending hundreds or thousands of messages.) Processing then continues in the template without notification. A mail message could fail perhaps days down the road. So how do you know that the mail message was sent? You don't.

Okay, not quite. A mechanism is available to review the status of messages that fail as well as a log of undeliverable messages. But these are not generally available to developers on a server — access is usually restricted to the ColdFusion Server administrator).

For more information on specifying mail servers, see Allaire's *Administering ColdFusion Server* manual. And for more information on resolving mail server problems, see the Allaire Knowledge Base articles 11335 and 1288, available at their Web site (www.allaire.com).

Dynamic E-Mail Using Variables

You've seen how easy it is to use the CFMAIL tag. You simply specify the same information you would when sending any e-mail message, most notably in the To, From, and Subject fields.

One of the nifty features of CFMAIL is that you can specify any of these as the value of a variable or other ColdFusion expression. For instance, suppose you want a simple form on your Web site for users to indicate their interest in receiving a one-time notification or document. The form simply prompts them for their e-mail address, perhaps in a field called email. Then your form's action page specifies that form field as the To field for the mail message, as in the following:

```
<CFMAIL TO="#form.email#" FROM="sales@ourcompany.com"
      SUBJECT="Message You Requested">
This is the message you requested from OurCompany.com.
Thanks for your interest.
. . .
(rest of message)
. . .
</CFMAIL>
```

You can substitute any or all mail header fields (To, From, CC, BCC, and Subject) in this way.

Using variables like this is even more useful when you consider driving the message content with variables. Consider a form that prompts a visitor for Web site feedback. This is a common type of form and a common Web site requirement; you could extend it to forms prompting for tech support and much more.

With CFMAIL, you simply use the data from the feedback field as well as the e-mail address and subject that visitors provide to create a message to be sent to the Web support staff, as in the following:

```
<CFMAIL TO="support@ourcompany.com" FROM=" form.email "
      SUBJECT="#form.subject#">
The following web site feedback was offered:
From: #form.email#
Subject: #form.subject#
Date: #dateformat(now())#
Message:
#form.message#
</CFMAIL>
```

You may use more than form variables in e-mail. For example, in this example, we use the value of the Dateformat(Now( )) function to indicate the date and time that the message was sent.

Note that when you use variables and other ColdFusion expressions inside a CFMAIL tag, you do not use CFOUTPUT as you might expect. You simply place the variables and expressions in the body of the message; ColdFusion replaces them with their value when the CFMAIL tag is processed.

Finally, remember that you may format the body of the message in whatever way you want.

You might be wondering why we bother with a form-driven process to accept feedback e-mail when we could provide a mailto link on the page that opens the user's e-mail program to send the e-mail. There are three potential problems: Visitors may not have a mail program; they may be on a machine other than their own that is not set up properly, or they may not want to identify themselves and therefore choose to not offer a From address. By using a Web form, we solve all three of these problems.

Dynamic E-Mail using Query Results

We can take the dynamic power of CFMAIL to yet another level by using query variables. The possibilities are much more exciting than simply using another type of variable.

Using a query column for the To field

When you use a query variable in the To field of a message, CFMAIL is smart enough to know that you want to loop over all the records in the query and create a single message for each recipient indicated by the named query column. (We assume that the column holds an e-mail address.)

Consider a process that searches a customer database for people living in a given state, so that you can send them a special sale notice. The combination of CFQUERY and CFMAIL solves this problem easily:

```
<CFQUERY DATASOURCE="Test" NAME="GetCust">
SELECT Email FROM Customers
WHERE State='MD'
</CFQUERY>

<CFMAIL TO="#GetCust.Email#" FROM="sales@ourcompany.com"
        SUBJECT="Special Offer for Maryland Customers">
Attention Maryland Customers:

We are happy to be able to offer you a special deal...
. . .
(rest of message)
. . .
</CFMAIL>
```

That's nifty enough. To think that one tag (okay, two tags) could create several, or dozens, or even thousands of messages in one fell swoop! And because the messages are spooled when CFMAIL passes them to the mail server, the process happens quickly.

But, as they used to say in those knife commercials, "Wait, there's more!"

Using query columns in the message body

Things get even more exciting when you find out that while looping through the creation of a message for each recipient found in the query, you may also refer to the other columns in the query within the body of the message. In other words, you can approximate the mail-merge processing performed in word processing. When used this way, you again use the query columns as variables within the body of the message. You can then customize each message to refer to specific details for each recipient.

Extending our last example, consider the following:

```
<CFQUERY DATASOURCE="Test" NAME="GetCust">
SELECT FirstName, LastName, Email FROM Customers
WHERE State='MD'
</CFQUERY>

<CFMAIL TO="#GetCust.Email#" FROM="sales@ourcompany.com"
        SUBJECT="#getcust.firstname# #getcust.lastname#'s
        Special Offer">
Dear #getcust.firstname# #getcust.lastname#,

We are happy to be able to offer you a special deal. . .
. . .
(rest of message)
. . .
</CFMAIL>
```

See how we are able to use the customer's first and last name within the body of the message? Now it's clear to the recipient that the message is not just spam being sent to everyone in the Internet world.

Note also that we have even used a query column to make part of the Subject query driven. Talk about personalization! When your customers receive an e-mail with their name in the subject, they may more likely notice it. (As more and more businesses have access to powerful query-driven mail processing, however, the novelty of a custom-addressed Subject line will wear off.)

Finally, keep in mind that you can use `startrow` and `maxrows` attributes to further control which records in the query result are used to create e-mails.

You can do more than just spit out the recipient's name in the body. You can refer to any query column. The query can be as complex as you need, can refer to any columns, and can even do multi-table joins. Imagine the types of reporting that are now possible!

Using grouped output for message processing

Another compelling reporting possibility is to use grouped output in much the same way as in CFOUTPUT GROUP processing, which we discuss in Chapter 12. The benefit there, as here, is that if several records have a matching characteristic, such as several orders placed by the same customer, you can display each of those multiple records within the message body.

Consider the following query and its results:

```
<CFQUERY DATASOURCE="Test" NAME="GetOrders">
SELECT Customers.CustomerId, FirstName, LastName, Email,
        OrderDate, OrderAmount FROM Customers, Orders
WHERE Customers.CustomerId = Orders.OrderId
ORDER BY CustomerID, OrderDate
</CFQUERY>
```

This might result in data that looks like Figure 8-1.

Figure 8-1:
Finding customers with more than one order.

1	Bob	Smith	Bsmith@mindfall.com	01-12-99	12.52
1	Bob	Smith	Bsmith@mindfall.com	05-30-99	54.00
1	Bob	Smith	Bsmith@mindfall.com	08-4-99	26.99
2	Jane	Doe	Jdoe@ballaire.com	06-1-99	432.08
3	Bill	Bloggs	Bbloggs@bilbo.com	02-14-99	23.23
3	Bill	Bloggs	Bbloggs@bilbo.com	02-14-99	23.23
3	Bill	Bloggs	Bbloggs@bilbo.com	02-14-99	23.23

This query found three customers (customer IDs of 1, 2, and 3). We have multiple records per customer because multiple order records existed for each customer and we joined the two tables to get the result.

If you want to produce a single e-mail for each customer that lists all orders for that customer, you need to add a little magic to the CFMAIL tag . . . we mean, you need to use the group attribute in the CFMAIL tag. The group attribute, which is case sensitive, eliminates adjacent duplicates when data is sorted by a specified field.

The trick works just as it does in CFOUTPUT processing: We sort the records by the column that will group the records in the way we want to send them (in this case, by the customer_id column). Then we refer to that column with the group attribute in the CFMAIL tag. Finally, we use a CFOUTPUT tag in the body to create an inner loop over the records found per recipient.

Our template could follow the query offered previously with this CFMAIL tag:

```
<CFMAIL TO="#GetCust.Email#" FROM="sales@ourcompany.com"
       SUBJECT="Your Order Status" GROUP="customer_id">
Dear #getcust.firstname# #getcust.lastname#,

Following is a statement of your orders with us this year:
. . .
(rest of message)
. . .
</CFMAIL>
```

As in CFOUTPUT `group` processing, the case of the `group` column's values is considered when the process attempts to find duplicates.

As mentioned in the syntax section, Version 4.5 has a `groupcasesensitive` Boolean option (Yes/No) that you can specify to change the default behavior regarding case. That is, you can now choose to ignore case sensitivity.

Sending Attachments

Another common mail processing feature that you can use with CFMAIL is sending attachments along with the e-mail. Doing so is as easy as everything else in CFMAIL. In the `mimeattach` attribute, you specify the name (and path) of a file to be sent along with the message. The file name can be a variable when appropriate. The file must reside on the ColdFusion server. The attached file is mime encoded, which is the standard for mail attachment processing.

ColdFusion 4.5 introduced CFMAILPARAM, which enables you to have more than one attachment file. You specify CFMAILPARAM inside the CFMAIL tag. See the ColdFusion 4.5 documentation for more details.

Part III
Creating ColdFusion Applications

The 5th Wave   By Rich Tennant

"Look, I've already launched a search for 'reanimated babe cadavers' three times and nothing came up!"

In this part . . .

*H*ere, you see how to turn your Web site into a full-fledged application, rather than a bunch of linked-together pages. Need to track a visitor from one page to another, even when neither page has a form? Need a members-only site? Perhaps you need to keep track of a shopping cart for your e-commerce site?

This part gives you skills from thinking like a programmer, to creating the right kind of variable for your application, to securing your site and maintaining state, to selecting and displaying data. These skills put you on the road to developing professional Web applications — and in a *For Dummies* book, at that!

Chapter 9

Thinking Like a Programmer

● ●

In This Chapter

▶ Understanding the basics of programming

▶ Making decisions with CFIF and CFSWITCH

▶ Looping with CFLOOP

▶ Uncovering some useful ColdFusion functions

● ●

"*W*ait a second," you're saying. "I don't *want* to think like a program-mer! Next thing you know, you'll want me to *be* a programmer." Quit worrying — it's not as bad as it sounds. You don't need to enjoy pizza, highly caffeinated soda, and *Star Trek* reruns to be a programmer (though it certainly helps). If you've programmed macros in Word, built formulas in Excel, or created JavaScripts on the Web, you're already heading down the programming path.

ColdFusion has many of the components of other high-level languages, such as C++, Visual Basic, and Java. This chapter demystifies the art of program-ming and covers the ColdFusion tags that add decision-making and looping to your ColdFusion templates, enabling you to build sophisticated Web applications.

Get with the Program

Programming is not an arcane art. Sure, programming involves a lot of jargon, such as *pointers* and *compiling*, as well as strange abbreviations and syntax, such as *println* and *x == 1 || die*. Underneath, however, programming has a remarkable simplicity and logic.

Programming is basically a way to automate things. It's about making the computer *do* things that don't require anything more than logical decision-making and calculation. It's about structuring the application to handle a problem. It's about controlling how the application works on the problem. And most importantly, it's about solving that problem.

It's about structure

All programming languages have some sort of formal structure. You're probably familiar with the *external* structure of a computer program — the nicely packaged executable file that you run to build a Web page, edit a photograph, or type a manuscript. Inside that computer program is a much richer *internal* structure.

Most computer programs have a number of independent components that work together to attack the various problems they are designed to solve. For example, a traditional data-entry application performs a variety of activities repeatedly, such as checking the format or contents of a data field.

Somewhere in the thousands of lines of programming that went into building the data-entry application is a set of instructions for making sure that the date is entered in the correct format (11/01/1999, for example). This component of the data-entry program might be a few lines or thousands, but it serves a single purpose. Others might call it a *procedure,* a *function,* a *subroutine,* an *object,* a *class,* or a *library,* but we'll call it a "chunk of code."

These chunks of code make it easier to build and maintain an application. If you need to add new data validation features to the data-entry program, for example, you must modify only the data validation chunk of code. It's also likely that you can recycle that same chunk of code when you create another application that handles data entry.

Breaking code into smaller chunks also reduces maintenance because you can focus on a particular action or behavior represented by the chunk of code without worrying about dozens of other actions and behaviors. Some folks call a program that hasn't been broken into smaller chunks *spaghetti code* because the program is a big mass of interconnected pieces without an obvious beginning, end, or path to follow.

In ColdFusion, a basic chunk of code is called a *template*. It's a single file of ColdFusion tags and functions and can also include text, HTML, JavaScript, and virtually anything else that can be displayed by a Web browser. An *application* in ColdFusion is one or more of these templates.

The nature of Web programming forces you to break your ColdFusion application into smaller pieces. The basic scenario for any Web application is that the client browser makes a *request* that generates a *response* from the server. This *request-response* cycle is a fundamental part of programming ColdFusion applications.

Each request and response is a separate ColdFusion template. A good example is the process of data entry: A user fills out a form that is submitted to the Web server (request), which processes the information and presents the appropriate feedback (response).

The request-response cycle also makes ColdFusion a little different than more traditional languages that allow custom subroutines, modules, and functions. ColdFusion implements custom subroutines and functions through an extensible *custom tags* framework. For example, you could create a custom tag that checks a text box on a Web form and makes sure that the contents are in the format 11/01/1999. You could then include that custom tag in any ColdFusion template that needs date-related data validation.

These custom tags can be written in CFML, or they can be created by using C++ or Java. Chapter 16 discusses custom tags and includes ten of the best custom tags created by the ColdFusion development community.

It's about control

In the ColdFusion templates you build in other chapters, each line of ColdFusion code is processed, and every bit of the resulting HTML is presented to the user. But what if you want to process only a *portion* of the template? Or what if you want to process only a portion of the template under certain conditions? For these types of scenarios, you need programmatic control over the execution of the template. With such control, the program can branch into different areas of itself to handle different requests, situations, and conditions, as shown in Figure 9-1.

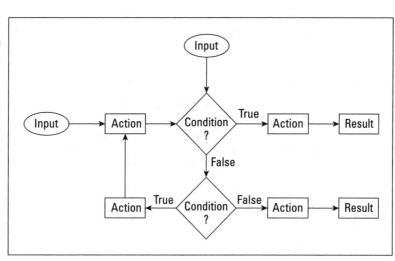

Figure 9-1: Conditional processing logic makes it easier to model complex real-world situations with a limited number of steps.

Returning to our data-entry example, the date needs to be validated only when the user *requests* that event. Somewhere in the data-entry program is a chunk of decision-making code that — in response to a signal (such as a menu item click) — selectively activates the chunk of action code that does the validation. In computer lingo, the decision-making chunk of code is *triggering* the date-validating chunk of code. In a ColdFusion application, the date-validation custom tag would be triggered only when the user requests a response (by submitting the form).

It's about solving problems

The goal of any computer program is to solve a problem. A program might be as simple as a backup program that copies a crucial set of files to a secure location at the end of each day or as complex as the core business application of a major company. In any case, programs are designed to solve problems.

The most important part of any programming project is outlining the problem. This crucial step of the application development process is often overlooked by those new to programming. **Don't skip this step!** Formal steps are available for needs analysis and project development, but you need only the following simple steps:

1. **Define the problem.**

   Be as specific as possible, such as keeping a list of names and e-mail addresses of the visitors to your site or creating an order-processing system for a CD site. A clear definition of the problem helps you keep on track as you work.

2. **Outline the steps to solve the problem.**

   We find that flowcharts or other sketches of problem-solving steps are crucial parts of designing an application. You'll be glad that you created a sketch, too, when you come back to the application later to make changes. You don't have to be fancy. (We often scribble little boxes and arrows in pencil on recycled computer paper.)

3. **Translate those steps into a rough program outline.**

   This is where the computer work starts. Create a rough draft of the chunks of code needed to handle each step you identified in Step 2.

4. **Code, debug, refine, and debug.**

   Start coding! Turn your plan into action. No one gets it right the first (or even second) time, so don't feel badly about refining the design and debugging the code (which we discuss in detail in Chapter 14). Repeat this step until your program works and is completely bug-free (or as close as you can get to that ideal).

For example, suppose that you created an online CD collection database and you want to produce a list of CDs from a specific genre of music. You've already accomplished Step 1, defining the problem: Find CDs that match a certain genre.

Step 2 is equally straightforward: The program needs to be able to select the genre to search for; search the database; and display the results. This example is simple, so the solution presents itself readily. Most problems, however, take more time and energy to solve.

The program outline for Step 3 is simple, too. You need one chunk of code to ask the user for the CD genre, another chunk of code to perform the search, and a final chunk of code to display the results. The outline could consist of two ColdFusion templates, one to get the search parameters and one to do the search and display the results. Listing 9-1 is the code in the search template.

Listing 9-1	Search-Entry Form for Selecting a CD by Genre from a Database Collection

```
<HTML>
<HEAD>
        <TITLE>Search CD Database</TITLE>
</HEAD>

<BODY>
<FORM action="do_search.cfm" method="POST" name="CDSearch">
<SELECT name="Genre">
        <OPTION value="R&B">R&amp;B</OPTION>
        <OPTION value="Jazz">Jazz</OPTION>
        <OPTION value="Hip-hop">Hip-hop</OPTION>
        <OPTION value="Techno">Techno</OPTION>
        <OPTION value="Classic Rock">Classic Rock</OPTION>
</SELECT>
<INPUT type="Submit">
</FORM>

</BODY>
</HTML>
```

It would be a lot more effective to create the SELECT list from a database query, possibly using the CFSELECT tag discussed in Chapter 13. But for this example, it's easier to focus on solving the problem by looking at the hand-coded HTML.

The template that actually performs the search might look like Listing 9-2.

Listing 9-2   **Code That Searches the CD Collection and Displays the Results**

```
<CFQUERY name="FindGenres" datasource="MusicCollection">
SELECT AlbumName, Artist FROM MusicCollection WHERE
        Genre='#Form.Genre#'
</CFQUERY>
<HTML>
<HEAD>
      <TITLE>Do CD Search</TITLE>
</HEAD>

<BODY>
<CFTABLE query="FindGenres" colheaders htmltable border>
      <CFCOL text="#AlbumName#" header="Album Name">
      <CFCOL text="#Artist#" header="Artist">
</CFTABLE>
</BODY>
</HTML>
```

Put these two listings together and you have a basic Web application. Figure 9-2 shows an example of search parameters; the results are shown in Figure 9-3. For more information on using the ColdFusion tags in this example, take a look at the chapters in Part II.

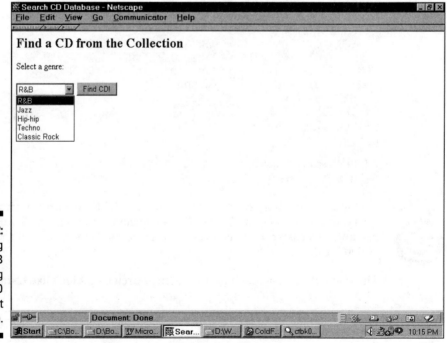

Figure 9-2: Searching for an R&B CD by using our basic CD management application.

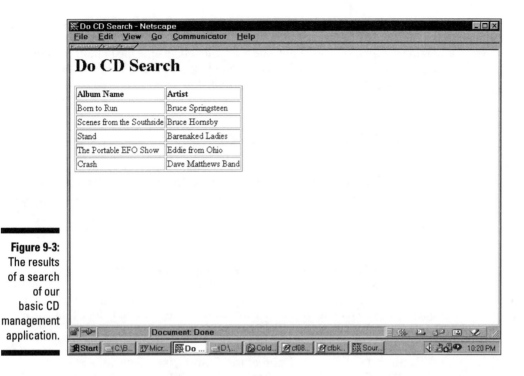

Figure 9-3:
The results
of a search
of our
basic CD
management
application.

The rest of the chapter outlines the major concepts in most programming languages: decision-making, controlling how the program executes, and producing values with functions. Take the design ideas in this section, add some of the programming ideas from the following sections, and you'll be well on your way to becoming a programmer, like it or not!

This or That?

Humans often find it difficult to make decisions, but computer programs have no such limitations — at least in situations they were programmed to handle. Computer programs reliably and infallibly do exactly what you tell them to do.

Expressing the conditions for making a decision is a crucial first step to controlling a computer program. The prerequisite for making a decision, however, is understanding (or evaluating) the expression that is crucial to making the choice. A good example is the relationship between your clothing choice and the weather forecast. Most people choose a raincoat or an umbrella when the chance of rain is high, but the value of a high chance of rain varies from person to person. Worrywarts might choose to carry an umbrella if the chance of rain is greater than 0 percent; children might fight against wearing a raincoat even if the chance of rain rises to 100 percent! A computer program that advises you about raingear will need a specific definition of *high* so that it can evaluate the information and help you make the decision whether to take an umbrella or leave it in the closet.

Comparison operators

To a computer, logic is at the core of decision making. Decisions in a ColdFusion template are made by evaluating logical expressions. These expressions consist of a comparison operator as well as any number of logical or arithmetic operators, or any number of ColdFusion functions, or both. The result of evaluating an expression is always either the value TRUE or FALSE.

The most basic type of expression is a simple comparison between two values. Most computer languages, including ColdFusion, offer a set of operators to handle this type of decision-making. Table 9-1 lists the comparison operators you can use in ColdFusion code. (They probably look familiar.)

Table 9-1	ColdFusion Comparison Operators	
Operator	*What It Means*	*Example*
EQ, IS	Equal (=)	Form.Name EQ "John"
NEQ, IS NOT	Not equal (<>)	Form.Name NEQ ""
LT	Less than (<)	Sales LT Expectations
LTE	Less than or equal (<=)	Sales LTE Expectations
GT	Greater than (>)	Expenses GT Revenue
GTE	Greater than or equal (>=)	SellPrice GTE BuyPrice
CONTAINS	String appears within	Form.Name CONTAINS "john"
DOES NOT CONTAIN	String does not appear	Form.Name DOES NOT CONTAIN "jane"

The operators in Table 9-1 make it possible to compare any type of numeric or string values.

Numeric values provide a variety of comparison possibilities. They can either be explicit, as in

```
X LTE 10
```

or implicitly created by using a combination of arithmetic operators or ColdFusion functions, such as the following examples:

```
X LTE 10+2

X+2 GT (2*X)/5

COS(x) EQ SIN(y)
```

Note that, in each case, the values on both sides of the operator evaluate to a numeric result.

Keep in mind that you'll usually compare a variable (such as X) to a value that's either a constant or another variable. Also remember that the evaluation of functions and any arithmetic take place *before* the comparison operator is evaluated.

Here's an example of how the comparison process works:

1. Start with the expression X LTE 10+2, where X is equal to 5.

2. Evaluate the expression X and the expression 10+2. The expression is now 5 LTE 12.

3. Compare the values to the right and left of the operator.

4. Determine the result of the comparison (TRUE or FALSE). Because 5 is less than 12, the expression is TRUE.

You can use the IS, EQ, IS NOT, NEQ, CONTAINS, and DOES NOT CONTAIN operators to compare not only numeric values but also text strings. You can use string functions to manipulate strings (for example, chopping off everything but the first two characters of a string) before they are compared, just as you can manipulate numeric values before their comparison. For example:

```
Form.Password EQ "Open Sesame"

Username NEQ "guest"

Permissions CONTAINS "Read"
```

Using comparison operators other than IS, EQ, IS NOT, NEQ, CONTAINS, and DOES NOT CONTAIN for text strings will probably give you unexpected results. ColdFusion tries to compare strings alphabetically when you use LT, GT, and the like, but it gets confused when it compares a numeric value and a string.

Logical (Boolean) operators

You can also use a set of logical, or *Boolean,* operators to connect logical expressions together to form more complex, or compound, statements. Check out the short list of Booleans in Table 9-2.

Table 9-2	ColdFusion Logic Operators Combined
Operator	*Example Logical Expression*
AND	(Sales GTE Target) AND (Profits GT 0)
OR	(Sales LT Target) OR (Profits LT 0)
NOT	Profit NOT 0, NOT IsNumeric(Form.Cost)

Compound expressions are evaluated in the same way as the simpler ones, except each part of the expression is analyzed individually, and then the results are compared to determine the value of the overall expression. For example:

1. Start with the expression (X LTE 10+2) AND (X GT 0), where X is equal to 5.

2. Mathematical operations and variable value checks happen first, so evaluate 10+2 and evaluate X.

3. Evaluate each of the expressions in parentheses. The left expression is now (5 LTE 12), and the right expression is now (5 GT 0).

4. Compare the values on the right and left of the operator in each expression. Because 5 is less than 12, the first expression is TRUE; 5 is also greater than 0, so the second expression is TRUE.

5. Determine the overall result of the comparison of both expressions. (TRUE) AND (TRUE) equals TRUE.

Table 9-3 lists the results of the combination of logical operators and the values TRUE and FALSE. If you need to figure out an expression with three or more compound statements, group two statements together and use the result of that comparison — you can eventually whittle anything down to a single value of TRUE or FALSE by using this process.

To avoid confusion, always use parentheses to group parts of an expression. If you string together a bunch of expressions using AND, OR, and NOT operators, you'll quickly become confused about how the various results are determined, plus you'll be at the mercy of the order of precedence ColdFusion uses to determine which expression to evaluate first. Parentheses should make everything crystal clear.

You must use the AND operator when combining two expressions with the NOT operator. The syntax NOT *expression* works fine by itself, but *expression* AND NOT *expression* is the appropriate way to combine two expressions to avoid errors.

Table 9-3		ColdFusion Logic Operators	
First Value	*Operator*	*Second Value*	*Overall Result*
TRUE	AND	TRUE	TRUE
TRUE	AND	FALSE	FALSE
FALSE	AND	FALSE	FALSE
TRUE	OR	FALSE	TRUE
TRUE	OR	TRUE	TRUE
FALSE	OR	FALSE	FALSE
TRUE	AND NOT	TRUE	FALSE
TRUE	AND NOT	FALSE	TRUE
FALSE	AND NOT	FALSE	FALSE

Together, the logical operators and comparison operators make it possible to create a variety of expressions that an application can evaluate to produce conditional results. But the expression alone isn't enough; you need to put the expression into a *control structure*. The value of the expression then percolates through the control structure and triggers the appropriate actions.

Houston, This Is Program Control

You can control the execution of a program in a wide variety of ways. More complex control, however, is typically made up of a combination of two simple control building blocks:

- ✔ **Decision statements** help the program choose between two (or more) alternatives
- ✔ **Repetition statements** repeat a certain set of code one or more times

Some complex control situations are so common that they've become new basic building blocks to make the programmer's life easier. One example is a block of code that must repeat until a certain condition is met — it's a combination of a repetition and a decision that might trigger another repetition, which starts the cycle again. In this section, we discuss all these fundamental building blocks, as expressed in the ColdFusion Markup Language.

To be or not to be (CFIF)

The most fundamental form of programmatic control in most computer languages is the IF statement. I bet you were thinking "if-then" thoughts as soon as you saw the phrase "IF statement." The two just seem to go together. The generic format of the IF statement is

```
IF (expression)
THEN (do something)
```

ColdFusion uses this basic structure with the inevitable CF prefix:

```
<CFIF expression>
     do something
</CFIF>
```

If the *expression* is TRUE, the *do something* instructions are performed. (Although some programming languages use a DO clause within an IF, ColdFusion does not.) This *something* could be ColdFusion commands, HTML, text, or whatever else you can display in a Web browser.

Note that the preceding ColdFusion command has both a start tag and an end tag. The expression to be evaluated is *inside* the CFIF-start tag, and the stuff to do is between the start and end tags.

ColdFusion doesn't use THEN in IF statements. The THEN clause is understood to be there, even though it isn't.

The expression can be any valid ColdFusion expression. Perhaps you are wondering why the engineers at Allaire decided to use text-based comparison operators, such as GT and LTE, instead of more traditional symbols. Look what happens if you use the traditional greater-than symbol in a CFIF:

```
<CFIF x > 2>
```

The extra angle bracket makes it devilishly difficult to figure out what is the expression and what is the tag end. One of the most common errors that new ColdFusion developers make is to accidentally use symbols (such as >) instead of the text equivalent (such as GT).

SQL uses symbols, such as >= and <>, instead of text equivalents. Because ColdFusion programming involves lots of database work in SQL, it's easy to become confused between the symbolic operators and the text comparison operators. Be alert to this type of mistake!

If the expression evaluates to FALSE, the block of code between the <CFIF> and </CFIF> tags is skipped. Basically, the expression turns a block of ColdFusion code on or off depending on the value of the arguments in the expression. You'll use CFIF statements regularly as you develop ColdFusion templates.

But what if?

The ColdFusion IF control structure has a few more parts, depending on the programming language. ColdFusion offers two more clauses that make more complicated control structures possible:

```
<CFIF expression1>
        do action1
<CFELSEIF expression2>
        do action2
<CFELSEIF expression3>
etc
<CFELSE>
        do action N
</CFIF>
```

The CFELSEIF clauses allow for control between additional sets of possibilities; the CFELSE clause catches everything else.

In an IF-THEN control block, only *one* action is executed. If, for example, both *expression1* and *expression3* are TRUE, only *action1* occurs. As far as the computer is concerned, only one part of the IF-THEN block can be TRUE, so it ignores everything else after it finds that TRUE statement. That's why the ELSE part is important — it triggers whenever all the other expressions are FALSE.

You can use the CFELSE block to catch errors. If you anticipate only three possible responses from a user, the CFELSE clause can catch the situation in which a user responds in an unanticipated (fourth) way and then inform the user that the response doesn't compute.

If, if, if . . .

You can probably think of many situations where you could have a large number of CFELSE statements in an enormous CFIF block of code. Nothing's wrong with that, except for the performance drain on your application.

Performance suffers because the program tests every single expression until it finds the one that's TRUE. This is especially galling when the expression being tested is basically the same format repeated over and over again — X

GT 7, X GT 10, X GT 200. The extra milliseconds don't matter if your application has a few users, but those milliseconds add up when hundreds or thousands of people are using your Web site.

In ColdFusion 4, Allaire added a control structure to deal with this problem: CFSWITCH. Basically, a single expression is evaluated, and all possible outcomes, or *cases,* are listed in the following block along with the appropriate instructions. Here's how it looks:

```
<CFSWITCH expression = "expression">
        <CFCASE value="value" delimiters="delimiters">
         stuff to do
        </CFCASE>
        <CFCASE value="value2">
         alternate stuff to do
        </CFCASE>
        <CFDEFAULTCASE>
         default stuff to do
        </CFDEFAULTCASE>
</CFSWITCH>
```

Here, one expression is evaluated, and one of a set of multiple possible values is quickly identified to find the appropriate response. If none of the values in the CFCASE statements match the value of the expression, the CFDEFAULTCASE block executes.

Most BASIC programmers will recognize this as a CASE control structure. The name *switch* comes from the C language.

On and On 'til the Break of Dawn

The final control structure that you'll examine is a wily character that comes in a number of different (but related) guises: the loop. Just like it sounds, a loop block repeats a command or set of commands over and over. This capability is useful in a number of situations:

✔ Performing a task a specific number of times, such as counting to 10

✔ Repeating a set of commands until a particular expression becomes TRUE (or FALSE), such as sending the user back to a data-entry form with missing required fields

✔ Outputting each item in a delineated list or set of values, such as the results of a query

The CFLOOP tag can handle each of these situations. Many traditional computer languages have several different loops, such as FOR-NEXT loops, WHILE-DO loops, and DO-UNTIL loops. In ColdFusion, the same tag handles all these different loops through the use of different sets of attributes. The CFLOOP tag provides five kinds of loops that correspond to the three general types of loops just mentioned. (You have five instead of three because the loop to handle sets of values comes in different flavors for sets of query results, lists, and object collections.)

The general syntax of CFLOOP is

```
<CFLOOP attributes>
        HTML/CFML code
</CFLOOP>
```

Like most ColdFusion tags, CFLOOP requires both a start tag and an end tag. The code between the tags can consist of any valid HTML or CFML. The attributes indicate which sort of loop is being requested and are discussed in the following sections. The structure is always closed by a plain old </CFLOOP>.

If you intend to display the value of ColdFusion variables within a CFLOOP, you still need to surround them with CFOUTPUT, whether within or outside of the CFLOOP. ColdFusion Server will treat anything in the format #variable# as a ColdFusion variable.

Drop and give me 20 (index loops)

The most basic flavor of the CFLOOP is the *index loop*. You use this construct to execute a block of code a specific number of times. After the start and end values are given, it takes an act of nature — well, a CFBREAK at least — to stop execution. The syntax is

```
<CFLOOP index="variable" from="start" to="end"
        step="interval">
```

The step attribute is optional and indicates a number by which to increment the index as it increases from start to end. The attribute is assumed to be equal to 1 unless otherwise specified.

For a basic example, you can make the program count from 1 to 10, as follows:

```
<CFOUTPUT>
<CFLOOP index="counter" from="1" to="10">
        This is iteration #counter#!<br>
</CFLOOP>
</CFOUTPUT>
```

For a more sophisticated use, you could dynamically configure the FROM and TO values by using a ColdFusion variable to set the value of those attributes.

Or you could make the program count backwards by using negative values for the step size. You never know what weird ways you'll need to use an index loop — luckily, the ColdFusion version provides a lot of flexibility.

If you've programmed before, you're probably familiar with the FOR-NEXT loop or some close relative. The syntax is similar here, but don't forget the double quotes around the FROM and TO values. Although ColdFusion some-times lets you get away with not specifying these, it's generally better to use them.

Grocery, laundry, and CFLOOP lists

The index loop is fine if you want to work your way through an orderly, con-tinuous set of numbers, but it falls short if you need to loop through a list of string values or some other irregular, non-numeric set. For these situations, CFLOOP allows looping over a *delimited* (clearly separated) list of values. The syntax looks like this:

```
<CFLOOP index="variable" list="list_of_values"
        delimiters="delimiter_list">
```

The index value is similar to the attribute for an index loop — except it holds the value of the current item in the list. *Delimiters* are characters that separate one item of the list from the next one. The most common example is the comma (,), which is the default if you don't include the delimiters attribute. If your set of data is delimited by another character, such as a semi-colon (;) or a pipe (|), including those characters in the delimiters list overrides the default delimiter, replacing it with the character or characters you desire.

Why would you want to use something other than commas to delimit data? Well, if the data itself contains commas, you would have no way to distin-guish between a comma and a delimiter.

Looping through a query

ColdFusion is all about databases, and databases are about queries, so it's probably no surprise that you can loop through a query as easily as a list of values. In Chapter 6, you use the CFOUTPUT tag with the QUERY="query_name" attribute to display the results of a query. The CFLOOP tag lets you do the same thing:

```
<CFLOOP query="query_name" startrow="start_row_num"
        endrow="end_row_num">
    CFML/HTML tags
</CFLOOP>
```

This tag is a good way to build an output table, just like you do in Chapter 6. But you're probably wondering why you need this type of tag when another tag in ColdFusion works perfectly well. Good question. The answer is that some ColdFusion tags can't be used inside a CFOUTPUT tag. Any tag is legal inside CFLOOP, so you can use it where you can't use CFOUTPUT.

A good example of a situation in which CFLOOP needs to replace CFOUTPUT is when you use CFINCLUDE to insert a number of dynamically chosen or created Web pages into a single master page. You'll get an error if you try to do that with CFOUTPUT.

I'll loop on one condition

The loops you've read about so far in this chapter have been predictable and restrictive. What do you do if you want to loop until a particular condition occurs or ends? You can use a *conditional loop,* which is somewhat like a combination of an IF-THEN statement and a loop. It's the most flexible of all the loops in this chapter. The basic format is

```
<CFLOOP condition="expression">
      CFML/HTML tags
</CFLOOP>
```

That's all there is to it. The expression is like the ones you'd use in CFIF:

```
X LT 5
Password NOT 'John'
(x GT 0) AND (y LTE 0)
```

As long as the expression is TRUE, the loop repeats.

If you need a loop to repeat as long as a condition is FALSE, turn the expression around by using NOT.

The variables in the CFLOOP condition must be *initialized* before the loop starts and then changed inside the loop. Suppose that you want a loop to repeat as long as x is larger than 0. Think through the following code:

```
<CFLOOP condition="x GT 0">
      T minus <CFOUTPUT>#x#</CFOUTPUT><br>
</CFLOOP>
```

What happens? Well, there are a few problems. We get an error unless x has been initialized. The correct way to create this type of loop is to use CFSET (or some other means to assign a value to x, such as input from a form variable) to set the value of x *before* the CFLOOP code. For example:

```
<CFSET x=10>
<CFLOOP condition="x > 5">
        T minus <CFOUTPUT>#x#</CFOUTPUT><br>
</CFLOOP>
```

The second crucial part of a conditional loop is changing the value of the variable(s) in the condition statement. In our example, we create an infinite loop because x is always greater than 5. To finish the countdown sample, we add one more line inside the loop:

```
<CFSET x=10>
<CFLOOP condition="x > 5">
        T minus <CFOUTPUT>#x#</CFOUTPUT>
        <CFSET x=x-1>
</CFLOOP>
<B>BLASTOFF!!!!</B>
```

Now we have all the pieces in place for a NASA-style countdown.

It would have been easier to create our countdown code by using an index loop with a step of –1. You'll find that you can often solve a problem using your choice of several looping structures.

Looping over a collection

For the sake of completeness, this section describes looping over collections, but you won't get a lot of use out of this type of looping because it involves types of collections that are beyond the scope of this book. Continue reading this section only if you're really into programming.

A *collection* can consist of either a ColdFusion structure, a COM or DCOM object, or a CORBA object. ColdFusion *structures* are data structures designed by a programmer, such as the collection of information that makes up an employee record (name, address, phone number, e-mail address, salary, and so on). This lets you loop through a structure looking for a particular data item without having to know how the raw data in the collection is organized.

For more on structures, check out the *Developing Web Applications with ColdFusion* manual that comes with ColdFusion Server (and is in the online help of Studio).

Collections of COM or DCOM objects are specialized components typically used to exchange data between different enterprise systems. CORBA is a similar technology with roots in the UNIX enterprise programming world. These technologies are typically used for high-level enterprise application design.

Functional Literacy

Computers are all about computations, and computations are all about functions. A _function_ is a tool that generates a value or a set of values, usually from some input. You might remember mathematics functions from your schooldays — cosines, arctangents, and their other less-than-memorable kin. Don't worry. Although all these mathematical functions are built into ColdFusion, you'll find many other nonmathematical functions useful in your development efforts.

The syntax of ColdFusion functions is straightforward. Table 9-4 shows you a few examples.

Table 9-4	Function Examples
Function	_What It Means_
`sin(x)`	Calculate the sine of the value x
`left(text,2)`	Find the leftmost 2 characters of the text value
`DayOfWeekAsString(`_number_`)`	Determine the word for the day of the week that is represented by the number (e.g., 1 yields Sunday)

The value produced by a function needs to be used, or it evaporates. In ColdFusion, you typically use functions as part of an expression in a conditional statement (such as CFIF or CFLOOP) or in a CFSET statement. In most cases, you'll use the function to generate a new value from an existing ColdFusion variable. Here are a few examples:

```
<CFSET x=arctan(2)>

<CFSET x=arctan(y)>

<CFIF Left(URL.HTTP_REFERER,7) NEQ "128.143">
```

ColdFusion contains hundreds of functions, which are divided into the thirteen categories listed in Table 9-5. Don't expect to remember them all — when you need them, just look them up in either the online documentation or the _CFML Language Reference_ that comes with ColdFusion. ColdFusion Studio users have the same information at their fingertips in Studio's Help documentation (see Chapter 3 for more). Check out Chapter 17 for the ten ColdFusion functions we find most useful.

TIP

ColdFusion Studio users can also use the dynamic Expression Builder, which is available on the CFML Basic toolbar or by right-clicking in the Edit window and choosing Insert Expression.

Table 9-5	Types of ColdFusion Functions		
Category	*What It Does*	*Example*	*Value*
Array	Operates on arrays	`ArrayLen(`*`arrayname`*`)`	Number of elements in *arrayname*
Date and Time	Manipulates date/time values	`CreateODBCDate(1999,20,5)`	{d '1998-05-20'}
Decision	Examines type of variable or value	`IsDefined("`*`variable`*`")`	TRUE if variable has been initialized; FALSE otherwise
Display and Formatting	Makes things look pretty	`DateFormat({d '1999-05-20'},` *"mmmm d, yyyy"*`)`	May 20, 1999
Dynamic Evaluation	Handles complicated conditional statements effectively	`IIf(sales< quota, "no bonus for you", "great job!")`	"no bonus for you" if sales<quota; "great job!" otherwise
International	Formatting commandsfor using local time, date, and currency conventions	`GetLocale()`	English(US)
List	Processes delimited lists of values	`ListFind ("George, Ringo, John, Paul","Paul")`	4
Mathematical	Standard math functions	`SQR(4)`	2 (square root of 4)
Query	Manipulates query objects	`QuerySetCell(`*`queryname, columnname, value`*`)`	Sets the value of *columnname* in the last row of the result set called *queryname*

Category	What It Does	Example	Value
String a test	Manipulates string data	`Trim (" This is a test ")`	This is a test
Structure	Manipulates data structures	`StructureNew()`	Allocates space for new structure
System	File and directory commands	`FileExists ("c:\autoexec .bat")`	TRUE if file exists
Miscellaneous	Everything else	`Encrypt (`*string,* *key*`)`	Encrypted version of *string* based on *key*

Putting it All Together

The essence of programming is to put together functions, decision-making elements, and program control structures to solve real problems. Right, you're probably thinking, it's easy for us to tell you that. But creating programs isn't as hard as you think. All you need is practice. Start with small projects, such as a phone number manager or an application to manage your CD collection. Use the steps discussed in the first section of this chapter to sketch out a solution, and go from there. You'll be surprised how quickly you start to crave Mountain Dew, pepperoni pizza, and *Star Trek* reruns!

Chapter 10

Storing Data with Variables

● ●

In This Chapter

▶ Understanding rules for variables

▶ Working with local variables

▶ Using form variables

▶ Passing URL variables

▶ Referencing query variables

▶ Making use of variables that persist naturally

● ●

*T*o store data within a page and pass data between pages in ColdFusion, you use variables. Variables are also a way to get at data that ColdFusion has about a visitor, such as what browser the visitor is using. Variables are your key to turning a Web site visit into a seamless Web application.

Normally, the server can't distinguish one click by a Web site visitor from another — that's why the Web is referred to as a *stateless system*. Unless you take action to maintain *state* for your visitors, you won't be able to track visitors from one page to another. ColdFusion makes it easy to maintain state, track the actions of a visitor, and maintain data, such as the visitor's preferences and security information.

Finally, some tags create variables that give you information about the results of the tag's action. For example, when you run a query, the `queryname. recordcount` variable is created and holds the number of records that the query returns.

This chapter explores the different types of variables and shows how you can use each type to store and pass data, maintain state, and determine the results of some ColdFusion tags.

General Rules about Variables

ColdFusion has quite a few variable types, each of which can be used under different circumstances. For example:

- ✔ Local variables exist only on the page on which they're created.
- ✔ Server variables exist across clients and applications.
- ✔ Form variables exist on the page that's processing the results of a form.

Despite these differences, all variables have to follow rules about scope and referencing.

Scope is the context in which a variable exists. All variables have scope. Because a variable can have the same name in different scopes, you might need to reference a variable by name and scope when you refer to it on a page.

For example, the CFOUTPUT tag takes an attribute called query, which holds the name of the query performed earlier on the page. This generally indicates that you mean to loop over the record set of the query, but it also changes the default scope for variables within the loop.

If a variable is not prefaced by a scope, ColdFusion tries to determine the scope of the variable by looking for a variable of that name in the following scopes, in the given order:

1. Local variables created using CFSET and CFQUERY
2. CGI variables
3. File variables
4. URL variables
5. Form variables
6. Cookie variables
7. Client variables

This is changed within a CFOUTPUT query loop, where the first scope inspected becomes the query itself. If you want to refer to a query variable within the CFOUTPUT tag pair, you don't need to preface the variable name with the query name. But if you want to refer to the variable outside the CFOUTPUT tag, you need to preface the variable name with the query name:

```
<CFSET last_initial = #left(GetMe.last_name,1)#>
<CFOUTPUT query="GetMe">
Your name is #first_name# #last_name#.
</CFOUTPUT>
<CFOUTPUT>Your last name begins with
        #last_initial#.</CFOUTPUT>
```

In the code, note the following:

✔ In the first line, the CFSET tag creates a local variable called `last_initial`, which is based on the leftmost character of the `last_name` variable. The `last_name` variable is a query variable from the `GetMe` query.

✔ The second line states that any variables within the CFOUTPUT tag pair are first considered to be variables from the `GetMe` query.

✔ In the third line, the `first_name` and `last_name` variables are referenced. These variables, unlike the `last_name` variable in the first line, don't have to be prepended with the `GetMe` query name because they are within the CFOUTPUT tag pair.

✔ In the last line, the CFOUTPUT tag isn't using output from a query, so it has no `query` attribute. Because `last_initial` is a local variable, no scope referencing is necessary.

Case doesn't matter with variables. For example, `File_Name` is the same as `file_name`. It pays to give your variables intuitive names. Calling variables (other than an index in a looping structure) x, y, or z might reduce the amount of typing but doesn't help you or another programmer remember the information that the variable contains.

Local Variables

Local variables exist only on the page on which they're created. They are often used as temporary storage for manipulating data in some way. If you've used the CFSET tag, you've created local variables.

When you create a local variable, unlike any other type of variable, you don't need to preface the variable name with the scope. In addition, you don't have to define local variables before you use them.

For most local variables, the first time you use them will be on the left side of a CFSET statement:

```
<CFSET newvariable = #Mid(form.variablename, start, length)#>
```

In this code, we create the local variable called `newvariable`, which is a substring of the `variablename` form variable. We use the Mid() function to extract a substring beginning at position `start` for a length of `length`. From the way that the variables `start` and `length` are used in the example, you can tell that they're likely local variables created previously on the page.

You can also create variables using the CFPARAM tag, as in

```
<CFPARAM name="page_name" default="this_page">
```

The CFPARAM tag creates a variable and sets a value, if the variable doesn't exist. If the variable already exists, the value of the variable doesn't change. You can use CFPARAM with many variable types, including local variables, server variables, client variables, session variables, and cookie variables.

To create a nonlocal variable using CFPARAM, include the scope in the variable name, as in

```
<CFPARAM name="cookie.merchant_ID" default="0001">
```

CFPARAM also has a third attribute: `type`. Although you're not required to specify the variable type for any variable you create — ColdFusion deduces the type based on the value — you can use CFPARAM to set the variable type or to discover the variable type.

The `type` attribute is beyond the scope of this book. For a complete discussion, refer to the *CFML Language Reference* that installs with ColdFusion Server or Studio.

Form Variables

To pass a page containing a form to the page that will process the form, you use `action="post"` in a FORM tag. To take action on the form fields from the form page, the form-processing page needs a way to reference the fields. That's why ColdFusion automatically turns your form fields into form variables. You can refer to them by prepending their field names with `form`.

You don't typically create form variables on the page on which they're used. If you want a form variable on the processing page and you already have that data on the form page, use a *hidden* form field to pass the data from the form page to the processing page. For instance, if you have an update page (which is the form page) on which visitors can update information about themselves, you probably already have the unique key to the data. You pass that key to the processing page to indicate which record should be updated.

Because visitors probably don't even know you have a unique key for their data, don't make the unique key part of any editable field on the visitors' form. However, you can pass the unique key from the form page to the processing page by including it in a hidden field, as follows:

```
<INPUT type="hidden" name="ID" value="#ID#">
```

The hidden field defined in the preceding code won't appear on the page on which the form is displayed, but will be visible to anyone who views the source of the page. That means you shouldn't put any information in a hidden field that you don't want a visitor to have. Treat hidden field data like public data that's irrelevant to the visitor's browsing experience. (You may want to look into the Encrypt() function to make the data unreadable by end users.)

URL Variables

You may pass information from one page to another in a way that doesn't use forms. Use URL (uniform resource locator) variables, which are specified following a URL (when building A HREF links or perhaps in the ACTION of a form). They are then visible in the location text field of your visitor's browser. You often see URL variables in action when you visit a search engine.

To use a URL variable, you simply place it after the page's URL (such as www.overtheweb.com), but preceded by a question mark. URL variables are listed as variable-value pairs, with an ampersand sign (&) separating each variable. For example:

```
www.overtheweb.com?client_id=otw&id=johnson
```

Unless you take specific action to encrypt URL variables and values — again, perhaps with the Encrypt() function — they are visible. Be careful that you don't expose confidential data, such as your data source, user name, or password, through the URL.

URL variables are valuable when you want a hyperlink from one page to provide data to the destination page.

On the processing page, you can use URL variables like any other variable by prepending the variable name with the scope, which is url. For example:

```
<CFOUTPUT>
You are signed in as: #url.id#.
</CFOUTPUT>
```

In this example, the last-visited-name variable is passed as a URL variable. Note that the CFOUTPUT tag doesn't need a query_name attribute if nothing within it refers to a query.

URL variables exist for the life of the page. If you want to pass URL variables to yet another page, be sure to do one of the following:

✔ Pass them as form fields using a form and action=get. They will be available as URL variables in the processing page.

✔ Pass them as hidden variables to the next page using a form and `action=post`.

✔ Pass them in an A HREF tag.

✔ Pass them in the `action` attribute of a FORM tag.

✔ Store them in a cookie, or some other form of persistent variable, such as session or client variables, so that you can read them from another page.

Query Variables

Query variables are created when you execute a query that selects data from a database. The names of the columns that you select become variables of the same name (which is why we recommend that a newly created database use column names that would work as valid variable names).

When you refer to query variables, you prepend them not with the word `query` (as you might think from the other variable types) but with the name of the query. In the following code, the query is named `GetMe`. If you want to refer to the results of the query, you do so by prepending a variable name with `GetMe`, like this:

```
<CFQUERY name="GetMe" datasource="mydata">
SELECT name, address, city, state, zip
FROM billing_address
</CFQUERY>
```

Referencing query variables

To display the fields we extracted in the preceding code, we use either this code:

```
<CFOUTPUT query="GetMe">
#name#<BR>
#address#<BR>
#city#, #state#   #zip#<BR>
</CFOUTPUT>
```

or this:

```
<CFOUTPUT>
#GetMe.name#<BR>
#GetMe.address#<BR>
#GetMe.city#, #GetMe.state#   #GetMe.zip#<BR>
</CFOUTPUT>
```

The difference between the two CFOUTPUT tags is that one includes the name of the query. If you include the name of the query in the CFOUTPUT tag, you are indicating that you want to loop over all the records in the query result set, and you don't need to specify the query name with each query variable.

If you don't include the `query` attribute in the CFOUTPUT tag, you will not loop over all the records in the result set, but you will have access to the first record in the result set. In that case, you need to be specific and tell ColdFusion the name of the query holding the query variable that you're referring to.

You can't create query variables outside a CFQUERY tag. When you either list field names after the key word `Select` or use an asterisk to indicate that all fields are selected, you create query variables for the fields you select.

Properties of a query

When you run a query, the query returns three properties in addition to the fields that you expect the query to create. They're all useful. You access these properties — `recordcount`, `currentrow`, and `columnlist` — in the same way you access variables. (In fact, they really are just variables.)

Recordcount

The `recordcount` variable is valuable because it permits you to determine whether any records are returned. Suppose you have a subscription service in which each subscriber has a unique ID. You want to know whether an ID is already in use before permitting another subscriber to use that ID. To accomplish that task, you could use the following code to determine whether to permit the new subscriber to have that ID:

```
<CFQUERY name="taken" datasource="mydata" dbtype="ODBC">
SELECT ID
FROM subscribers
WHERE ID = '#form.ID#'
</CFQUERY>
<CFIF taken.recordcount GT 0>
        ...return the new subscriber to the "choose an ID"
page, tell him or her that the requested ID is already taken,
and suggest possible alternate IDs
<CFELSE>
        ...assign the new ID to the new subscriber because
            the ID is not already in use
</CFIF>
```

Currentrow

The `currentrow` variable tells you which row of the query the CFOUTPUT tag is processing. If you're displaying a lot of records from a database, you can use the `currentrow` variable to control the display of multiple columns of records on a page.

The following code shows how you might display three records across in a listing of many records. The trick is to calculate which is the third, sixth, ninth, and so on record and place a BR tag after those records:

```
<CFOUTPUT name="GetAll">
#city#
<CFIF currentrow MOD 3 IS 0><BR></CFIF>
</CFOUTPUT>
```

The `MOD` operator gives the remainder when the number to the left of `MOD` is divided by the number to the right of `MOD`. In standard arithmetic, this would be phrased `curentrow/3 = integer + remainder`. `MOD` returns only the remainder. We use that to determine every third row.

Columnlist

The `columnlist` variable displays the column name of every column returned in a query. If you specify the column names in the SELECT statement, you know which columns are being returned.

If you use the wildcard (*) to return every column (field) in a table, however, it can be useful to know which columns are returned. The following code displays a comma-delimited list of all columns returned by the query `GetAll`:

```
<CFOUTPUT>
The following fields were returned:<BR>
#GetAll.columnlist#.
</CFOUTPUT>
```

Variables That Persist Naturally

Do you need to keep information about your visitors across multiple templates, so that your site acts more like an integrated application than like a series of posters? If the answer is yes, you need persistent variables — or you need to take pains to use URL or form variables to pass visitor data from page to page.

Naturally persistent variables — that is, variables that exist outside the confines of one page — consist of server variables, application variables, client variables, session variables, and cookie variables.

Table 10-1 compares the six types of persistent variables and whether you can only read them or read and write to them, whether you can create each type, how long they persist, and whether you need to have application management, client management, and session management enabled to use them.

Table 10-1			Comparison of Persistent Variables				
Variable Type	*Read/Write*	*Fixed/Dynamic**	*Persistence*	*Application Names*	*Client IDs*	*Client Management*	*Session Management*
Server	R/W	Dynamic	Until server is restarted	-	-	-	-
Application	R/W	Dynamic	Until server is restarted	Required	-	-	-
Client	R/W	Dynamic	Set by you	Optional	Yes	Yes	-
Session	R/W	Dynamic	20 minutes or through session	Optional	Yes	Yes	Yes
Cookie	R/W	Dynamic	Set by you	-	-	-	-

*Fixed/Dynamic: If you can't create variables in this scope, the variables from which you can choose are fixed. If you can create variables in this scope, the variables are dynamic.

Server variables

Server variables can be used to track information that should be persistent for all users *in all applications* within a server. In other words, they are truly global variables. Once set, they can be seen by every user on the server.

The following example uses a server variable:

```
<CFSET Server.TimeZone = "Eastern">
```

Don't confuse this type of server variable with another type that consists of several predefined server variables that tell you specific configuration information about the server on which ColdFusion runs. You can't update those server variables, but you can read them. Table 10-2 lists the available predefined server variables.

Table 10-2	Server Variables
Variable Name	*What It Returns*
Server.ColdFusion.ProductName	ColdFusion at this point (because this is the only server product); this variable will be useful if ColdFusion ever produces more than one engine
Server.ColdFusion.ProductVersion	Version of the ColdFusion engine running
Server.ColdFusion.ProductLevel	Type of ColdFusion product: Professional or Enterprise
Server.ColdFusion.SerialNumber	Serial number
Server.OS.Name	Operating system: Windows NT or Solaris
Server.OS.AdditionalInformation	Service pack number
Server.OS.Version	Operating system version
Server.OS.BuildNumber	Operating system build

In addition to server variables, some CGI environment server variables also reveal information about the server, as described later.

Application variables

Application variables exist across an application for all pages and for all clients under control of that application. Application variables are stored in server memory, so they're easily accessible.

To use an application variable, you have to enable an application using the CFAPPLICATION tag. The CFAPPLICATION tag can be as simple as this:

```
<CFAPPLICATION name="employees">
```

Because you generally want this command to be in effect for every template in the associated group of templates, you should place it in the special application.cfm file, which is automatically executed (if it exists, in the current directory or any parent between that directory and the root) before every template is itself executed.

If you're publishing ColdFusion code to a WPP server or an ISP server, make sure that they have enabled support for application variables. It's possible to disable application variables support from ColdFusion Administrator.

You create your own application variables using the CFSET or CFPARAM tag or any tag that can create local variables, including CFQUERY. (Yes, that means you can make a query result that can be shared by all users of an application!) You simply prepend any reference to the variable name with application.

Because application variables exist across the application, you can refer to them in any page that's part of the directory structure for the application. They aren't unique to either a visitor or a session, so don't use them to store personal information. They're better suited to storing site information and data source information.

Client variables

Client variables persist for a client across all sessions. Client variables are ideal for storing a visitor's preferences or a shopping list that should persist from session to session.

You store client variables in the system registry, a data source, or cookies. Storing client variables in the system registry (which was the only choice before Release 4 and which gave them a bad name) can slow server performance, so some WPPs and ISPs still won't permit you to do that. Where you can store client variables, whether session and application variables are enabled, and the default timeouts for these variables are all controlled in ColdFusion Administrator, under Server⇨Variables. Browser limits exist on how many cookies you can create, so if you'll be relying heavily on client variables for maintaining state, store them in a data source rather than in cookies. Chapter 11 discusses tracking state through the use of session and client variables.

To use client variables, you enable them in the CFAPPLICATION tag, using the clientmanagement attribute. You can also indicate how you want client variables to be stored using the clientstorage attribute. Finally, you can set the setclientcookies attribute in the CFAPPLICATION tag.

Setclientcookies defaults to yes, which means CFID and CFTOKEN cookies will be stored on the client's computer. If you set setclientcookies to no, you must see to it that you pass CFID and CFTOKEN throughout the application using URL variables or hidden variables in forms. State management is handled through the use of CFID and CFTOKEN. These two variables tell the server who you are on every page, so that it knows you're the same person who clicked on the previous page. You can't enforce any type of site security without them. If you ever lose one or the other, your application framework is broken.

The following code shows how you might enable client variables, storing them in the ecom data source:

```
<CFAPPLICATION name="employees"
        clientmanagement="yes"
        clientstorage="ecom"
        setclientcookies="yes">
```

Don't set setclientcookies to no unless you realize the effects of doing so. If you turn off the storage of client variables in cookies, you have to make sure that any clicks through your application will pass CFID and CFTOKEN onto the next page through either URL parameters or hidden form fields.

Again, you can create client variables using CFSET or CFPARAM or any tag that creates variables. To refer to client variables, preface the variable name with client.

Session variables

Session variables, like application variables, are stored in system memory. Session variables are a perfect way to store information that relates to only the current visit, such as a shopping cart.

Unlike application variables, which hold, when set, the same value for all users of the application, the value of session variables is unique. And unlike client variables, which can persist for days or even months, depending on how they are created and configured, session variables can never be expected to last that long (because they're stored in server memory). Instead, session variables have a predetermined lifespan, known as their *timeout,* which is often specified in a time frame as small as minutes.

The duration of the timeout of session variables is specified in ColdFusion Administrator or in the `sessiontimeout` attribute of the CFAPPLICATION tag.

To enable session variables, use the `sessionmanagement` attribute of the CFAPPLICATION tag. The following code shows the CFAPPLICATION tag for an application called `employees`, with session variables that time out after 20 minutes:

```
<CFAPPLICATION name="employees"
      sessionmanagement="yes"
      sessiontimeout="#CreateTimeSpan(0, 0, 20, 0)#">
```

In the preceding command, we use the CreateTimeSpan() function to specify how long session variables will last for the user. We've set the duration to 20 minutes.

After a page sets a session variable, a countdown begins. If the user doesn't return to another page in that application before that countdown expires, the server simply deletes all remnants of any session variables for that user (for that application).

Because timed-out session variables delete themselves, you shouldn't refer to them until you make sure they do indeed exist, such as with the IsDefined() function, which is discussed in Chapter 17.

Support for using session variables, as with application variables, may be turned off for the entire server in ColdFusion Administrator, so make sure that your WWP or ISP permits their use. Also, even if you specify a timeout of 2 hours on your CFAPPLICATION tag, the administrator can define a maximum (as well as a default) value. If your specified time exceeds that maximum, you'll simply get that maximum, with no message to you or your user.

You can create session variables in the same way you create application and client variables, with either CFSET or CFPARAM or any tag that creates variables. To refer to a session variable, prepend the variable name with `session`.

The notion of timeouts, including specifying timeouts in CFAPPLICATION and in the Administrator, applies to application variables as well. ColdFusion has an `applicationtimeout` attribute, just as it has a `sessiontimeout` attribute.

Cookie variables

Cookies have always been a topic of controversy. Simply put, *cookies* are a tiny text file on the visitor's computer that you can use to store data about the visitor or actions he or she has taken on your page. Without cookies, maintaining state is considerably more difficult.

Generally, cookies are a convenience for you as a Web developer because you can track the actions of visitors and store data about their actions right on their computer. Cookies are a convenience for visitors as well because they can navigate more easily through your site, and the next time they visit, the site recognizes them when they arrive.

Many Web merchants use a feature that relies on cookies, called one-click ordering, which saves shoppers the trouble of re-keying their billing and shipping information. Cookies have received a bad name, though, and some visitors have cookies turned off in their browsers. Also, some older browsers don't support them.

You can create a cookie variable by using the CFCOOKIE tag:

```
<CFCOOKIE Name="ID" Value="#GetMe.ID#">
```

Note that like the other variables we have discussed, you can create a cookie variable also using CFSET, CFPARAM, or any other tag that creates variables. But the CFCOOKIE tag has many other useful attributes specifically for creating cookies, such as specifying the time frame in which the cookie should expire on the browser.

In the following line of code, the ID cookie variable is set to hold the value of the ID query variable. To use the ID variable later on that page or another page, simply refer to it by prepending the variable name with cookie:

```
<CFQUERY datasource="dsn1" name="UpdateMe" dbtype="ODBC">
Update member
Set last_name = '#last_name#',
    first_name = '#first_name#',
    address = '#address#',
    city = '#city#',
    state = '#state#',
    zip = '#zip#'
where ID = #cookie.ID#
</CFQUERY>
```

In the preceding code, last_name, first_name, address, city, state, and zip are all form variables (take our word for it), and ID is a cookie variable.

CGI environment variables

CGI environment variables are created not by ColdFusion but by the Web
server software and the browser. They're a set of variables that describe
both the browser and the Web server environment in ways that might be
useful to you as a ColdFusion programmer. CGI client and server environment
variables are listed in Table 10-3.

Table 10-3	CGI Environment Variables
Environment Variable	*What It Returns*
	CGI client
HTTP_Referer	Document that submitted the form data or linked to the script being executed; it's empty if the user typed the URL or used a bookmark
HTTP_User_Agent	Browser and version of software on the client
	CGI server
Server_Software	Name and version of the Web server software
Server_Name	Hostname, DNS, or IP address of the server
Gateway_Interface	CGI revision specification of this server
Server_Protocol	Protocol of this request to the server with revision information
Server_Port	Port number that answered the request
Request_Method	Method of requesting data: get, head, post (useful for determining whether a page is acting as a form submission)
Path_Info	Virtual path of the page that made the request
Path_Translated	Absolute path of the page that made the request
Script_Name	Path and name of script being executed
Query_String	URL variables
Remote_Host	Hostname making the request, if this information exists
Remote_Addr	IP address of the host making the request
Auth_Type	Type of authentication used to validate the user, if the script requires authentication for execution

(continued)

Table 10-3 (continued)

Environment Variable	What It Returns
CGI server	
Remote_User	Username for authentication (also called Auth_User), if the script requires authentication for execution
Remote_Indent	Remote username retrieved from the server, if the server supports FRC 931 identification
Content_Type	Mime type of the attached data, such as images uploaded with CGI Post
Content_Length	The length of the content uploaded from the client

Most software that tracks Web site traffic relies on the same data that's available to you through CGI environment variables. The number of unique visitors to a site, the types of browsers using the site, and the length of time a visitor stays at a site are derived from the data you can access in CGI environment variables. Web site tracking software, such as WebTrends, relies on the Web server logging this data. Not all Web servers log data at this level of detail, but if you need it, ask your WPP or ISP whether the data can be made available to you. Because this level of detail about your site traffic is available to you through CGI environment variables, and to the Web server logs as well, surfing the Web is not as anonymous as most people believe.

Chapter 11

Applications, Security, and State

● ●

In This Chapter

▶ Discovering the inner workings of ColdFusion Server

▶ Figuring out the ColdFusion Application Framework

▶ Deciphering ColdFusion security issues

▶ Maintaining the client state

▶ The whole application enchilada

● ●

ColdFusion does a lot of neat things, but the core reason to use
ColdFusion is to build Web applications. To understand how to build
effective applications, you need to understand the application framework
that provides the architecture for your Web development projects.

Wait! Don't skip to another chapter! This isn't as difficult — or as boring — as
it sounds. We provide plenty of diagrams and explanations to help you
through it. This chapter provides an important opportunity to dramatically
increase the usefulness of your applications as well as to greatly simplify
some tasks that might otherwise seem daunting.

Two related topics follow from discussing ColdFusion applications: security
and state. You're probably aware of the importance of security for Web
applications — a client tends to get upset if his or her credit card number or
confidential medical information is readily available to the outside world.
Security is tightly integrated into the ColdFusion application framework at
every level, and we discuss those security features throughout this chapter.

You might be wondering what *state* has to do with a Web application. The
simple answer is that good security requires that you constantly know the
state of the user. For example, you should know whether the user has logged
on with the right password before serving up secure pages. In computer programming lingo, keeping track of the user between screens or pages of an
application is called *maintaining state*. And maintaining state is important for
security and other programming tasks, as you'll see.

This chapter has a strong underlying theme of security; some might say it
borders on paranoia. Don't be rattled. A few simple steps can increase the dif-
ficulty of cracking your site and decrease the likelihood that someone will

take the time to break in — he or she can just move on to a site that isn't as vigilant! By the end of the chapter, you'll know how ColdFusion works with your server components to provide a secure application environment, and you'll know how to secure specific applications.

Behind the Scenes with ColdFusion

The first step to understanding how to build a ColdFusion application is to understand more about how ColdFusion Server works. Figure 11-1 depicts the process involved in serving a ColdFusion template to a client Web browser. In a nutshell, ColdFusion Server intercepts any ColdFusion template requested by a Web browser and processes it into an HTML page for the Web server to deliver. The processing can consist of database queries, file and directory manipulations, interactions with COM or CORBA objects, and Internet protocol functions — in any combination. This wide-ranging functionality provides an incredibly rich foundation for designing sophisticated Web applications.

Figure 11-1:
ColdFusion
Server
makes it
possible to
interface
Web pages
with a
number of
different
services.

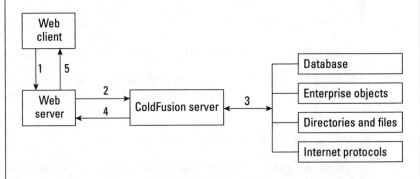

Stuck in the middle with you

ColdFusion Server is an example of a class of software known as *middleware*. This evocative name accurately describes the function of this type of tool — it's in the middle of different technologies and connects them together. You could also think of ColdFusion as the *glue* that bonds your Web server to other services quickly, easily, and cheaply. ColdFusion makes it possible for disparate software components to interact.

ColdFusion Server participates in two types of interactions: the interaction between ColdFusion and the Web server and the interaction between ColdFusion and the various software components it can access. Although these interactions might seem similar at first glance, you need to be aware of their differences when designing applications.

ColdFusion and the Web server

Chapter 4 describes the relationship between ColdFusion Server and your Web server in some detail; for this chapter, you need to remember only a few facts. The first is that ColdFusion can work with your Web server in two drastically different ways:

✔ Through the **Web server API,** just like ColdFusion Server built into your server software

✔ As a **CGI application,** no different than a Perl script, for example

When ColdFusion accesses the Web server through the server API , you gain the following advantages:

✔ **Speed,** because ColdFusion can directly access the internal functions of the Web server

✔ **Efficiency,** because most Web servers have multithreaded processing

✔ **Security,** through the innate Web server security model

If, instead, you must use ColdFusion as a CGI application, you will take a noticeable performance hit and must provide stronger security measures. Because this book focuses on the Windows platform, in which Microsoft IIS is ubiquitous (and free), we assume that you're using IIS.

When possible, choose a Web server with an API that ColdFusion understands. Currently, only servers from Microsoft, Netscape, and O'Reilly meet this criterion.

The performance gains of API integration are useful, but the security integration is crucial. The capability to use the sophisticated security measures in commercial Web servers means that you have to secure your application from only those users who already have access to your Web server. This situation increases your odds of foiling hackers and offering a secure site.

Make sure that your Web server has the latest security patches to ensure the utmost in protection.

Integrating ColdFusion, Internet protocols, and enterprise objects

For those not acquainted with all the technologies that ColdFusion can access, check out the following brief rundown:

- ✔ **COM** is Microsoft's enterprise Component Object Model. This protocol allows ColdFusion to share data with complex enterprise software in the NT environment. It also provides hooks into ActiveX components.

- ✔ **CORBA,** or Component Object Request Broker Architecture, is the UNIX predecessor of COM. Enterprise software, such as SAP and Peoplesoft, can be accessed through CORBA.

- ✔ **FTP,** or File Transfer Protocol, provides a way to move files between servers easily. However, you can't use FTP for file upload and download applications.

- ✔ **HTTP** is the technology that underlies the Web. ColdFusion can gather Web pages from other Web servers for further processing or analysis using the HTTP protocol.

- ✔ **LDAP,** or Lightweight Directory Access Protocol, is often used in larger organizations to store user name, address, and phone number information. You can build an application to access or validate users from the records in an LDAP server.

- ✔ **POP,** or Post Office Protocol, is the most common protocol for receiving electronic mail. POP enables ColdFusion to get mail from a remote mail server.

- ✔ **SMTP,** or Simple Mail Transport Protocol, is the other half of the electronic mail capability of ColdFusion. Your applications can use SMTP to send e-mail.

This long list spans nearly all network and Internet technologies typically in use. Now you can see why ColdFusion is an ideal platform for building robust and complex Web applications — virtually any technology can be integrated into a ColdFusion application.

The 4.5 Enterprise release of ColdFusion also includes software for load balancing, failover, and clustering, which increase uptime and improve the performance of large-scale applications. Those topics are beyond the scope of this book, but it's good to know that you're working with a system that can scale to large organizations and busy Web sites.

Cracking the CFML code

Now that you have an idea of the way ColdFusion interacts with the Web server and other technologies, it's time to focus on how ColdFusion server itself works. ColdFusion server reads the template, processes all CFML code, and returns the resulting HTML into the template without affecting non-CFML code. The resulting page is then sent to the Web server as if it were a static page of HTML living on the server. All complex programming is hidden in simple ColdFusion tags.

ColdFusion processes CFML *before* the rest of the page. This means that you can use ColdFusion variables or functions to modify, create, or manipulate JavaScript, HTML, or other similar (client-side) technology. One great example of HTML dynamically generated with ColdFusion is the creation of HTML tables based on the results of a query (discussed using CFOUTPUT in Chapter 6 and using CFLOOP in Chapter 9).

You could do the same type of dynamic code generation with JavaScript, as in the following example:

```
<CFQUERY name="GetEmployeeName" datasource="Employees">
SELECT Employeename FROM Employees WHERE
        Username=#Form.Username#
</CFQUERY>
<CFOUTPUT query="GetEmployeeName">
    <SCRIPT>
    alert('Welcome to work,
        #GetEmployeeName.Employeename#!');
    </SCRIPT>
</CFOUTPUT>
```

The resulting page creates a JavaScript alert box (Figure 11-2) including the employee's name after he or she has logged on to the intranet application that this fragment of code is part of. This isn't a fancy example, but you should get the idea.

Figure 11-2:
A dynamically generated JavaScript alert box.

Another point to remember is that because ColdFusion processes all CFML in the template before sending it to the Web server, your ColdFusion code isn't visible to users when they view the page's source code. As a result, no one will know what CFML code you're using to create the effect on the page, so you don't have to worry about someone stealing your code. People will know that you used ColdFusion, however, because the template name (.cfm) is a dead giveaway.

Templates versus applications

Individual ColdFusion templates can drastically improve the quality of your Web site by adding features ranging from dynamic page creation to credit-card processing to e-mail capabilities. But single ColdFusion templates will take you only so far.

To truly unlock the power of ColdFusion, it's important to realize that you can write entire applications with ColdFusion. But applications require several capabilities that are missing from the Web — security and maintaining state in particular. Have no fear! The engineers at Allaire built ColdFusion with the realization that it would be used for application development, so they provided an entire framework for building robust and scalable ColdFusion applications.

Building Applications

The ColdFusion Web Application Framework provides a schematic for building the crucial functionality of a traditional application with the added advantages of browser-based delivery and tight integration with other Internet technologies (such as e-mail, FTP, and LDAP). The framework has four fundamental components:

- **Application-level settings and functions**, discussed later in this section
- **Client state management**, one of the prime topics later in this chapter
- **Custom error handling**, a topic briefly discussed in the sidebar
- **Web server security integration**, the focus of the majority of this chapter

These components provide the basic scaffolding to help you erect a full-fledged Web application. They are also integral parts of any professionally designed application — you should consider all four components when designing an application.

Catching errors when they're thrown

Want to generate nicer error messages? Use the ColdFusion CFERROR command in the application.cfm file to create custom error pages for typical ColdFusion server error messages.

The CFERROR tag makes it easy to create friendlier error message screens than the default errors generated by ColdFusion, ODBC drivers, and other components of Web applications.

The process of implementing the tag is straightforward and discussed in detail in the Allaire *Developing Web Applications with ColdFusion* manual that ships with ColdFusion.

ColdFusion 4.0 introduced a set of tags for developing messages for errors generated by your

Web application itself. You can use the CFTRY, CFTHROW, and CFCATCH tags together to create a set of messages that are thrown when specific application errors occur and then caught by your application for special handling. This is a good step towards creating more professional-looking applications. These tags are discussed in *Developing Web Applications with ColdFusion*. The development of this sort of error-handling is beyond the scope of this book.

Because it's a better idea to avoid errors in the first place than to create a pretty error-handling system, we cover debugging techniques in Chapter 14 and common ColdFusion errors in Chapter 15.

Allaire has a white paper on its application framework that you can download at the following address:

```
http://www.allaire.com/products/coldfusion/Whitepapers/index
        .cfm
```

You need a general idea about how the application framework is organized because it's integral to how ColdFusion handles security for your application.

You can explicitly define ColdFusion applications using a standard directory structure. The easiest approach is to include in a single directory or directory tree all the templates in the application. In the root directory of the application, you define a special file called application.cfm that contains all the crucial information about the application, such as application-wide variables and constants. That directory and all its subdirectories are then considered a single application. Figure 11-3 shows an overview of the application file structure.

For more on application directory structures and the processing of the application.cfm file, see the *Developing Web Applications with ColdFusion* manual that ships with ColdFusion Server.

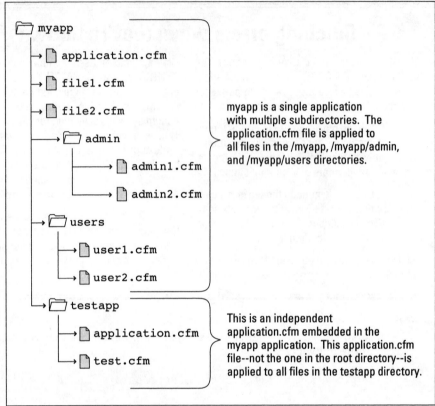

myapp is a single application with multiple subdirectories. The application.cfm file is applied to all files in the /myapp, /myapp/admin, and /myapp/users directories.

This is an independent application.cfm embedded in the myapp application. This application.cfm file--not the one in the root directory--is applied to all files in the testapp directory.

Figure 11-3:
ColdFusion applications are defined by directory structures and the application .cfm file.

The application.cfm file is automatically processed at the beginning of every page of your application, just as if you had explicitly typed the entire contents of the application.cfm file into the template. It's useful for setting application-level variables and controlling settings that affect the entire application. Because the file is effectively included at the beginning of every page in your application, it's also a good place to include security if you need it.

Application variables

Often a set of values must be available to every part of an application. These values could be the physical location of files for use with the CFFILE tag (C:\MyApp\SpecialFiles), version information (MyApp Revision 1.2), the datasource name for an application (CFExamples), or any other value that is a constant for the application *regardless of the particular client or user.*

ColdFusion offers application-level variables that are available to every page in the application every time the page is browsed.

Two types of application-level variables (that are often confused) are available. The first type is simply any variable created in the application.cfm file using the CFSET tag. Because anything you do in application.cfm is performed for all templates under its control, any variables set in that file are, in effect, application-level and are available in all related templates.

A separate type of application variable is prefaced with the word *application*. These variables, once set, are available also to all users of that application. They can be set in any template in the application and remain set to that value until they are changed again (or until the Web server is restarted).

As you can probably guess, the syntax follows the general ColdFusion style of *VariableType.VariableName,* as shown in the following code example:

```
<CFSET Application.Version="1.2">
```

One useful example of an application variable is for application-wide settings that vary between machines or installations. Suppose you're building an e-commerce application that includes thumbnail images for each item in a catalog. On your development machine, these images are located in the /images Web directory, but you don't know where users of your application would want the images to reside when they install the application on their server — they might even have a machine to serve the images that's separate from the machine that serves the ColdFusion templates. By using an application variable, it's easy to modify that location, either automatically during the installation of your application or manually later. This approach is especially important if your templates are encrypted, and therefore uneditable, by the user installing your application.

The CFAPPLICATION tag

Each ColdFusion application on a particular server should have a unique name to differentiate it from other applications. In that way, application variables for a particular application name can remain distinct from those of different applications. The CFAPPLICATION tag contains several crucial global ColdFusion settings for an application, including the name of the application. These attributes are discussed in more detail in the final section of this chapter.

An application name is required if you intend to use application or session variables.

ColdFusion Security Model

For the most part, ColdFusion expects the native security of the underlying technology (such as the Web server, database, or mail server) to control access and permissions. But ColdFusion itself needs to be secure to prevent exposing the Web server to easy access by crackers. Your application must be secure as well to prevent unauthorized users from using the applications you create.

This section provides guidance on configuring these different levels of security. Make sure you *always* consider security when designing and deploying sensitive applications.

This section is by no means the authoritative guide to ColdFusion Web application security. The techniques in the following sections should help you avoid making your system easily crackable, but they won't guarantee invulnerability. Each component of the application (templates, the Web server, ColdFusion, and the database) must be secure to make the entire application secure.

Securing a ColdFusion application requires four basic steps:

1. Secure the Web server.

2. Secure ColdFusion Server.

3. Secure the resources that interact with your application (including database servers, mail servers, and so on).

4. Secure your application.

The first step is mainly beyond the scope of this book (see Chapter 4 for more information on Web server configuration), but the remaining steps are straightforward and covered in the following sections.

Securing ColdFusion Server

Protecting ColdFusion Server from unauthorized users is one of the most critical components of a good security environment. ColdFusion has adequate built-in security, but since version 4.0, it offers an even more sophisticated and granular (highly configurable) model of advanced security for mission-critical systems (see the sidebar). The major security areas to configure in the basic ColdFusion security model are the Administrator settings, ColdFusion Studio access, and the use of some potentially dangerous ColdFusion tags.

Advanced ColdFusion security

ColdFusion 4.0 introduced a powerful set of Advanced Security features for applications requiring sophisticated security measures. The specifics of advanced security services are far beyond the scope of this book, but here's a quick overview of the basic components:

✔ **Administrator security** allows different administrative functions (such as registering data sources and registering custom tags) to be secured so that administrative functions can be assigned to different (and multiple) individuals.

✔ **RDS security** is aimed at developers. When using RDS with ColdFusion Studio, only a single password is available in the Basic Security model, which means every developer could have access to the directories and data sources of other developers. RDS security in the Advanced Security model makes sure that these separate development areas are individually protected.

✔ **Server sandbox security** is of interest mainly to ISPs who host ColdFusion. It allows each application to run in the equivalent of a virtual ColdFusion server. This protects applications from each other and

provides much stronger security for other applications running in different *sandboxes* (security areas) on the server. It might also be useful in a corporate environment with multiple disparate and unrelated application development groups.

✔ **User security,** probably the most useful component of advanced security in ColdFusion, allows individual users of a ColdFusion application to be validated using a Microsoft NT domain or LDAP directory service. This allows ColdFusion applications to be integrated with enterprise security databases. (Version 4.01 added the capability to perform this authentication against an ODBC data source.)

For more information on the advanced security services in ColdFusion, consult the *Administering the Application Server* manual included with ColdFusion Server. *Note:* Many people think these advanced security features are available only in the Enterprise version of ColdFusion, but the Server Sandbox option is the only Advanced Security feature specific to the Enterprise version of the ColdFusion Server.

Administrator security

The ColdFusion Administrator application is available only through a Web browser. It's protected by a password (created at installation). Any person with access to this password effectively has the ability to manipulate the ColdFusion Server configuration and could gain access to your entire machine through some of ColdFusion's features. *Guard this password carefully!* Make sure that you change it on a regular basis.

If you don't mind using Internet Explorer as your browser (and you're using IIS as the server), you can use the more secure NT challenge-response encrypted password security instead of the more generic clear-text version available with Netscape. Talk to your system administrator for more information.

Studio security

ColdFusion Studio offers tightly integrated access to the server through Remote Development Server (RDS). For instance, RDS allows you to edit ColdFusion templates on a remote server, as well as view databases and perform debugging against ColdFusion templates on that remote server. By default, ColdFusion Server requires an RDS password when connecting. (The password is created during the ColdFusion Server installation, as discussed in Chapter 4, and can be changed in the Administrator). It's not a good idea for the administrator to remove this protection for two reasons:

- ✔ The Remote Files tab in Studio allows access to virtually any file on the server when connected through RDS, which means the Studio user can *delete* almost any file on the server.

- ✔ The Database tab in Studio allows any query (including DELETE *) to be run on any data source on an RDS-connected server, even those owned by other users.

If you have an incorrectly or poorly maintained database and file security permissions, any Studio user can accidentally (or purposely) wreak havoc on your application. Make sure you don't remove that RDS Studio password.

For more flexible security arrangements, such as assigning different developers individual access through Studio to different data sources and file areas, use the Remote Development security features of Advanced Security or the Server Sandbox services in ColdFusion Enterprise (see the sidebar for more).

Tag security

Some ColdFusion tags offer a lot more potential for abuse or security problems than others do. The ColdFusion administrator can selectively enable or disable these tags to implement a more secure production environment. This setting is global — you have to convince your ColdFusion administrator if you want him or her to enable or disable one of these tags.

Table 11-1 lists these more dangerous tags. Currently, an administrator can't place restrictions on other ColdFusion tags.

Table 11-1	Tags an Administrator Might Disable
Tag	*What It Can Do*
CFCONTENT	Download and delete server files
CFDIRECTORY	Manipulate directories on the server
CFFILE	Upload or manipulate files on the server
CFOBJECT	Allow manipulation of COM and CORBA objects
CFREGISTRY	Read, write, and delete registry keys on the server

Securing Internet services and enterprise objects

Previously in the chapter, you saw an overview of the broad range of services that ColdFusion Server can interact with. Keep in mind, however, that this interaction can lead to security breaches if you're careless. Anyone with access to your ColdFusion application has access to anything that application interacts with — such as the mail server, databases, or files on the server. For example, if you build an application that lets someone send an e-mail message to an arbitrary e-mail address (such as billclinton @whitehouse.gov), anyone who finds your application can use it to send e-mail to anyone. With a little scripting, someone could turn your simple application into a spam engine (or cause a visit from the Secret Service).

Table 11-2 lists the various Internet and enterprise components and the available security measures. Most of the services that ColdFusion interacts with have their own security systems — you should use them.

Table 11-2	Security Options for ColdFusion Components
Component	*Security Options*
COM/CORBA	These types of objects require the CFOBJECT tag, which can be disabled by the ColdFusion administrator; in addition, each object has its native security system
FTP	Standard FTP username and password protection
HTTP	Standard Web server security (such as .htaccess on Apache and permissions on NT)
LDAP	Username and password protection for different types of actions and levels of data access
ODBC database	Varies by database, but generally includes username and password security or group-based security; also can control which SQL functions are not allowed (such as DELETE)
POP	None; use standard POP server username and password security for an e-mail account
SMTP	None; need to implement security in the SMTP mail server itself or limit access to the ColdFusion application using the SMTP service

Securing your application

The first line of defense in protecting your application from misuse is keeping unauthorized people out of it in the first place. This sort of security isn't an issue if you're building a phone book application, for example. But it becomes important if you're creating an intranet application that provides access to personal information (such as a social security number or credit card number) or confidential corporate data (such as sales reports or product marketing strategy).

The fundamental rule for designing any secure application is simple: Make sure that only the people who are supposed to use the application can use it.

Securing an application basically means that you need to know the identity of the person making a request at any given time. This is fairly easy in typical client/server environments, but this is difficult on the Web for two simple reasons:

- ✔ Web browser (client) sessions are anonymous.
- ✔ The Web server treats each page request as a new user — the server doesn't remember who did the requesting or what he or she previously requested.

To implement any type of security in a Web application, you need to uniquely identify a given user *and* keep track of what that user is doing in your application. You need to maintain the *state* of the Web browser (client) at all points in your application to ensure that it is secure. ColdFusion provides several ways of maintaining state, as you discover in the next section.

ColdFusion has a number of advanced security features that provide robust protection for your applications, but these security features typically require administrative access to the Web server, ColdFusion Administrator, and possibly other systems. This situation is far removed from the typical environment of a commercial host but possible if you're developing in-house and running your own server. These security features are beyond the scope of this book, but to get a rough idea of what's possible, look at the Advanced Security chapter in Allaire's *Administering the App Server* manual.

Matters of State

The nature of the Web is chaos — anonymous users freely jumping from page to page around a Web site and around the world. This chaotic organization might be great for the user, but it's the antithesis of a secure system. Since the early days of HTML+ and HTML 1.2, however, when the capability to fill out forms was added to the specification, you've been able to track a single user between pages. Maintaining the state of the user connection in this manner is important not only for security but also for a personalized and convenient Web experience. But this sort of tracking from one page to another is often not enough. Sometimes, you also need to track users between visits.

Consider the successful Amazon.com site. One crucial competitive advantage it has is the convenience of 1-Click Purchasing, as shown in Figure 11-4. If you register with Amazon.com and enable this feature, the browser and server keep track of you during a visit and even between visits if you request. Amazon has enough information to know who you are and to access your information stored on its server, such as your name and credit card information. That way, whenever you visit Amazon.com, you're only a click away from an impulse buy!

User information like this is typically tracked over the Web using a cookie. A *cookie* is a value or a set of values associated with a particular Web site that the browser stores somewhere on your computer. A script on the server checks the value of the cookie stored on the browser and then reacts based on the information the browser provides. Check out Listing 11-1 for an example of a Netscape cookie file.

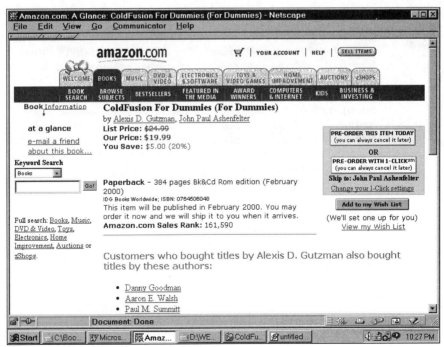

Figure 11-4:
A 1-Click purchase on Amazon.com.

Listing 11-1	Contents of Cookie File for Amazon.com

```
# Netscape HTTP Cookie File
# http://www.netscape.com/newsref/std/cookie_spec.html
# This is a generated file!  Do not edit.
.amazon.com     TRUE    /       FALSE   9316529538
        session-id-time
9322524200
.amazon.com     TRUE    /       FALSE   9316529538
        session-id
002-9876910-5575417
.amazon.com     TRUE    /       FALSE   20827354
        x-main
Em52OrtC2lzqimMjYYs3i4WG?2F6Tmp1rM
.amazon.com     TRUE    /       FALSE   20827354
        ubid-main
002-1785330-3420629
```

In Amazon.com, the cookie stores a number that identifies you so that Amazon can find more important information (such as your credit card number) on the secure servers it uses for its commerce systems. This approach is almost as good as logging onto its server directly.

In Netscape Navigator, cookies are stored in a single file named cookies.txt in the Users directory. Internet Explorer stores each cookie individually in the Temporary Internet Files folder (in the Windows directory) with names such as `cookie:user@website.com`. Feel free to look at these files with a text editor, but don't expect to understand them — and don't expect your visit back to the related sites to work properly if you modify them.

ColdFusion includes a tag that makes it easy to set, modify, and access cookie information. The CFML language also includes additional ways to track information through a single session (or visit) to a site and to track client information between visits to a site. All three methods — cookies, session information, and client information — help you build more secure and friendly ColdFusion sites.

Plain vanilla cookies

The CFCOOKIE tag provides a quick way to set or modify a cookie. It has the following syntax:

```
<CFCOOKIE
    name="cookie_name"
    value="text"
    expires ="period"
    secure="Yes/No"
```

```
        path="urls"
        domain=".domain">
```

name	The name used to refer to the cookie variable in your code.
value	The value of the cookie variable.
expires	The date that the cookie expires.
secure	A Yes/No value indicating whether the variable data must be transferred securely using SSL (secure socket layer).
path	The URL subdirectory path(s) in the Web site where the cookie is active.
domain	The Web site domain where the cookie is active.

Again, like most tags, you don't need all these attributes (just name and value are typically needed). This code, when executed on a page called by a given browser, will set the named cookie with the given value in that browser. If an expires attribute is offered, the cookie will expire in the given time frame.

Once set, the cookie is sent along with all subsequent calls to templates on the server that set the cookie. The value of the cookie is accessible like any other ColdFusion variable: You use the prefix *Cookie* and the variable name. For example, a cookie called UserName could be accessed with Cookie.Username in any application within the specific domain and path. If no path or domain was specified on CFCOOKIE, the cookie variable created will be available to any application on the server that set the cookie. If you've dealt with cookies through JavaScript or Perl, you probably think this syntax is pretty slick compared to the gymnastics required to use cookies in those languages.

Note one fundamental point about using cookies with ColdFusion:

> Think twice about using cookies.

Don't get us wrong — nothing is wrong with cookies *per se,* but ColdFusion is optimized for using more sophisticated means of keeping track of the user. Designing ColdFusion applications that use plain vanilla cookies properly can be difficult. You'll find it easier and more efficient to use ColdFusion client and session variables instead. Both of these variable types rely on small cookies residing in the client's Web browser, but manipulation of the cookies takes place behind the scenes, letting you focus on developing the application instead of managing the cookies.

State tracking with ColdFusion

You enable ColdFusion session and client variables in the CFAPPLICATION tag, typically specified in the application.cfm file of your application. To turn on client and session management, you set the corresponding attributes to Yes.

Timeout values determine how long the variables exist. You can use any values you want, but default and maximum values are set in the ColdFusion Administrator application (see Chapter 4 for more). The typical default is 20 minutes for session variables and 2 days for client variables. If you set a time period in your CFAPPLICATION that's greater than the maximum value specified in ColdFusion Administrator, the maximum value overrides your decision.

You can use either or both types of variables in your application.

You can use the CFAPPLICATION tag to enable session and client variables as well as to set default timeout values:

```
<CFAPPLICATION
    name="Name"
    clientmanagement="Yes/No"
    clientstorage="Storage Type"
    setclientcookies="Yes/No"
    sessionmanagement="Yes/No"
    sessiontimeout=#CreateTimeSpan(days,hours,minutes,
        seconds)#
    applicationtimeout=#CreateTimeSpan(days,hours,minutes,
        seconds)#>
```

name	The unique name on the server for the application.
clientmanagement	A Yes/No value indicating whether client variables are enabled in the application.
clientstorage	If client variables are enabled, this attribute determines whether they are stored in cookies, the server registry, or a datasource. The default is cookies.
setclientcookies	Allows ColdFusion to maintain client state using cookies. If this is set to No, the CFID and CFTOKEN client information must be manually passed through the URL in each page of the application.
sessionmanagement	A Yes/No value indicating whether session variables are enabled in the application.

sessiontimeout	The length of time that session variables persist between accesses. The default and maximum are set by ColdFusion Administrator.
applicationtimeout	The length of time that application variables persist between accesses. The default and maximum are set by ColdFusion Administrator.

All client and session variables are stored by relating the application to a specific user. The user is assigned a pair of values that uniquely and securely identify him or her to the server. The first value is CFID, a numerical identifier for that particular user. The second value, CFTOKEN, is a key that, in association with a particular CFID, opens the door to the client and session variables associated with the particular user for that application.

CFTOKEN is generated by a complex algorithm that incorporates information about the application, the CFID value, and possibly even the IP or network address. This makes it difficult to *spoof* (artificially create) a valid pair of values that would work with your application.

Session state

Session variables store information about the user of an application from the time the variables are set (typically when the user logs on) until the variables are deleted or cleared (typically when the user logs out), or the session times out, or the server is restarted, as described later. These variables are normally used to store information that does not change during a session but that could change *between* sessions.

After you enable session variables in the application.cfm file, you can set them using CFSET, which might look familiar:

```
<CFSET Session.Day=DayofWeekAsString(DayOfWeek(Now))>
```

This code snippet assigns the name of the day (Thursday, for example) to the `Session.Day` variable. Throughout the application, whenever you want the program to display the day of the week, you can avoid repeating that complex set of nested functions on the right side of the equals sign by accessing this session variable instead.

Session variables can also take the place of passing data among templates by way of FORM and URL variables. (See Chapter 10 for more on variables.) Suppose you build a string that is the WHERE part of a SQL query, and you need to pass the string between two pages (to refine a search, for example). You could use a hidden form field, but then you'd have to include buttons to submit the form. Or you could pass the text as a URL, but spaces and special characters in the string could cause problems. Instead, simply assign the variable to a session variable, such as `Session.Querystring`, which you can then use on the following page by referencing it. Another useful application for session variables is to track whether a user has logged on to an application.

The downside of using session variables is that they are stored in the server's memory. This makes your application vulnerable to system crashes because the variables disappear when the server is rebooted. This disadvantage isn't crucial because lots of problems occur if your server goes down, but it's important to remember. (Note that the ColdFusion Server application alone can be restarted in some situations, without the entire physical server being restarted. In that case, session variables — as well as application and server variables — are lost.)

A more germane disadvantage is that extensive (and careless) use of session variables can impede the performance of the server. If the size of simultaneous session variables starts to max out server memory, then the server has to use overflow disk-based pagefile memory, which is several orders of magnitude slower than system memory.

To avoid running out of memory, make sure you reassign session variables that could contain a lot of information back to a default value, such as an empty string, after you're finished with them.

Client state

Client variables are similar to session variables but are typically used to keep track of information about a user (client) that persists between sessions (instead of during sessions). Client variables are typically user names and other permanent information.

You create client variables in the same way you create session variables, by using the CFSET tag:

```
<CFSET Client.UserID=GetCustomerInfo.UserID>
```

You could use this example to get the primary key from a customer table when the user logs on. (GetCustomerInfo is a query that has already been performed.) Later in the application, when you need to get the user's address and billing information for a purchase, you can automatically pull the information into the appropriate areas of the order form using the `Client.UserID` variable instead of asking the user to fill in the information again.

You can store client variables in any one of three places, but session variables are stored only in server memory. Table 11-3 lists the possible storage areas for client variables, along with the advantages and disadvantages of each. Regardless of the method you choose, use client variables sparingly. They are best suited for saving permanent information that will reduce the number of database queries required by your application.

Table 11-3	Storage Options for Client Variables	
Option	*Advantages*	*Disadvantages*
Registry	Default setting. Provides server-side storage, which can be moved from machine to machine if necessary (though not easily).	Registry size is predetermined on the server. Overuse can crash the system.
ODBC data sources	Can use for other database applications. Easy to manage and analyze.	Works well with clustering. Slower than other methods. Must be configured by the administrator.
Cookie	Not constrained by server-side issues. Can also access with Perl scripts or other CGI applications.	Users can turn cookies off, and knowledgeable users can modify the cookie on their browser.

Putting It All Together

In this section, we present the skeleton of an application that uses both client and session variables to manage security on a set of ColdFusion templates. Here's an overview of the high points:

- The application stores the UserID (the primary key in the user information table) in a client variable on the server.

- The application.cfm file checks for the `Session.LoggedIn` variable on each page to prevent unauthorized access.

- The password is stored in the database along with the username.

Figure 11-5 shows an overview of how the application works.

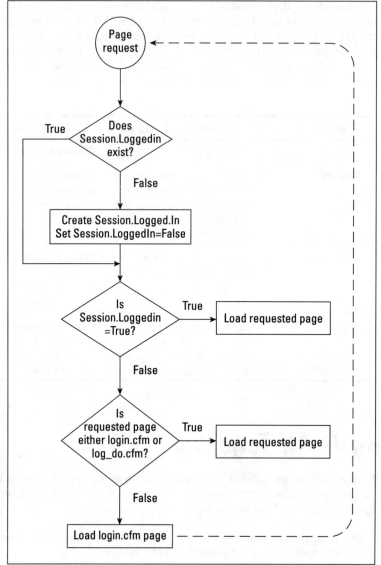

Figure 11-5:
The security
application
follows a
specific
series of
steps to
govern
access to
your
application.

Listing 11-2 is the source code for the application.cfm file that's executed at
the beginning of every ColdFusion page in the application. If the user has not
logged on, the `Session.LoggedIn` variable is not defined and the user is
redirected to the login.cfm page, shown in Listing 11-3. Listing 11-4 processes
the login.cfm page using the database to verify whether the username and
password combination is correct and then forwards the user to the index.cfm
page.

These files are all located on the *ColdFusion 4 For Dummies* CD.

Listing 11-2   **The Application.cfm File**

```
<CFAPPLICATION name="SecureApp" clientmanagement="Yes"
          sessionmanagement="Yes" setclientcookies="Yes">

<CFIF NOT IsDefined("Session.LoggedIn")>
  <CFSET Session.LoggedIn=False>
</CFIF>

<CFIF Session.LoggedIn EQ FALSE>

  <CFIF NOT (CGI.PATH_INFO EQ "/login.cfm" OR CGI.PATH_INFO
          EQ "/login_do.cfm")>
<CFLOCATION url="login.cfm" addtoken="No">
  </CFIF>
</CFIF>
```

The CFLOCATION tag is used to force the Web browser to jump to another page. It's similar to a GOTO statement in many programming languages.

Listing 11-3   **The Login.cfm File**

```
<!DOCTYPE HTML PUBLIC "-//W3C//DTD HTML 4.0
          Transitional//EN">

<html>
<head>
   <title>Login Page</title>
</head>

<body>

<FORM action="login_do.cfm" method="POST">
      Username: <INPUT type="Text" name="Username"
          value="test"><BR>
      Password: <INPUT type="Password" name="Password"
          value="test"><BR>
      <INPUT type="Submit">
</FORM>

</body>
</html>
```

Listing 11-4	The Login_do.cfm File

```
<!DOCTYPE HTML PUBLIC "-//W3C//DTD HTML 4.0
          Transitional//EN">

<html>
<head>
   <title>Logged in</title>
</head>

<body>

<CFQUERY name="DoLogin" datasource="Login" dbtype="ODBC">
SELECT      UserID, loginid, password
FROM        Users
WHERE       (loginid = '#FORM.Username#') AND (password =
            '#Form.Password#')
</CFQUERY>

<CFIF DoLogin.RecordCount EQ 1>
   <CFSET Session.LoggedIn=True>
   <CFLOCATION url="index.cfm" addtoken="No">
<CFELSE>
   Bad password<BR>
   Click <A HREF="login.cfm">here</A> to try again
</CFIF>

</body>
</html>
```

The only code that might be a little confusing is the following line from the application.cfm file in Listing 11-2:

```
<CFIF NOT (CGI.PATH_INFO EQ "/login.cfm") OR (CGI.PATH_INFO
          EQ "/login_do.cfm")>
```

This code prevents the application.cfm file from redirecting the user to the login.cfm page when the login.cfm or login_do.cfm pages are being processed. This corrects the endless loop that would occur because login.cfm includes application.cfm, which includes login.cfm, and so on. The CGI.PATH_INFO variable contains the name of the ColdFusion template (you could also use the CGI.SCRIPT_NAME variable), which enables you to check the page being processed so that you can selectively activate or deactivate portions of the application.cfm file required for a particular page.

Chapter 12

Selecting and Presenting Data

● ●

In This Chapter

▶ Selecting data from the database

▶ Finding the perfect match

▶ Handling partial matches on a single field

▶ Handling partial matches on multiple fields

▶ Displaying data from the database

▶ Showing the results of your query

▶ Displaying grouped query results

▶ Understanding how to nest with CFOUTPUT

● ●

*Y*ou seldom want to display all records in a database. More likely, you want to select records based on the values of fields and on whether those values match the criteria you or your visitors are providing.

As you will see, selecting data from a database is straightforward if a visitor's request and the database's contents match perfectly, but what if they don't? This chapter delves into SQL to show you how to extract data from a database when the criteria and the data match only partially.

The CFTABLE and CFCOL tag set is great for displaying tabular data. But if you want to thank visitors by name, for example, or format a billing address next to a shipping address, you need a different tag: CFOUTPUT. In this chapter, you see how to display query results using CFOUTPUT, how to group query results, and how to nest CFOUTPUT to display grouped query results.

Data Selection Fundamentals

When you use a Web search engine, you provide search criteria, such as one of the following:

```
ColdFusion and book

database and web

+"ColdFusion classes" -"web-based"
```

Have you thought about how a search engine handles the data you enter? You need to decide how flexible you'll be when you accept search criteria. The easy way to develop your search page is not to be overly flexible. To provide your visitors with a way to search your database, you need to let them enter information that you can match against the data in your database.

Unlike a search engine, your search page doesn't need to cram all search criteria into one big field. When you enter search criteria at a search engine, it searches the URLs, file names, titles, meta tags, and contents of the pages it indexes. In your search page, you can provide field names for search criteria, and ask the visitor for values on which to search for one or more of those fields.

If you do provide more than one criterion on which visitors can search, make sure your code returns data if the visitors don't provide *any* criteria. For instance, if you provide no criteria to the form created by the ColdFusion Studio Drill Down wizard, it returns no records, which is counter-intuitive. Most people think in terms of their criteria narrowing the pool, so providing no criteria should display all the data.

Creating the Possibility of a Perfect Match

The easiest way to let visitors select records from a database is to offer a drop-down list containing all the options in the database. Suppose your database contains ColdFusion contract programmers in the United States, and all records have states with two-character codes. Offering to let visitors see the state of their choosing makes sense for those looking for local assistance with ColdFusion programming.

Limiting visitors to one state shouldn't be too inconvenient. Even visitors from the New York metropolitan area who want to see listings for New York, New Jersey, and Connecticut, for example, would have to run through the search and result pages only three times.

To extract from a database each unique value of a field — such as each state for which there is a developer — use the Distinct( ) function in SQL, as shown in the following CFQUERY tag. The alternative to extracting each unique value is to have states with multiple developers appear in the list multiple times.

```
<CFQUERY name="AllStates" datasource="ecom" dbtype="ODBC">
SELECT Distinct(State)
FROM Developers
ORDER BY State
</CFQUERY>
```

This query gives us the sorted state list for the form page in which the visitor selects the search criteria. When we pop the results of the query into a CFOUTPUT tag nested inside a SELECT tag on the form page, the visitor has a complete (and unique) list of states. That list is created by the following SELECT tag, in which ColdFusion contract programmers are located:

```
<SELECT name="state">
<OPTION value="*">Any
<CFOUTPUT query="AllStates">
<OPTION value="#state#">#state#
</CFOUTPUT>
</SELECT>
```

The select list created by the preceding code displays all the states in the database. Limiting the selection to states for which there is data makes this approach better than just giving visitors the opportunity to select from a list of all states. Before visitors even submit their queries, they'll know that if the state isn't listed, no developers are in the state.

If we were using a relational approach with a lookup table of states and state codes, we could instead join that state codes table to the developers table to achieve this limited list of states.

The select list also has a value of Any, which allows a visitor to see all records for all states. Note that the value of Any is "*", which we can use in determining whether to find all records or just those for the chosen state.

If the only field in your criteria-selection form is the select list created in the preceding code, the following SQL extracts the records the visitor has requested:

```
<CFQUERY name="GetMatches" datasource="ecom" dbtype="ODBC">
SELECT name, address, city, state, zip, phone, email
FROM developer
<CFIF form.state is not "*">
    WHERE state = '#state#'
</CFIF>
ORDER BY city
</CFQUERY>
```

Limiting your search criteria to values in just a single select list isn't useful for most applications. Consequently, we look at more flexible ways for handling search data in the rest of the chapter.

Searching for a Field Based on Partial Matches

When you can't expect an exact match on the data, such as when the visitor is looking for the words *ColdFusion* and *developer* in a large text field or in a memo field, you have to use a more advanced query to let ColdFusion match the term in the field.

You might want your visitor to be able to search in other ways, based on the following:

- ✔ The first part of a field, such as the beginning of a company name
- ✔ The last part of a field, such as the end of a last name
- ✔ Any part of the field, such as the word *developer* in a job title

To compare only part of a text field, you need to use wildcard characters in your SQL as well as a different operator, called `like`. You can use wildcard characters before, after, or on both sides of the value.

Using like as an operator

In algebra, you learned all sorts of equations with either an equal sign (=), a greater than sign (>), or a less than sign (<) as the operator. SQL is more flexible than your algebra teacher in evaluating equations because it can accept `like` as an operator.

Note that you can use `like` as an operator only when you're evaluating text strings.

Using % as a wildcard character

The `like` operator requires some vagueness in the search string. Use the percentage sign (%) to indicate whether the part of the search results about which you're unsure precedes, follows, or both precedes and follows the part about which you are sure.

The following code illustrates the use of the percentage sign as a wildcard character:

```
SELECT *
FROM Developers
WHERE Name Like '%John%'
AND City Like '%Park%'
```

This query returns John Smiths as well as Mary Johnsons who live in Park Ridge or Lincoln Park. If you were sure that the person's name was John *something* and he was definitely from *something* Park, the following is a better query:

```
SELECT *
FROM Developers
WHERE Name Like 'John%'
AND City Like '%Park'
```

The values *John* and *Park* are likely to be stored in variables set previously in your application, so your query might look more like the following:

```
SELECT *
FROM Developers
WHERE Name Like '#form.name_begins_with#%'
AND City Like '%#form.City_ends_with#'
```

Using dynamic operators

ColdFusion Studio created the page in Figure 12-1. As you can see, the select list that contains the operator for the search includes *begins with, ends with,* and *contains.*

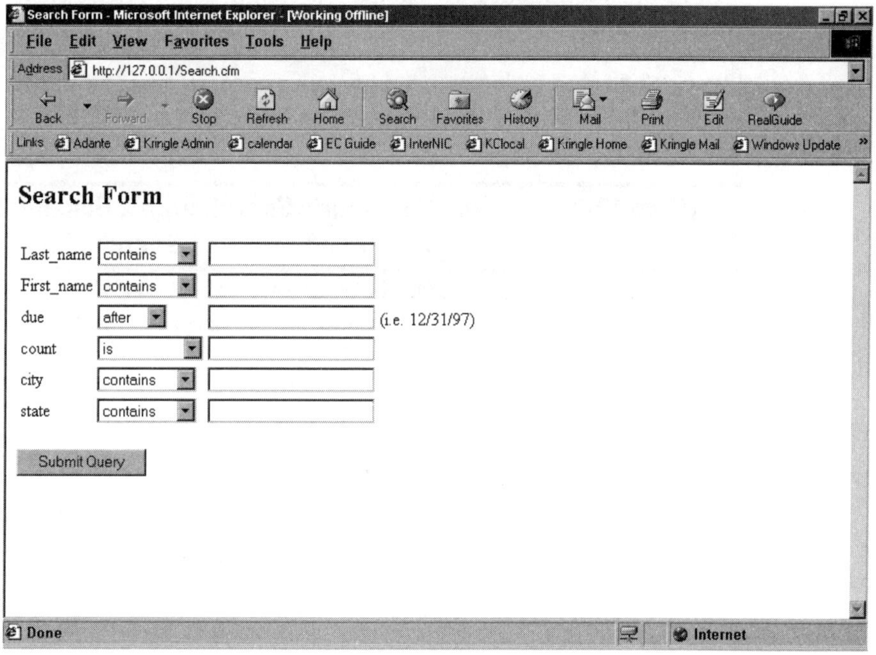

Figure 12-1: The search page generated by ColdFusion Studio with a select list for the operator.

To use a dynamic operator (one provided by visitors based on the form they complete), you need to use conditions in your query.

Listing 12-1 shows how you might both create the select list for the page containing the form in which the visitor provides the criteria and have ColdFusion return useful information on the result page.

Listing 12-1   **A Form with a Single Search Field and a Dynamic Operator**

```
<FORM action="process.cfm" method="post">
<B>Last name</B>
<SELECT name="last_name_operator">
<OPTION value="Is">Is
<OPTION value="Contains">Contains
<OPTION value="Begins">Begins with
<OPTION value="Ends">Ends with
</SELECT>
<INPUT type="text" name="last_name"><P>
<INPUT type="Submit">
</FORM>
```

In Listing 12-1, the values in the select list are shorthand for the complete operator name displayed to the visitor. They don't perfectly match the values sent to the server, but they have enough information to be clear without requiring unnecessary typing on your part.

Listing 12-2 is the code you need on your processing page if the last name field is the only search field on your page, as is the case in Listing 12-1.

Listing 12-2   **The Query for a Search with a Dynamic Operator and only One Search Field**

```
<CFQUERY name="FindMatches" datasource="ecom">
SELECT *
FROM Developers
WHERE Last_name
<CFSWITCH Expression="#last_name_operator#">
    <CFCASE VALUE="Is">
        = '#last_name#'
    </CFCASE>
    <CFCASE VALUE="Contains">
        Like '%#last_name#%'
    </CFCASE>
    <CFCASE VALUE="Begins">
        Like '#last_name#%'
    </CFCASE>
    <CFCASE VALUE="Ends">
```

```
        Like '%#last_name#'
    </CFCASE>
</CFSWITCH>
ORDER BY Last_name
</CFQUERY>
```

This is just beginning to get interesting, but you probably want more than
one search field. If that's the case, read on.

Searching for Multiple Criteria Using Partial Matches

If you want to search your database based on one or more of several criteria,
permitting partial matches on the data, you probably want to build a more
flexible approach than hard-coding the field names into the query.

Using variables for field names might sound complicated. But many Web sites
provide this type of flexibility — where the visitor can provide one or more
criteria or no search criteria — so you should, as well. Figure 12-2 shows a
form with multiple search criteria and dynamic operators.

Figure 12-2:
The form
that permits
the visitor to
provide mul-
tiple search
criteria and
dynamic
operators.

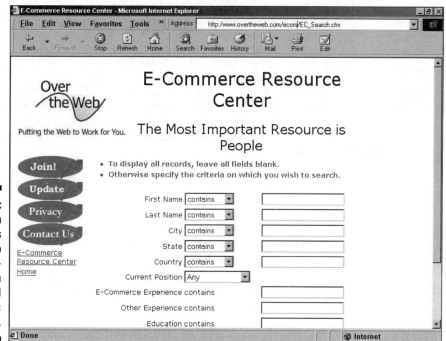

The numbered field technique

One way to search for more than one criterion is to use the *numbered field technique,* in which you assign each field a number in addition to a name. For the database and for purposes of knowing what's in a field, you need a meaningful field name. The way to have your cake and eat it, too, is to use the Evaluate( ) function to translate the numbered field into the field name on the processing page.

Both naming and numbering your field sounds more complicated than it really is. Using this technique requires three steps:

1. Use the database field name on the form page.

   ```
   <INPUT type="text" name="FirstName" size="20">
   <INPUT type="text" name="LastName" size="20">
   <INPUT type="text" name="City" size="20">
   <INPUT type="text" name="State" size="2">
   <INPUT type="text" name="Country" size="20">
   ```

2. Create a hidden field for each form field on the form page, assigning the numbered field the value of the form field name.

   ```
   <INPUT type="hidden" name="field_1" value="FirstName">
   <INPUT type="hidden" name="field_2" value="LastName">
   <INPUT type="hidden" name="field_3" value="City">
   <INPUT type="hidden" name="field_4"value="State">
   <INPUT type="hidden" name="field_5" value="Country">
   ```

3. Use the Evaluate( ) function on the form-processing page to translate the numbered field into the name of the field.

With the Evaluate( ) function, you can convert `field_i` (where *i* is a number) into the field name. You can then convert the field name into the value of the field by nesting Evaluate( ) statements! The expression looks like a mess when you type it, but it can save you a lot of code lines — lines that require debugging.

Using this numbered field technique, you can also add fields without making your processing code any longer. Consider the code in Listing 12-3.

Listing 12-3	**A Query Using the Numbered Field Technique to Find Multiple Fields with a Dynamic Operator Matching on Partial Values**

```
<CFQUERY name="SearchResult" dataSource="ecom">
  SELECT *
  FROM Developers
```

```
<CFIF (Len(Trim(FirstName)) GT 0) OR (Len(Trim(LastName)) GT
        0) OR    (Len(Trim(City)) GT 0) OR
        (Len(Trim(State)) GT 0) OR    (Len(Trim(Country))
        GT 0) OR    (Len(Trim(Ecommexp)) GT 0) OR
        (Len(Trim(OtherExp)) GT 0) OR
        (Len(Trim(Education)) GT 0)>
    WHERE deleted = 0 AND (1=0
    <CFLOOP index="i" from="1" to="5">
    <CFSET field_name= Evaluate("field_#i#")>
    <CFSET field_operator= Evaluate("field_#i#_operator")>
    <CFSET field_value= Evaluate(field_name)>
    <CFIF Len(field_value) GT 0>
    OR #field_name#
    <CFSWITCH expression="#field_operator#">
        <CFCASE value="is">
        = '#field_value#'
        </CFCASE>
        <CFCASE value="contains">
        Like '%#field_value#%'
        </CFCASE>
        <CFCASE value="begins">
            Like '#field_value#%'
        </CFCASE>
        <CFCASE value="ends">
            Like '%#field_value#'
        </CFCASE>
    </CFSWITCH>
    </CFIF>
</CFLOOP>
<CFLOOP index="i" from="1" to="3">
    <CFIF Len(Evaluate(Evaluate("memo_#i#"))) GT 0>
    OR #Evaluate("field_#i#")# Like
        '%#Evaluate(Evaluate("memo_#i#"))#%'
    </CFIF>
</CFLOOP>
    )
<CFELSE>
WHERE deleted=0
</CFIF>
</CFQUERY>
```

Returning all records if criteria aren't provided

The CFIF statement that begins on the fourth line of Listing 12-3 makes sure all the fields weren't left blank:

```
<CFIF (Len(Trim(FirstName)) GT 0) OR (Len(Trim(LastName))
        GT 0) OR
```

If all the fields are left blank, no records match. (This is the problem with the search page that Studio produces when you use the Drill Down wizard.) But if visitors don't provide any search criteria, they often expect all fields to match and thus be returned. We prevent the return of no records by assuming that if no criteria are provided, every record should be returned.

In ColdFusion, we use the Len( ) function to check that the length of every returned field is 0. If all returned fields are empty, we make sure that we return all records (at least all but those with a deleted value of 1, which means they've been deleted).

If any field has a value (meaning at least one field isn't empty), we proceed with the WHERE clause, which begins as follows:

```
WHERE deleted = 0 AND (1=0)
```

The first condition checked is that the record hasn't been deleted (deleted = 0). Next begins the most confusing but also most elegant section of code. We don't know how many criteria were provided by the visitor. We do know that at least one criterion was provided (or we wouldn't have made it through the CFIF statement on line 4). Rather than address why your code contains 1=0, step through the way you might have tried to code this example.

If only one value were provided, the code could read

```
deleted = 0 AND this = that
```

But what if the visitor provided two values? You'd need the following:

```
deleted = 0 AND (this = that OR this2 = that2)
```

If you're dynamically constructing the OR clause because you don't know how many values you're going to receive from the form page, deciding where to put the OR is a problem. Should it go after each search criterion, in which case there'd be a dangling OR at the end? Or should the OR go before each criterion, in which case there'd be an extra OR at the beginning?

Consider the following code:

```
SELECT *
FROM Developer
WHERE deleted = 0 AND
    <CFIF A>(This = That OR</CFIF>
    <CFIF B>This2 = That2 OR</CFIF>
    <CFIF C>This3 = That3)</CFIF>
```

In this code, we created A, B, and C as Boolean values out of thin air. What if condition B is false (the test CFIF B fails)? The WHERE clause works because the result of the evaluation of CFIFs is

```
deleted = 0 AND (This = That OR This3 = That3)
```

But what if B is false? The WHERE clause then fails because the clause ends with B (and the parentheses don't match)! So you might try the following approach:

```
SELECT *
FROM Developer
WHERE deleted = 0 AND
        <CFIF A>(This = That</CFIF>
        <CFIF B>OR This2 = That2</CFIF>
        <CFIF C>OR This3 = That3)</CFIF>
```

Even placing the operator before the conditions, your logic will fail if B is false. Plus, you'll have problems with parentheses in almost any case.

What should you do? Create code that parses correctly if any line is missing. This is where 1=0 , which is always false, comes in. Because we're stringing together OR clauses, we need to use a value that will always be false. If we were stringing together AND clauses, we'd use 1=1, instead.

```
SELECT *
FROM Developer
WHERE deleted = 0 AND (1=0
        <CFIF A>OR This = That</CFIF>
        <CFIF B>OR This2 = That2</CFIF>
        <CFIF C>OR This3 = That3</CFIF>)
```

Now if A and B and C are all false, the WHERE clause reads

```
deleted=0 AND (1=0)
```

No records are returned, so the code is working, but it may not be exactly what you want. If any of A, B, or C is true, the WHERE clause won't cause an error and will return a value if a value in the database meets the criteria.

Finally in Listing 12-3, you see that we have a few loops. The loops are for the two types of fields in the form and the number of fields for each type that are offered.

Notice also that several Evaluate( ) functions are within the loops, such as

```
Evaluate("field_#i#")
```

Some of these Evaluate( ) functions are even nested inside Len( ) functions. The #i# is a variable that takes its value from the CFLOOP statement. If the value of i is 1, the value of the first Evaluate( ) function is FirstName and the value of the third Evaluate( ) function is the value of the FirstName variable.

Displaying Data that the Query Delivered

You can use the CFTABLE and CFCOL tags to return data in tabular format, but that's limiting because you can show data only in a horizontal table. What if you want to show data displayed down the page, rather than across? You need to use CFOUTPUT instead of CFTABLE to display data that way. Consider Figure 12-3, which shows data in a vertical table.

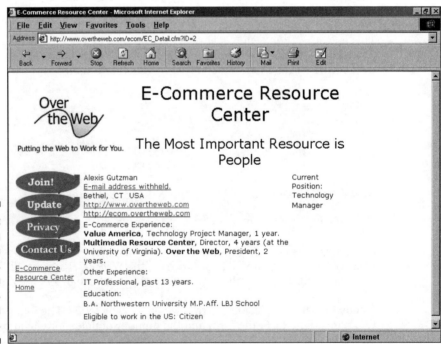

Figure 12-3: Displaying data down the page, rather than across, using CFOUTPUT.

The CFOUTPUT tag, which follows, takes only a few attributes:

```
<CFOUTPUT
    query="query_name"
    maxrows="number"
    startrow="number"
    group="field_name">
    . . . output here
</CFOUTPUT>
```

query	**Optional.** The name of the query for which you want to loop over and display output, if the output is the result of a query. If the output is for a variable, you don't need the query name.
maxrows	**Optional.** The maximum number of rows from the query that you want to display. It can be used with the startrow attribute to get a set of 20 rows (or whatever you set maxrows to be).
startrow	**Optional.** Defaults to 1. Permits you to return rows beginning somewhere other than with the first record in a record set.
group	**Optional.** Using the ORDER BY clause in your SQL statement, you can nest CFOUTPUT tags to show grouped output. Simply specify the name of the ORDER BY field as the value of the group attribute.

The next section shows an example of using the CFOUTPUT tag to display query results.

Displaying Query Results

You can use the CFOUTPUT tag without attributes. If you simply want to display the value of a variable, such as a local variable, you don't need any attributes. If you're using the CFOUTPUT tag to display the results of a query, however, adding the query attribute makes the tag act as both a looping structure and a way to display the contents of query variables.

The following code loops through the result set of the getall query and displays the first 20 rows in the table:

```
<CFQUERY name="getall" datasource="universe" dbtype="ODBC">
    SELECT first_name, last_name, created_date
    FROM list
    WHERE client_id='otw'
</CFQUERY>
<TABLE>
    <CFOUTPUT query="getall" maxrows="20">
```

```
      <TR>
            <TD>#first_name# #last_name#
            <TD>#DateFormat(created_date, "mm/dd/yyyy")
      </TR>
      </CFOUTPUT>
</TABLE>
```

In the preceding code, the CFQUERY tag gets all records from the list table of the universe database where the client_id field is otw. Then the CFOUTPUT tag loops through the results within the TABLE tag, showing one row for each record returned, up to a total of 20 rows. Although the table has two columns, it could have had as many as you wanted. We use the DateFormat( ) function to format the created_date field as mm/dd/yyyy.

You can use the CFTABLE tag to create a simple table like that created in the preceding code. For more on CFTABLE, check out Chapter 6.

Displaying Query Results in Groups

If you include in your query the ORDER BY clause — which sorts the data in the record set before it's returned to your page — you can display the results grouped by the unique values of the column using the group attribute of the CFQUERY tag.

In the code that follows, we request data grouped by city, and then we display the city name on its own line, followed by the records within that group:

```
<CFQUERY name="getbycity" datasource="aug99">
      SELECT first_name, last_name, siblings, city
      FROM Mom
      ORDER BY city, last_name, first_name
</CFQUERY>
<CFOUTPUT query="getbycity" group="city">
      <b>City:  #city#</b><br>
      <CFOUTPUT>
      #first_name# #Left(last_name, 1)#<br>
      Other Children: #YesNoFormat(siblings)#<br>
      </CFOUTPUT>
      <hr>
</CFOUTPUT>
```

The preceding code uses nested CFOUTPUT tags. The outer CFOUTPUT tag contains the group name; the inner CFOUTPUT tag contains all the data to be displayed for that group. Each tag is a looping structure. The outer tag loops through the group names, and the inner tag loops through the records within the group. We use the YesNoFormat( ) function to force the Boolean variable siblings to display as either Yes or No. Figure 12-4 shows how the results look.

Figure 12-4:
Grouping by
city using
nested
CFOUTPUT
tags.

```
http://127.0.0.1//ch10-group.cfm - Microsoft Internet Explorer - [Working Offline]

File   Edit   View   Favorites   Tools   Help

Address   http://127.0.0.1//ch10-group.cfm

Back   Forward   Stop   Refresh   Home   Search   Favorites   History   Mail   Print   Edit
```

City: Albany
Carrie S
Other Children: Yes

City: Altamonte (Orlando)
Jane A
Other Children: Yes

City: Auburn
Aurica M
Other Children: Yes

City: Austin
Alison D
Other Children: No
Kirsten M
Other Children: Yes

City: Baltimore
Dianna G
Other Children: No

City: Bargersville
Martha B
Other Children: Yes

Notice that the outer CFOUTPUT tag has the `query` and `group` attributes set, and the inner CFOUTPUT tag has no attributes. ColdFusion understands that the inner CFOUTPUT should loop through and display all the records within the group specified in the outer CFOUTPUT tag.

You aren't limited to one group. If you want to group first by state and then by city, for example, simply use three sets of CFOUTPUT tags — in which case the first two would have `group` attributes.

Because CFOUTPUT with a `query` attribute is a looping structure — in addition to being a way to indicate to the server that the values of variables should be displayed — you can't nest CFLOOP in a CFOUTPUT. You can put CFOUTPUT in a CFLOOP tag, however, if you need to show the results of a variable in a loop.

Some folks have been confused by the CFOUTPUT `group` attribute and thought it required that they use the GROUP BY clause rather than ORDER BY in SQL. The two clauses have different purposes. ORDER BY simply orders the results. GROUP BY is generally used along with SQL aggregate functions to perform calculation based on the GROUPed results. Although the two clauses can produce similar results in some cases, more often GROUP BY is *not* the appropriate clause.

Part IV

Serious about ColdFusion

The 5th Wave   By Rich Tennant

"Your database is beyond repair, but before I tell you our backup recommendation, let me ask you a question. How many index cards do you think will fit on the walls of your computer room?"

In this part . . .

In the first chapter in this part, we discuss how to use the CFFORM tag to build cooler forms than HTML can give you. In Part II, you see how easy it is to create simple pages. In this part, you see how to spiff up simple pages; one big way is to use the CFFORM field.

You also find out what to do when something goes wrong. You may have already turned to Chapter 14 to figure out why (oh why!) your page wasn't working, when everything was obviously right (oops, didn't notice those extra quotes). We compiled a list of the things we wish we had known when we first started out, and we made sure the list included things we still forget to check when our pages don't work the first time we test them.

Chapter 13

Building Better Forms

• •

In This Chapter

▶ Dissecting the anatomy of a form

▶ Searching for some validation

▶ Building forms with ColdFusion

▶ Waking up tired old forms with Java

• •

*W*eb forms are the common denominator of virtually every type of Web database application. Forms can be used to collect information from a user (using a guestbook or an order form), to provide a search interface, or for any other type of database interactivity.

We use HTML forms in a number of examples in other chapters in this book, but here we focus on a set of special form elements built into ColdFusion. In this chapter, we cover the CFFORM tag and the related ColdFusion form element tags you can place inside it. The majority of these tags are enhancements of existing HTML tags with better formatting and data validation functions. The remaining tags are a set of Java-based controls that provide functionality missing from the current implementation of HTML forms. These ColdFusion form elements can help you design more robust and user-friendly interfaces for your application.

Anatomy of a Form

Forms are simply a way of making Web pages interact dynamically with a Web server. The most common role for forms in a Web site is to gather data from the user; you then use that data to help generate additional Web pages that the user requests.

One of the simplest examples of using forms to make a dynamic Web application is a search engine such as Yahoo!, which is shown in Figure 13-1.

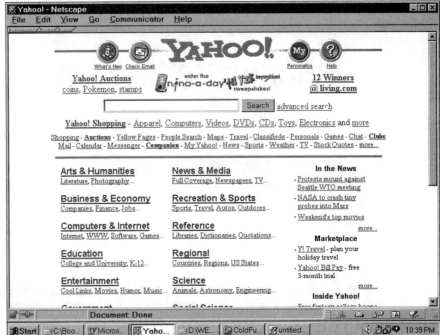

Figure 13-1:
Yahoo! uses
a simple
HTML form
to search an
enormous
database of
Web sites.

Notice the input box jumping out from the top center of the page — that box is part of a simple form. Following is the HTML source for that page (edited for clarity). Check it out and you should notice two pieces of HTML right away, the FORM and INPUT tags:

```
<HTML>
<HEAD>
 <TITLE>Yahoo!</TITLE>
</HEAD>
<BODY>
<CENTER>
<FORM action=" http://search.yahoo.com/bin/search>
<TABLE border="0" cellspacing="0" cellpadding="4"
        width="600">
    <TR>
       <TD colspan="3" align="middle">
          <INPUT size="30" name="p">
          <INPUT type="submit" value="Search"><A
          href="r/so">advanced search</A>
       </TD>
    </TR>
 </TABLE>
</FORM>
</CENTER>
```

The FORM tag is basically a container that makes it possible to collect a set of information from the user. The individual *form elements* that make up the form include the INPUT text box and other common interface components (such as buttons and lists). Form elements were part of the first revision to the HTML standard back in the dark ages of the early 1990s. Since then, few substantial changes have been made to the way forms work.

For more on the HTML FORM tag and various form elements, see Chapters 5, 6, and 7. For even more information, take a look at *HTML 4 For Dummies* by Ed Tittel and Natanya Pitts (published by IDG Books Worldwide, Inc.).

FORM versus CFFORM

Forms are the core of most ColdFusion applications, so it shouldn't be surprising to find that the engineers at Allaire souped up the standard HTML form and form elements. They also went a step further and added new elements of their own that are "missing" from HTML. These CFFORM tags, like all other tags in CFML, are converted into plain-vanilla HTML tags, but this time JavaScript and Java play a role as well. The result is far more efficient data entry, form manipulation, and database integration.

The CFFORM tag is used solely as a container for CFML and HTML form elements. The syntax for the tag follows.

```
<CFFORM
    name="form_name"
    action="ColdFusion_template"
    method="POST"
    enablecab="YES/NO"
    onsubmit="javascript_function"
    target="frame_name"
    enctype="mime_type"
    passthrough="HTML attributes"
```

name   **Optional.** The name of the form.

action   **Required.** The name of the ColdFusion template that will process the information entered on this page. If the CFFORM page sets up the parameters for a database search, for example, the template named in this attribute will do the search and present the results to the user.

method   **Optional.** You almost always want the POST method for ColdFusion form processing and rarely the GET method. With the CFFORM tag, unlike the FORM tag, you can leave off this attribute because it will default to POST.

enablecab	**Optional.** Allows Microsoft Java cabinet (*.cab) versions of Java-based CFFORM elements to be downloaded to improve the performance of the page on subsequent visits. If this option is enabled and users run the Internet Explorer browser, they never have to download the Java code for that particular ColdFusion tag again. There is no Netscape equivalent, so Navigator and Communicator users have to wait for the browser to download the Java code for these pages at the beginning of each browser session that uses the templates. Using this tag significantly reduces page download times, particularly for users connected on slower modems. If Yes, users are asked on opening the page whether they want to download the CAB file.
onsubmit	**Optional.** The JavaScript to execute just before the page is submitted; this is great for additional validation routines.
target	**Optional.** The window or frame that receives the output of the form-processing page.
enctype	**Optional.** This attribute describes the MIME type of the form submitted when the Submit button is clicked. The value defaults to `application/x-www-form-urlencoded`, which you shouldn't change unless you *really* know what you're doing.
passthrough	**Optional.** HTML attributes that are not explicitly supported by CFFORM. If you specify an attribute and its value, the attribute and value are passed to the HTML code generated for the CFFORM tag.

When ColdFusion Server processes the CFFORM tag, the result is a normal HTML FORM tag. The tags are almost identical, though their contents differ significantly if you use CFFORM elements instead of plain old HTML. The CFFORM tag simply signals that one or more form elements in the current form are special CFML form elements — no more, no less.

CFFORM elements

The new form elements that you can include in CFFORM come in two flavors: enhanced HTML form elements and new Java-based controls. Both are designed to make development easier and applications more powerful. The tags are discussed individually in the following sections; Table 13-1 gives a quick overview.

Table 13-1	New Form Elements in ColdFusion	
Name	*Type*	*What It Is*
CFSELECT	HTML	Drop-down list with auto-fill from queries
CFINPUT	HTML	Greatly improved data validation for text values (and radio buttons and check boxes)
CFTEXTINPUT	Java	Text input with validation and formatting control
CFTREE	Java	Hierarchical display (Explorer style) of data, files, and so on
CFGRID	Java	Spreadsheet-like data grid with validation as well as database manipulation
CFAPPLET	Java	Mechanism for embedding custom Java controls in a form

All HTML-based CFFORM tags use a combination of JavaScript and HTML to improve data validation and enhance the user interface. The Java components provide powerful display options that are impossible with HTML and JavaScript, and include data validation routines and an improved visual display and layout.

Seeking Validation?

The main improvement to all CFFORM elements is the capability to *validate* data more efficiently. The validation process ensures that the data you collect for a database record fits the format you envisioned for that record.

Suppose you just built an online shopping cart and a user is filling the basket. What happens if the user leaves the quantity of an item blank? With no data validation, the user could type anything — or nothing. How will your order fulfillment software handle an order for what might be interpreted as NULL items? Don't even think about it!

The amount of time it takes to get your ColdFusion application up and running is nothing compared to the work to clean up your data if it's been entered without reasonable validation. The primary types of validation issues you need to worry about are

✔ **Required fields,** which must be filled out, selected, or checked

✔ **Appropriate ranges for numeric data** (or lengths for text fields)

✔ **Consistently formatted values,** particularly dates and currency

✔ **Use of numbers only,** optionally with or without decimals

A number of shortcuts are available for validating data on the server after a form is submitted. CFFORM elements can also perform client-side validation of form input values to address any or all of these issues and more, including checking phone numbers, zip codes, social security numbers, and even credit card numbers!

The adage "Garbage in, garbage out" is applicable to data validation. Make sure any data input by the user is not garbage.

Server-side validation

The new ColdFusion form elements can do a lot of validation tasks for you using client-side JavaScript (as discussed later in the chapter), but ColdFusion also makes *server-side* validation simple. In this process, you use HTML to build the form and include hidden fields that contain validation information. When the server processes the form, any errors are displayed and the user is advised to use the Back button in the browser to return to the original form and correct the problem.

Table 13-2 lists the type of data validation that can be performed server side.

Table 13-2	Server-Side Validation Options
Suffix	*Validation Format*
date	Common date formats, including 9/9/99, 9/9/1999, and Sept. 9, 1999; the year defaults to the current one if not specified. Also converts date to valid ODBC date format.
eurodate	European date format, with the year preceding the month and day. Also converts date to valid ODBC date format.
_float	Numeric, including decimal.
_integer	Numeric, without decimal.

Suffix	Validation Format
range	Minimum, maximum, or both minimum and maximum numeric value; specified in the value attribute of the hidden field "MIN=1,MAX=10".
_required	Value is required.
_time	Common time formats of HH:MM or HH:MM:SS.

You activate server-side validation by including a hidden variable named for a form element followed by the type of validation. For example, to require that a value be entered on a form with a field named Lastname, you would add a hidden form field named Lastname_required. You can perform multiple validations (such as requiring a variable that also must be a date value) on a single form variable, but you need a separate hidden variable for each.

This validation is automatic and will occur for any form field whose name follows this convention. Be careful if you create a form field for a database column named, for instance, order_date. This form field will cause the form to be validated as a date field. That might not be a problem, though it might lead to unexpected results.

The value attribute of the INPUT tag provides a means of overriding the default error message presented if the validation fails.

Listing 13-1 is the source code for a form that requires an integer guess between 1 and 10. The resulting form is shown in Figure 13-2. Figure 13-3 shows the error message generated by leaving the text box blank and clicking the Submit button.

Listing 13-1   Server-side Validation Code Example

```
<FORM action="SSideValidate.cfm" method="POST">
<INPUT type="Hidden" name="guess_required" value="A guess is
        required">
<INPUT type="Hidden" name="guess_range" value="MIN=1,MAX=10">
<INPUT type="Hidden" name="guess_integer" value="Guess must
        be an integer">
Guess<INPUT type="Text" name="Guess">
<INPUT type="Submit" value="Make a Guess">
</FORM>
```

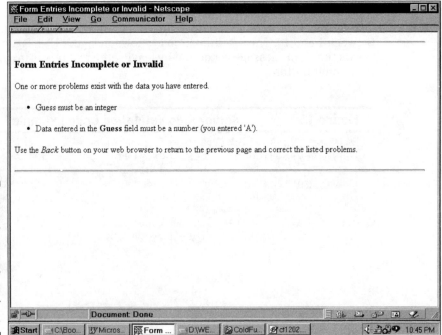

Figure 13-2:
This form is validated on the server side to make sure the input values are correct.

Figure 13-3:
Here's the error message generated by ColdFusion Server for invalid data.

Do you want more control over the display of the validation error message, as well as the formatting of the page displaying such errors? If so, use the CFERROR tag, which allows you to specify a special page to use to display error messages from such server-side validation errors. See the Allaire documentation for more details.

Client-side validation

Client-side validation is preferable to server-side validation, but it's also harder to implement. The problem is that ColdFusion can operate only on information submitted to the server — client-side ColdFusion isn't an option! But fear not, there is a solution — and that solution is JavaScript.

JavaScript is a client-side programming language that is often used for developing validation routines. Unfortunately, this isn't a book on JavaScript; for that you need *JavaScript For Dummies*, 2nd Edition, by Emily A. Vander Veer (published by IDG Books Worldwide, Inc.).

The folks at Allaire have thought about this problem, however, and have provided a set of ColdFusion tags that actually *create* JavaScript validation code! These custom validation routines are pretty good for typical types of data and simple forms; we discuss them in the next section.

Improved Form Elements

Two of the most useful elements on forms are the ubiquitous *text input box* and its close cousin, the *select* (or *drop-down*) *box*. Both of these user interface elements have been with the Windows operating system (as well as other graphical user interfaces) since the beginning and are intuitive to most computer users. These two workhorses of data entry forms are obvious choices for a little improvement with ColdFusion!

The upgraded CFINPUT text box and CFSELECT list box include several optional attributes that automatically generate client-side JavaScript for various types of validation. These tags make the requirement for a properly formatted data field in an input form trivial. In addition, you can perform this task and others without any knowledge of JavaScript. When the CFINPUT or CFSELECT tag is processed, the result is a plain-vanilla HTML INPUT or SELECT box, respectively, with associated JavaScript.

TIP

If you want to generate JavaScript-validated forms with ColdFusion, but need to implement the Web page on a machine without ColdFusion Server, you can easily convert the ColdFusion page to pure HTML. Simply create the page in CFML, browse it on ColdFusion Server, and then save the resulting page from within the browser, to store it as an HTML file that you can use separately. ColdFusion Server converts the CFFORM tags into normal HTML FORM tags when the page is rendered by the browser and creates the appropriate JavaScript. The resulting source code is 100 percent transportable and no longer requires ColdFusion.

CFINPUT

The INPUT box, shown in Figure 13-4, is the form-based user interface element probably used most often. CFINPUT can greatly enhance the plain-vanilla HTML text box and can provide marginal improvements for password boxes, check boxes, and radio buttons. In all cases, the improvement over the HTML INPUT tag takes the form of automatically generated JavaScript that can help with data validation.

```
Untitled - Netscape                                                _ □ ×
 File   Edit   View   Go   Communicator   Help

  Input Box examples

         Text box control:    [_____]

         using preset size:   [_____]

        using preset value:   [Preset Value_____]




 [≡]  Document: Done                              [icons]
 Start  C:\Boo...  Micros...  Untitl...  D:\WE...  ColdFu...  cf1203...        10:58 PM
```

Figure 13-4:
HTML input
boxes.

The attributes for the CFINPUT tag follow:

```
<CFINPUT
    type="input_type"
    name="input_name"
    value="initial_value"
    required="Yes/No"
    range="min_value, max_value"
    validate="data_type"
    onvalidate="javascript_function"
    message="validation_message"
    onerror="error_message"
    size="integer"
    maxlength="integer"
    checked="Yes/No">
```

name **Required.** The name of the input element. You'll save lots of development time and avoid confusion if you use the same name for the input element as any database column for which its value will be used.

type **Required.** The type of input element: `text`, `radio`, `checkbox`, or `password`. These are all standard HTML form elements.

value **Optional.** The initial (default) value for the element.

required **Optional.** A Yes/No value indicating whether the field is required. If this option is set to Yes, ColdFusion Server generates JavaScript code to ensure that the form element has a value when the form is submitted.

range **Optional.** The minimum and maximum ranges for the text box in "Min,Max" format. If this attribute exists, ColdFusion Server generates JavaScript validation code to ensure that the value of this input field is between the Min and Max values specified here. Only numeric values are allowed.

validate **Optional.** A check for a specific type of input (text boxes only): `date`, `eurodate`, `time`, `float`, `integer`, `telephone`, `zipcode`, `creditcard`, `social_security_number`. If this attribute exists, ColdFusion Server generates a JavaScript function to ensure that the input data is consistent with the chosen format.

message **Optional.** A message for a failed validation check. This replaces the default error message.

onvalidate	**Optional.** A JavaScript function to execute instead of the `validate` attribute. If you use this attribute, *you* need to create the appropriate JavaScript validation routines.
onerror	**Optional.** A JavaScript function to execute on a failed `onvalidate` validation.
size	**Optional.** The size (in characters) of a text or password box.
maxlength	**Optional.** The maximum number of characters in a text or password box.
checked	**Optional.** The Yes/No value for the initial state of check boxes and radio buttons.

The number of attributes might seem overwhelming, but for the most part, you use the CFINPUT tag to make sure that a text box is properly filled out. The only reason to use CFINPUT for a check box or a radio button is so you can use the `onvalidate`, `message`, and `onerror` attributes to help set up a validation routine.

Although the `validate` attribute causes ColdFusion to create JavaScript for you, the `onvalidate` attribute causes execution of custom JavaScript you have created. If you need a more sophisticated validation routine, check out *JavaScript For Dummies*, 2nd Edition, by Emily A. Vander Veer (published by IDG Books Worldwide, Inc.) to find out how to create your own validation routines.

A great example of CFINPUT in action is the validation of a credit card number on a Web order form. Listing 13-2 shows the source code of such a form.

Listing 13-2 Source Code Generated by CFINPUT for Validating a Credit Card Number

```
<html>
<head>
    <title>Enter a Credit Card number</title>
</head>

<body>
<CFFORM action="process_order.cfm" method="POST">
Enter your credit card number <CFINPUT type="Text"
        name="creditcard" message="Enter a valid credit
        card number" validate="creditcard"
        required="Yes"><BR>
```

```
<INPUT type="Submit"><INPUT type="Reset">
</CFFORM>

</body>
</html>
```

When you view the source code of the output in a browser, notice that ColdFusion builds several dozen lines of JavaScript for you! The good news is that you don't need to understand it. It just works! (You might want to review it, however, for an example of some complex JavaScript.) Listing 13-3 shows the appropriate output.

Listing 13-3   Source Code Generated by CFINPUT to Validate a Credit Card Number Entered in a Text Box

```
<script LANGUAGE=JAVASCRIPT>
<!--

function _CF_onError(form_object, input_object, object_value,
         error_message)
  {
  alert(error_message);
    return false;
  }

function _CF_hasValue(obj, obj_type)
  {
  if (obj_type == "TEXT" || obj_type == "PASSWORD")
    {
    if (obj.value.length == 0)
        return false;
      else
        return true;
    }
  else if (obj_type == "SELECT")
    {
    for (i=0; i < obj.length; i++)
      {
      if (obj.options[i].selected)
        return true;
      }
        return false;
    }
  else if (obj_type == "SINGLE_VALUE_RADIO" || obj_type ==
        "SINGLE_VALUE_CHECKBOX")
    {
    if (obj.checked)
      return true;
```

(continued)

Listing 13-3 *(continued)*

```
    else
      return false;
    }
  else if (obj_type == "RADIO" || obj_type == "CHECKBOX")
    {
    for (i=0; i < obj.length; i++)
      {
      if (obj[i].checked)
        return true;
      }
        return false;
    }
  }

function _CF_checkinteger(object_value)
  {
  //Returns true if value is a number or is NULL
  //Otherwise returns false
  if (object_value.length == 0)
      return true;

  //Returns true if value is an integer defined as
  //    having an optional leading + or -.
  //    Otherwise containing only the characters 0-9.
var decimal_format = ".";
  var check_char;

  //The first character can be + -  blank or a digit.
  check_char = object_value.indexOf(decimal_format)
  //Was it a decimal?
  if (check_char < 1)
      return _CF_checknumber(object_value);
  else
      return false;
  }

function _CF_checknumber(object_value)
  {
  //Returns true if value is a number or is NULL
  //Otherwise returns false

  if (object_value.length == 0)
      return true;

  //Returns true if value is a number defined as
  //    having an optional leading + or -
  //    having at most 1 decimal point
  //    Otherwise containing only the characters 0-9
var start format = " .+-0123456789";
```

```
    var number_format = " .0123456789";
    var check_char;
    var decimal = false;
    var trailing_blank = false;
    var digits = false;

    //The first character can be + - .  blank or a digit.
    check_char = start_format.indexOf(object_value.charAt(0))
    //Was it a decimal?
    if (check_char == 1)
       decimal = true;
    else if (check_char < 1)
      return false;

    //Remaining characters can be only . or a digit, but only
          one decimal
    for (var i = 1; i < object_value.length; i++)
    {
       check_char =
            number_format.indexOf(object_value.charAt(i))
       if (check_char < 0)
          return false;
       else if (check_char == 1)
       {
          if (decimal)         // Second decimal.
             return false;
          else
             decimal = true;
       }
       else if (check_char == 0)
       {
          if (decimal || digits)
             trailing_blank = true;
         // ignore leading blanks
       }
           else if (trailing_blank)
          return false;
       else
          digits = true;
    }
    //All tests passed, so...
    return true
    }

function _CF_checkcreditcard(object_value)
    {
    var white_space = " -";
    var creditcard_string="";
    var check_char;
```

(continued)

Listing 13-3 *(continued)*

```
    if (object_value.length == 0)
        return true;

    // squish out the white space
    for (var i = 0; i < object_value.length; i++)
    {
        check_char = white_space.indexOf(object_value.charAt(i))
        if (check_char < 0)
            creditcard_string += object_value.substring(i, (i +
                1));
    }
    // if all white space, return error
     if (creditcard_string.length == 0)
        return false;

    // make sure number is a valid integer
    if (creditcard_string.charAt(0) == "+")
        return false;
    if (!_CF_checkinteger(creditcard_string))
       return false;
     // now check mod10
    var doubledigit = creditcard_string.length % 2 == 1 ?
            false : true;
    var checkdigit = 0;
    var tempdigit;
    for (var i = 0; i < creditcard_string.length; i++)
    {
        tempdigit = eval(creditcard_string.charAt(i))
        if (doubledigit)
        {
            tempdigit *= 2;
            checkdigit += (tempdigit % 10);
            if ((tempdigit / 10) >= 1.0)
            {
                checkdigit++;
            }
            doubledigit = false;
        }
        else
        {
            checkdigit += tempdigit;
            doubledigit = true;
        }
    }
    return (checkdigit % 10) == 0 ? true : false;
    }

function _CF_checkCFForm_1(_CF_this)
   {
```

```
    if (!_CF_hasValue(_CF_this.creditcard, "TEXT" ))
        {
        if  (!_CF_onError(_CF_this, _CF_this.creditcard,
            _CF_this.creditcard.value, "Enter a valid credit
            card number"))
            {
          return false;
            }
        }
    if (!_CF_checkcreditcard(_CF_this.creditcard.value))
        {
        if  (!_CF_onError(_CF_this, _CF_this.creditcard,
            _CF_this.creditcard.value, "Enter a valid credit
            card number"))
            {
          return false;
            }
        }
    return true;
    }

//->
</script>
```

Wow! The few attributes in the following code fragment generate 182 lines of JavaScript automatically:

```
<CFINPUT type="Text" name="creditcard" message="Enter a valid
        credit card number" validate="creditcard"
        required="Yes">
```

If you understand JavaScript, you probably recognize most of Listing 13-3. If you're not JavaScript-savvy, you need to know that the code basically performs the following tasks:

- ✔ Ensures that the credit card input box is filled in

- ✔ Strips any spaces or hyphen (non-numeric) characters from the contents of the input box

- ✔ Checks the number to make sure it's a valid credit card number and not simply a made-up string of numbers

Credit cards must be validated, authenticated, and authorized before a transaction is complete. ColdFusion can *validate* the credit card number to ensure that it's a legitimate number using the standard mod10 algorithm (credit card numbers are generated with this same algorithm). In the authentication and authorization steps, you make sure the real owner is using the credit card and that funds are available. These steps *are not* part of the validation routine, although third-party ColdFusion tags can help you connect to major online authentication and authorization systems, such as MerchantNOW and CyberCash (see Chapter 16 for more).

ColdFusion generates JavaScript code that is cross-browser and cross-platform, so it should cause few problems for most users of your site — and should greatly improve the functionality of your page with minimal effort.

CFSELECT

The traditional select box, which is shown in Figure 13-5, provides an excellent way to force users to choose a value from a limited set of values for a field on a form. The main advantage of using a select box over a text box is that validation is a snap — as long as something from the appropriate list is selected, the value is by default within the acceptable range of values. Lists of values are static, however, which can be a problem when data changes quickly.

For example, suppose you have an order form in which the client can choose from a list of products in a discount warehouse's online catalog. The contents of the warehouse turn over quickly, so a user could order something from the list that is no longer in stock. Conversely, the customer might want something that's in the warehouse but hasn't yet made it onto the list. Now think about what would happen if that list of products was generated dynamically using the most recent warehouse contents data.

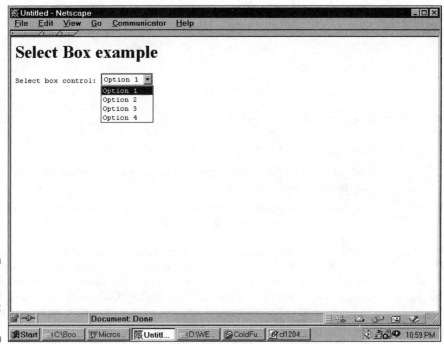

Figure 13-5:
A simple
HTML select
box.

The primary innovation of the CFSELECT box is that you can automatically generate the contents of the list from a database query. As shown in the following CFSELECT syntax, you can use the `query`, `value`, and `display` attributes to automatically generate the HTML code to build the list. The `onerror`, `required`, and `message` attributes are equivalent to the same attributes for CFINPUT.

```
<CFSELECT
    name="name"
    required="Yes/No"
    message="text"
    onerror="text"
    size="integer"
    multiple="Yes/No"
    query="query_name"
    selected="column_value"
    value="text"
    display="text"
    passthrough="HTML_attributes">
```

name   **Required.** The name of the form element.

required   **Optional.** A Yes/No value indicating whether the field is required. If this option is set to Yes, ColdFusion Server generates JavaScript code to ensure that the form element has a value when the form is submitted.

message   **Optional.** An error message that appears if `required` is set to `Yes` and no list item is selected.

onerror   **Optional.** A JavaScript function to execute on a failed validation.

size   **Optional.** The number of entries in the drop-down list box.

multiple   **Optional.** Yes if multiple list selections are allowed. No if only a single value can be selected.

query   **Optional.** The name of the query to use in populating the select box. This option makes it possible to generate dynamic select lists from the current contents of the database.

selected   **Optional.** If this attribute's value matches any element in the select list, that element is preselected (highlighted).

value	**Optional.** The query column to use for the value of the list element. This attribute can be used only if the query attribute is also present.
display	**Optional.** The query column to use for the display value of the list element. This attribute can be used only if the query attribute is also present. If you use the display attribute with the value attribute, you can display a field (such as a user's name) as a label in the browser's select list. That field, however, actually corresponds to a less-friendly value (such as a database key) that needs to be passed in this input element.
passthrough	**Optional.** HTML attributes that are not explicitly supported by CFSELECT. If you specify an attribute and its value, they are passed to the HTML code generated for the CFSELECT tag.

It's instructive to compare the results of one of the improved CFFORM tags to see how much work the tag is doing for you. Listing 13-4 shows the source code for a ColdFusion template that uses CFSELECT to automatically create a select list from a query. The resulting raw HTML code is shown in Listing 13-5. The OPTION elements are built from the query by the query, value, and display attributes. (Note that we have also added another OPTION tag for a choice that's not generated from the query.)

Listing 13-4   ColdFusion Template that Uses CFSELECT to Automatically Generate a Select List from a Database Query

```
<CFQUERY name="GetEmployees" datasource="cfsnippets">
SELECT   Emp_ID, FirstName, LastName, EMail, Phone,
         Department
FROM     Employees
</CFQUERY>
<CFFORM action="cfselect.cfm" method="POST">

<!-- Use CFSELECT to present the contents of the query by
         column -->
<H3>Employee List</H3>
<CFSELECT name="EmployeeNames" message="Select an Employee
         Name" size="#getEmployees.recordcount#"
         query="GetEmployees" value="LastName"
         required="No">
<OPTION value="">Select All
</CFSELECT>
```

Listing 13-5 Source Code Generated by CFSELECT in Listing 13-4

```
<SELECT name="EmployeeNames" SIZE=15>
<OPTION>Peterson
<OPTION>Heartsdale
<OPTION>Stewart
<OPTION>Smith
<OPTION>Barken
<OPTION>Jennings
<OPTION>Jacobson
<OPTION>Frankin
<OPTION>Smith
<OPTION>Manley
<OPTION>Cabrerra
<OPTION>Leary
<OPTION>Branden
<OPTION>Reardon
<OPTION>Barnes
<OPTION value="">Select All

</SELECT>
```

The HTML code that CFSELECT generated is not complex, but it certainly saves time and has the benefit of presenting the user with information as fresh as the last database update.

ColdFusion Form Elements, Now with Java

The engineers at Allaire didn't stop at improving existing HTML form element tags — they added several new types of form elements that were "missing" from HTML.

Navigating a database (as opposed to traditional Web page information) can be too complex for traditional form elements such as SELECT boxes. ColdFusion includes tags for both grid-based (spreadsheet) and tree-based (file and disk navigation) data layout formats as well as a data slider. It also includes a custom text input box that provides more control over the visual effect of the form element than the HTML INPUT box.

All of these special ColdFusion tags share one important feature: They're implemented through Java. The ColdFusion tags in the previous sections — CFSELECT and CFINPUT — are more powerful than the traditional HTML equivalents, but only because ColdFusion Server automatically generates JavaScript routines that are combined with standard HTML elements to provide additional functionality. The ColdFusion tags in this section are all little Java applets that execute inside the form to provide functionality outside the realm of HTML.

Java and JavaScript are not related. JavaScript is a scripting language that interacts with HTML in a Web page to manipulate the contents of the Web page and the browser. Java is a full-fledged programming language (such as C++ or Visual Basic) that can be used to develop executable applications, many of which are delivered or run inside a browser window (referred to as *applets*).

The Java-based controls in ColdFusion provide a number of nifty display, formatting, and user-interface features, but those features come at a cost. The biggest disadvantage of using these Java-based form elements is that they require that the user have a browser that can run a Java applet. This isn't a problem for the newer versions of Netscape Navigator and Internet Explorer (4.0+), but can cause problems with older browsers as well as users who surf on nontraditional platforms such as WebTV, PalmPilot, and palmtop computers.

The other major disadvantage of using these form elements is that the browser needs to download the code to produce the control each time the user visits your site. Downloading might take a few seconds on a fast connection, but as long as 10 to 15 seconds (or even longer) on a slow computer with a slow modem, which is a turnoff for many users. In general, though, the interface improvements provided by these Java tools more than outweigh the concerns. (The `enablecab` attribute of the CFFORM tag, explained at the start of this chapter, can help alleviate this download problem, but currently only for those using Microsoft Internet Explorer.)

As of this writing, all ColdFusion Java controls use Java 1.02 compliant code. Earlier versions of Java might have problems running form elements, but newer versions of Java (even 2.0) should run everything without a hitch.

CFTEXTINPUT

As mentioned, the text box is probably the most-used user interface component on Web-based forms. CFINPUT solved a number of fundamental problems with validating data in an HTML INPUT box using JavaScript, but it does nothing to address the design problems of the INPUT control.

The INPUT box provides virtually no control over the look and feel of the visual control that it produces on the screen. This lack of control is not a roadblock for designing functional Web database applications, but it certainly puts a damper on designing visually pleasing ones! The CFTEXTINPUT control addresses all the visual concerns of the designer while including the equivalent validation functionality of CFINPUT.

The CFTEXTINPUT attributes follow. Notice that `required`, `onerror`, and `validate` are all included, just like in the CFINPUT syntax. Most additional attributes control the font and spacing on the page. The big change here is that everything is accomplished using Java instead of the more limited JavaScript.

```
<CFTEXTINPUT
    name="name"
    value="text"
    required="Yes/No"
    range="min_value, max_value"
    validate="data_type"
    onvalidate="script_name"
    message="text"
    onerror="text"
    size="integer"
    font="font_name"
    fontsize="integer"
    italic="Yes/No"
    bold="Yes/No"
    height="integer"
    width="integer"
    vspace="integer"
    hspace="integer"
    align="alignment"
    bgcolor="color"
    textcolor="color"
    maxlength="integer"
    notsupported="text">
```

name   **Required.** The name of the form element.

value   **Optional.** The initial value of the element.

required   **Optional.** A Yes/No value indicating whether the user must enter or change the value. If this option is set to Yes, ColdFusion Server generates JavaScript code to ensure that the form element has a value when the form is submitted.

range   **Optional.** The minimum and maximum ranges for numeric data in "Min,Max" format. If this attribute exists, ColdFusion Server generates JavaScript validation code to ensure that the value of this input field is between the Min and Max values specified here. Only numeric values are allowed.

validate   **Optional.** The data format (`date`, `eurodate`, `time`, `float`, `integer`, `telephone`, `zipcode`, `creditcard`, `social_security_number`) used to validate user input. If this attribute exists, ColdFusion Server generates a JavaScript function to ensure that the input data is consistent with the chosen format.

onvalidate	**Optional.** A JavaScript function for validating user input. If you use this attribute, *you* need to create the appropriate JavaScript validation routines.
message	**Optional.** A message to display on failed validation. This replaces the default error message.
onerror	**Optional.** A JavaScript function to execute on failed validation.
size	**Optional.** The number of characters to display before adding a horizontal scroll bar to the form element.
font	**Optional.** The font face for text.
fontsize	**Optional.** The font size for the text.
italic	**Optional.** A Yes/No value indicating whether text should be italicized.
bold	**Optional.** A Yes/No value indicating whether text should be bold.
height	**Optional.** The height of the control, in pixels.
width	**Optional.** The width of the control, in pixels.
vspace	**Optional.** The vertical spacing of the control, in pixels.
hspace	**Optional.** The horizontal spacing of the control, in pixels.
align	**Optional.** The type of alignment for the element with respect to other elements.
bgcolor	**Optional.** The background color of the control. Choices are `black`, `magenta`, `cyan`, `orange`, `darkgray`, `pink`, `gray`, `white`, `lightgray`, and `yellow`. You can also use a hexadecimal value for the color, which must be in the form "`##rrbbgg`" because ColdFusion interprets a single number symbol as the beginning of a ColdFusion variable. The red (`rr`), blue (`bb`), and green (`gg`) values range from 0 (`00`) to 255 (`ff`). Be careful not to use the same color for the text and the background!
textcolor	**Optional.** The text color. Choices are the same as for the `bgcolor` attribute.

maxlength	**Optional.** The maximum length of input in characters.
not-supported	**Optional.** The message that appears if the browser does not support Java.

Figure 13-6 shows a comparison between the results of INPUT, CFINPUT, and CFTEXTINPUT tags with default attributes. Some splashier CFTEXTINPUT is included as well to show the range of possibilities.

CFSLIDER

Computer interfaces have indoctrinated users to expect interface components such as menus, text boxes, buttons, check boxes, and a host of other form elements that are reproducible (at least in basic form) using HTML. But what about a slider control? You might have used a slider to adjust the volume of your sound card, the color components in an image-editing or graphics tool, or the speed of opponents in a game.

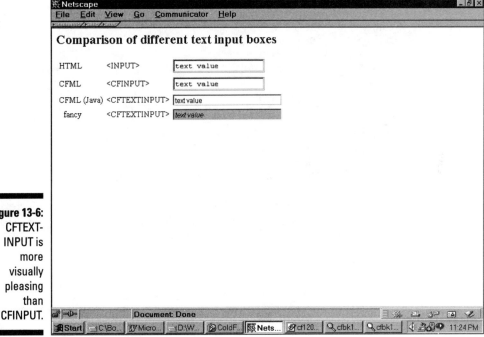

Figure 13-6:
CFTEXT-
INPUT is
more
visually
pleasing
than
CFINPUT.

Although we readily admit that a slider control is not an everyday component such as a text box, when you do need a slider in an application, there isn't an effective substitute. The CFSLIDER control provides this functionality in an HTML form.

Along with the attributes specific to the slider (shown next), a number of validation and formatting attributes produce a visually pleasing, as well as functional, form element.

```
<CFSLIDER
    name="name"
    label="text"
    refreshlabel="Yes/No"
    img="filename"
    imgstyle="style"
    range="min_value, max_value"
    scale="integer"
    value="integer"
    onvalidate="script_name"
    message="text"
    onerror="text"
    height="integer"
    width="integer"
    vspace="integer"
    hspace="integer"
    align="alignment"
    groovecolor="color"
    bgcolor="color"
    textcolor="color"
    font="font_name"
    fontsize="integer"
    italic="Yes/No"
    bold="Yes/No"
    notsupported="text">
```

name   Required. The name of the form element.

label   Optional. The label that appears on the control. The keyword %value% can be used to include the current value of the slider in the label string.

refreshlabel Optional. A Yes/No value determining whether the label is updated when the slider is moved. In most cases, you should set this value to Yes when you specify the %value% option in the label attribute so that the users get feedback when they adjust the slider.

img   Optional. The name of the image file to use in the groove of the slider. This attribute makes it possible to make more colorful and unusual sliders.

imgstyle	**Optional.** The style of the image in the groove (scaled, tiled, centered). If the img attribute is used, this attribute determines whether the image is scaled, tiled, or simply centered in the groove of the slider.
range	**Optional.** The minimum and maximum ranges for numeric data in "Min,Max" format. The default is 0,100.
scale	**Optional.** Defines the increments on sliders with a numeric scale. This works with the range attribute to determine how big the change is for one increment on the slider.
value	**Optional.** The initial value of the element.
onvalidate	**Optional.** A JavaScript function for validating user input. If you use this attribute, *you* need to create the appropriate JavaScript validation routines.
message	**Optional.** A message to display on failed validation. This replaces the default error message.
onerror	**Optional.** A JavaScript function to execute on failed validation.
height	**Optional.** The height of the control, in pixels.
width	**Optional.** The width of the control, in pixels.
vspace	**Optional.** The vertical spacing of the control, in pixels.
hspace	**Optional.** The horizontal spacing of the control, in pixels.
align	**Optional.** The type of alignment for the element with respect to other elements.
groovecolor	**Optional.** The color of the slider groove. Choices are black, magenta, cyan, orange, darkgray, pink, gray, white, lightgray, and yellow. You can also use a hexadecimal value for the color, which must be in the form "##rrbbgg" because ColdFusion interprets a single number symbol as the beginning of a ColdFusion variable. The red (rr), blue (bb), and green (gg) values range from 0 (00) to 255 (ff).
bgcolor	**Optional.** The background color of the control. Choices are the same as for the groovecolor attribute.

textcolor	**Optional**. The text color. Choices are the same as for the `groovecolor` attribute.
font	**Optional**. The font face for the text.
fontsize	**Optional**. The font size for the text.
italic	**Optional**. A Yes/No value indicating whether text should be italicized.
bold	**Optional**. A Yes/No value indicating whether text should be bold.
not-supported	**Optional**. The message that appears if the browser does not support Java.

Figure 13-7 shows two types of sliders that you could include on a form.

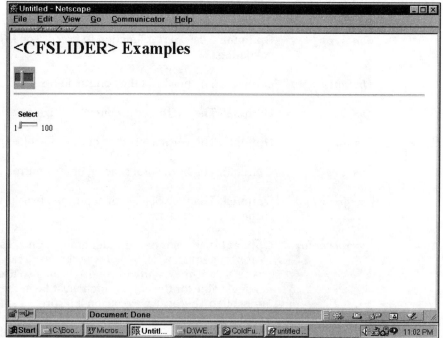

Figure 13-7:
CFSLIDER
elements
can range
from simple
to complex.

CFTREE

One common way that Windows displays hierarchical information is in a tree. Using the My Computer icon to drill-down to a particular file in a directory is the most common example of using a tree control. The various file and directory dialogs in Windows 95, 98, and NT all provide the capability to select an item from a tree, expand it to show all its subtrees, and continue to expand the tree until the final branch (usually a file) is found.

Tree-based navigation is the perfect way to navigate hierarchical information stored in a database. Employee information, contents of music CD collections, and many other types of data can be presented effectively in an expandable tree interface. This type of interface is exceedingly difficult to build in HTML and JavaScript, but easy to build with the CFTREE and CFTREEITEM tags. And if you're building the tree elements based on query information, CFTREE is especially powerful and effective. An example of a complete CFTREE interface is shown in Figure 13-8.

The CFTREE tag, shown next, is mainly a container to hold the various branches that contain the data in the tree. Also available are a wide range of display and formatting attributes, which should be familiar by now.

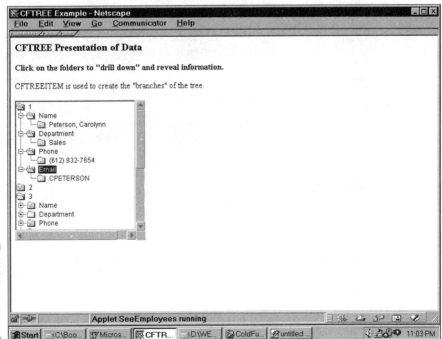

Figure 13-8:
A CFTREE
employee
information
example.

```
<CFTREE
    name="name"
    required="Yes/No"
    delimiter="delimiter"
    completepath="Yes/No"
    appendkey="Yes/No"
    highlighthref="Yes/No"
    onvalidate="script_name"
    message="text"
    onerror="text"
    font="font"
    fontsize="size"
    italic="Yes/No"
    bold="Yes/No"
    height="integer"
    width="integer"
    vspace="integer"
    hspace="integer"
    align="alignment"
    border="Yes/No"
    hscroll="Yes/No"
    vscroll="Yes/No"
    notsupported="text">
</CFTREE>
```

name Required. The name of the form element.

required Optional. A Yes/No value indicating whether the user must enter or change the value.

delimiter Optional. A character used to separate elements in the form variable path (defaults to \).

completepath Optional. A Yes/No value indicating whether or not the root level is passed to the processing template when the form is submitted.

appendkey Optional. A Yes/No value indicating whether the CFTREEITEMKEY variable should be passed to the form in the action attribute of the CFFORM tag. Used only with the CFTREEITEM href attribute. The default is Yes.

highlighthref Optional. A Yes/No value indicating whether links associating a CFTREEITEM with a url attribute value should be highlighted. The default is Yes.

onvalidate	**Optional.** A JavaScript function for validating user input.
message	**Optional.** The message to display on failed validation.
onerror	**Optional.** A JavaScript function to execute on failed validation.
font	**Optional.** The font face for text.
fontsize	**Optional.** The font size for text.
italic	**Optional.** A Yes/No value indicating whether text should be italicized.
bold	**Optional.** A Yes/No value indicating whether text should be bold.
height	**Optional.** The height of the control, in pixels.
width	**Optional.** The width of the control, in pixels.
vspace	**Optional.** The vertical spacing of the control, in pixels.
hspace	**Optional.** The horizontal spacing of the control, in pixels.
align	**Optional.** The type of alignment for the element with respect to other elements.
border	**Optional.** A Yes/No value indicating whether a border should be placed around the CFTREE control.
hscroll	**Optional.** Permits horizontal scrolling.
vscroll	**Optional.** Permits vertical scrolling.
notsupported	**Optional.** The message to display if the browser does not support Java. The default text is "Browser must support Java to view ColdFusion Java Applets!"

You use the CFTREEITEM tag to build the contents of the tree control. The branches of the tree can be generated from queries or directly coded into the ColdFusion template (for data that rarely changes).

The complete syntax for the CFTREEITEM tag is shown next; we cover a few slightly unusual attributes a little more completely.

```
<CFTREEITEM
    value="text"
    display="text"
    parent="parent_name"
    img="filename"
    imgopen="filename"
    href="URL"
    target="URL_target"
    query="query_name"
    quervasroot="Yes/No"
    expand="Yes/No">
```

value   **Required.** Value passed when CFFORM is submitted. When populating CFTREE with data from CFQUERY, columns are specified in a comma-separated list, as in `value="dept_id,emp_id"`.

display   **Optional.** Default is `value`. When populating CFTREE with data from CFQUERY, display names are specified in a comma-separated list, as in `display="dept_name,emp_name"`.

parent   **Optional.** The value for the parent of this item.

img   **Optional.** The name of the image file to use for this item (such as a folder icon). When populating CFTREE with data from CFQUERY, images or file names for each level of the tree are specified in a comma-separated list.

imgopen   **Optional.** The image to use for an opened tree item (such as an open folder icon).

href   **Optional.** The URL to associate with the tree item. If `href` is a query column, the `href` value is the value populated by the query. If `href` is not recognized as a query column, the `href` text is assumed to be an actual HTML HREF.

target   **Optional.** The target frame for the URL in the `href` attribute. When populating CFTREE with data from CFQUERY, targets are specified in a comma-separated list.

query   **Optional.** The query name to use for the tree item data.

queryasroot **Optional.** A Yes/No value that indicates whether `query` is the root query for the tree.

expand	**Optional.** A Yes/No value indicating whether tree item expands to show children. Most tree items should expand unless the data item is the last "leaf" of a tree or if application security allows only certain users access to certain information.

One of the biggest differences between the CFTREE form element and more traditional display options is that each CFTREEITEM and branch are visually represented with a small icon. These icons can also exist in open and closed states, which serve to expand or compress the data display. Figure 13-9 shows the icons included with ColdFusion; you can also use custom images for your own applications.

You can use CFTREE tags to create interfaces in which the user can quickly navigate through data to select a particular item. One problem with this approach, however, is that the user can select only a single item. Another problem is that the data can't be directly edited using this display method. For applications in which a spreadsheet-style presentation better fits the data display, read on and find out about the snazzy CFGRID control.

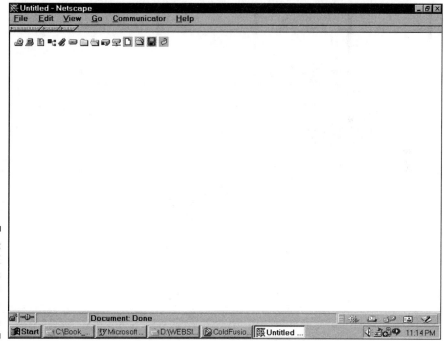

Figure 13-9:
The CFTREE
icons
provided
with
ColdFusion.

CFGRID

When most people think of data, a grid pops to mind — employee phone lists, accounts receivable lists, CDs in a music collection, spreadsheets, or other types of tabular information. You can certainly use ColdFusion queries with a TABLE or CFTABLE block of code to create a grid-like structure to display database information. The result, however, doesn't compare to a traditional application in which data can be presented in a visually pleasing manner with instant updating of data in the grid.

The CFGRID tag and its related subtags make grids possible inside an HTML form. For many applications, this tag is the single most important additional form component in ColdFusion.

The CFGRID tag, shown next, is a container that creates a spreadsheet-like area in the form that can be populated by query data. CFGRIDCOLUMN provides a great deal of control over the visual layout and display of the column. The CFGRIDROW tag can manipulate data in a row of the grid. Most importantly, the CFGRIDUPDATE tag allows direct database record manipulation using Java. The combination of all these tags can create a live database display in which records can be freely sorted, inserted, updated, and deleted efficiently and intuitively.

```
<CFGRID
    name="name"
    height="integer"
    width="integer"
    vspace="integer"
    hspace="integer"
    align="value"
    query="query_name"
    insert="Yes/No"
    delete="Yes/No"
    sort="Yes/No"
    font="column_font"
    fontsize="size"
    italic="Yes/No"
    bold="Yes/No"
    href="URL"
    hrefkey="column_name"
    target="URL_target"
    appendkey="Yes/No"
    highlighthref="Yes/No"
    onvalidate="javascript_function"
    onerror="text"
    griddataalign="position"
    gridlines="Yes/No"
```

```
rowheight="pixels"
rowheaders="Yes/No"
rowheaderalign="position"
rowheaderfont="font_name"
rowheaderfontsize="size"
rowheaderitalic="Yes/No"
rowheaderbold="Yes/No"
rowheaderwidth="col_width"
colheaders="Yes/No"
colheaderalign="position"
colheaderfont="font_name"
colheaderfontsize="size"
colheaderitalic="Yes/No"
colheaderbold="Yes/No"
bgcolor="color"
selectcolor="color"
selectmode="mode"
maxrows="number"
notsupported="text"
picturebar="Yes/No"
insertbutton="text"
deletebutton="text"
sortascendingbutton="text"
sortdescendingbutton="text">
</CFGRID>
```

name	**Required.** The name of the grid element.
height	**Optional.** The height of the control, in pixels.
width	**Optional.** The width of the control, in pixels.
vspace	**Optional.** The vertical spacing of the control, in pixels.
hspace	**Optional.** The horizontal spacing of the control, in pixels.
align	**Optional.** The type of alignment for the element with respect to other elements.
query	**Optional.** The name of the query to associate with the grid control.
insert	**Optional.** A Yes/No value indicating whether users are allowed to insert rows. The default is No.
delete	**Optional.** A Yes/No value indicating whether users are allowed to delete rows. The default is No.

sort	**Optional.** A Yes/No value indicating whether users are allowed to sort rows. The default is No.
font	**Optional.** The font face for text.
fontsize	**Optional.** The font size for text.
italic	**Optional.** A Yes/No value indicating whether text should be italicized. The default is No.
bold	**Optional.** A Yes/No value indicating whether text should be bold. The default is No.
href	**Optional.** The URL to associate with the grid item or a query column for a grid that's populated from a query. If `href` is a query column, the `href` value displayed is populated by the query. If `href` is not recognized as a query column, the `href` text is assumed to be an actual HTML HREF.
hrefkey	**Optional.** The name of a valid query column when the grid uses a query. The column specified becomes the key regardless of the grid's select mode.
target	**Optional.** The target frame for the HREF URL.
appendkey	**Optional.** A Yes/No value indicating whether the CFGRID-KEY value is appended to the HREF URL. The default is Yes.
highlight-href	**Optional.** A Yes/No value that indicates whether HREF values should be highlighted. The default is Yes.
onvalidate	**Optional.** A JavaScript function for validating user input.
onerror	**Optional.** A JavaScript function to execute on failed validation.
griddata align	**Optional.** The position of data in the grid within the column. Values are `Left`, `Right`, and `Center`. The default is `Left`.
gridlines	**Optional.** A Yes/No value that determines whether gridlines are displayed. The default is Yes.
rowheight	**Optional.** The height of each row in pixels.

rowheader	**Optional.** A Yes/No value that determines whether row headers are displayed. The default is Yes.
rowheader align	**Optional.** The position of data within the row header. Values are Left, Right, and Center. The default is Left.
rowheader font	**Optional.** The font face for row header text.
rowheader fontsize	**Optional.** The font size for row header text.
rowheader italic	**Optional.** A Yes/No value indicating whether row header text should be italicized. The default is No.
rowheader bold	**Optional.** A Yes/No value indicating whether row header text should be bold. The default is No.
rowheader width	**Optional.** The width of the row header in pixels.
colheaders	**Optional.** A Yes/No value that determines whether column headers are displayed. The default is Yes.
colheader align	**Optional.** The position of data with respect to the column header. Values are Left, Right, and Center. The default is Left.
colheader font	**Optional.** The font face for column header text.
colheader fontsize	**Optional.** The font size for column header text.
colheader italic	**Optional.** A Yes/No value indicating whether column header text should be italicized. The default is No.
colheader bold	**Optional.** A Yes/No value indicating whether column header text should be bold. The default is No.
bgcolor	**Optional.** The background color of the control.
selectcolor	**Optional.** The background color of the item when selected.
selectmode	**Optional.** The selection mode for grid items. Choices are Edit, Single, Row, Column, and Browse. The default is Browse.

maxrows	**Optional.** The maximum number of rows to display in the grid.
notsupported	**Optional.** A message that appears if the browser does not support Java. The default text is "Browser must support Java to view ColdFusion Java Applets!"
picturebar	**Optional.** A Yes/No value indicating whether image buttons of Insert, Delete, and Sort are used instead of text buttons. The default is No.
insertbutton	**Optional.** The text to use for the Insert button. The default is Insert.
deletebutton	**Optional.** The text to use for the Delete button. The default is Delete.
sort ascending button	**Optional.** The text to use for the AscendingSort button. The default is A -> Z.
sortdescending button	**Optional.** The text to use for the DescendingSort button. The default is Z -> A.

CFGRIDCOLUMN

The CFGRID tag provides lots of visual control over the entire grid and determines the available interface characteristics. But what if you need fine-grained control over every display parameter for each column in a grid? The CFGRIDCOLUMN tag, up next, provides an almost overwhelming collection of attributes that can determine almost any visual aspect of a column of data. Few of the attributes are required, and visual preferences can vary from column to column in a single grid.

```
<CFGRIDCOLUMN
    name="column_name"
    header="header"
    width="column_width"
    font="column_font"
    fontsize="size"
    italic="Yes/No"
    bold="Yes/No"
    href="URL"
    hrefkey="column_name"
    target="URL_target"
    select="Yes/No"
    display="Yes/No"
    type="type"
    headerfont="font_name"
    headerfontsize="size"
```

```
headeritalic="Yes/No"
headerbold="Yes/No"
dataalign="position"
headeralign="position"
numberformat="format">
```

name	**Required.** A name for the grid column element. If the grid uses a query, the column name must specify the name of a query column.
header	**Optional.** Text for the column header. The value of header is used only when the CFGRID colheaders attribute is Yes (or omitted, because it defaults to Yes).
width	**Optional.** The width of the column, in pixels. By default, the column is sized based on the longest column value.
font	**Optional.** The font name to use for data in the column. Defaults to a browser-specified font.
fontsize	**Optional.** The font size for text in the column. Defaults to a browser-specified font size.
italic	**Optional.** A Yes/No value indicating whether the text should be italicized. The default is No.
bold	**Optional.** A Yes/No value indicating whether the text should be bold. The default is No.
href	**Optional.** The URL to associate with the grid item.
hrefkey	**Optional.** This column serves as a URL key variable if the HREF option is specified.
target	**Optional.** A frame to use when opening the HREF link.
select	**Optional.** A Yes/No value that indicates whether users can select a column.
display	**Optional.** A Yes/No value that determines whether the column is displayed. Used to hide columns. The default is Yes.
type	**Optional.** Either image or numeric. The image attribute means the column should display a specified image; the numeric attribute means data in the grid can be sorted as numbers instead of as text.

headerfont	**Optional.** The font face for the header of the column. Defaults to a browser-specified font.
headerfont size	**Optional.** The font size for the header of the column. Defaults to a browser-specified font size.
headeritalic	**Optional.** A Yes/No value indicating whether header text should be italic. The default is No.
headerbold	**Optional.** A Yes/No value indicating whether header text should be bold. The default is No.
dataalign	**Optional.** The alignment format for column data. Possibilities are `Left`, `Center`, and `Right`. The default is `Left`.
headeralign	**Optional.** The alignment format for column header text. Possibilities are `Left`, `Center`, and `Right`. The default is `Left`.
numberformat	**Optional.** A number format mask for displaying numeric data.

CFGRIDROW

You use the CFGRIDROW tag to create data from scratch, without the use of a database query. This tag can be particularly useful to create blank rows in the grid. The tag is straightforward, consisting of a string of column values for the row it will create.

```
<CFGRIDROW
    data="col1, col2, ...">
```

data	**Required.** A comma-delimited list of data values for each column of the grid. Make sure you have one value for each column of the grid!

CFGRIDUPDATE

The most useful CFGRID-related tag has nothing to do with displaying grid data — it allows database updates, additions, and even deletions directly from the browser window! The CFGRIDUPDATE tag can use Java to connect to the ColdFusion data source directly, bypassing the process of submitting a Web form for ColdFusion to process.

The tag applies *all* the changes made to the editable data in the CFGRID since the last CFGRIDUPDATE or page download. Whereas the other GRID tags are placed on the form, this tag is placed on the form's action page.

Grid changes are applied to the database in a specific order: DELETEs first, then INSERTs, and finally UPDATEs. This ordering minimizes database errors.

```
<CFGRIDUPDATE
    grid="gridname"
    datasource="data source name"
    dbtype="type"
    dbserver="dbms"
    dbname="database name"
    tablename="table name"
    username="data source username"
    password="data source password"
    tableowner="table owner"
    tablequalifier="qualifier"
    provider="COMProvider"
    providerdsn="datasource"
    keyonly="Yes/No">
```

grid   **Required.** The name of the CFGRID form element that is the source for the update action. This attribute simply links the CFGRIDUPDATE command to the proper grid.

datasource   **Required.** The name of the valid data source to update. This can be any valid ColdFusion data source name.

tablename   **Required.** The name of the database table to update.

dbtype   **Optional.** The database driver type. Unless you're running Oracle or Sybase as your database, don't use this attribute. You can set it to ODBC (the default), but if your ColdFusion Server (or the one at your ISP or WPP) is not ColdFusion 4, your page won't work. If you're running Oracle or Sybase, you'll find that using the appropriate dbtype will give you faster queries than using an ODBC connection.

dbserver   **Optional.** The name of the database server machine; for use with native database drivers only (not ODBC).

dbname   **Optional.** For a Sybase System 11 driver only: the name of the database.

username   **Optional.** The database username. Necessary only if database security is enabled in this particular data source.

password   **Optional.** The database password. Necessary only if database security is enabled in this particular data source.

tableowner	**Optional.** The owner of the table (for databases that require this parameter).
table qualifier	**Optional.** The qualifier for the table (for databases that require this parameter).
provider	**Optional.** OLE-DB access only. The COM provider.
providerdsn	**Optional.** OLE-DB access only. The data source name for the COM provider.
keyonly	**Optional.** A Yes/No value that determines whether the key field is the only criterion in the WHERE clause of the SQL UPDATE command or whether all original field values are included in the WHERE clause as well. The default is Yes.

The combination of CFGRID tags makes it easy to create sophisticated (and good looking) Web applications that approach the look-and-feel of native Windows database applications. Figure 13-10 shows an employee information database in which all information is actively updateable.

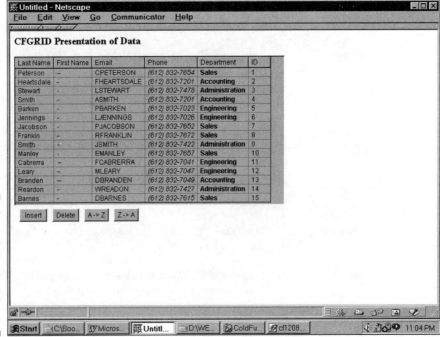

Figure 13-10: CFGRID can compactly display employee information in a Web page.

CFAPPLET

The engineers at Allaire realized that the world has a lot of good Java programmers, so they introduced the CFAPPLET tag, which allows the use of virtually any Java applet inside a ColdFusion form. You'll probably never have to create Java applets, but it's certainly good to know that doing so is possible if you need a special form element and know Java (or know someone who can code Java).

The ColdFusion Administrator must register any applets accessed through the CFAPPLET tag.

```
<CFAPPLET
    appletsource="applet_name"
    name="form_variable_name"
    height="pixels"
    width="pixels"
    vspace="pixels"
    hspace="pixels"
    align="alignment"
    notsupported="text"
    param_1="value"
    param_2="value"
    param_n="value">
```

appletsource	**Required.** The name of the Java applet registered in ColdFusion Administrator. This can be any sort of Java applet, but in most cases these custom tags are used to either display some sort of query result in the page (as a graph, for example) or to provide an alternative way to enter data (such as a random spinner).
name	**Required.** The variable name used to refer to the applet in other code in the form.
height	**Optional.** The height in pixels of the applet display space.
width	**Optional.** The width in pixels of the applet display space.
vspace	**Optional.** The space in pixels above and below the applet display space.
hspace	**Optional.** The space in pixels to the left and right of the applet display space.

align	**Optional.** Alignment values; possible values are `left`, `right`, `bottom`, `top`, `texttop`, `middle`, `absmiddle`, `baseline`, and `absbottom`.
notsupported	**Optional.** The text printed when the browser does not support Java. The default text is "Browser must support Java to view ColdFusion Java Applets!"
param	**Optional.** 0 to *N* parameters expected by the Java applet. For each parameter in the Java applet, you must have a `param_N` attribute.

Chapter 14

Troubleshooting

*I*n this chapter, we assume that you've embarked on your first attempt at creating a useful ColdFusion application. You've created your ColdFusion template(s), fired up your trusty Web browser, surfed to your application — and received an error message. Fear not, loyal reader, errors are a normal part of developing any computer application. Don't be hard on yourself. Microsoft (which can afford to hire the best programmers in the business) touted that its Windows 98 fixed several thousand bugs in Windows 95. Several *thousand* bugs?

This chapter describes methods for testing the quality of your programming as well as squashing bugs in your ColdFusion applications. We focus on application design, basic debugging techniques, ColdFusion Studio tools for debugging, and common server configuration problems. For more on the most common CFML programming mistakes, check out the list in Chapter 15.

Finding de bug

The term *bug* really does refer to creepy-crawly creatures. Back in the days of transistors and room-sized computers, so the story goes, a program wasn't working as expected. After an exhaustive check of the logic of the application and the accuracy of the punch cards (the way instructions were delivered to the computer), no cause for the problem could be established.

During a check of the computer hardware, however, technicians found a moth that had shorted a connection. After the machine was *debugged*, everything operated normally.

Technology has advanced a great deal from the days of punch cards and transistors, but computer programs still need debugging.

Good Design Is the First Step

The first step in creating an error-free application is to plan the application. Beginning and even experienced programmers often take a "seat of the pants" approach to programming by just jumping in and starting to create an application. Although the enthusiasm of such an approach is laudable, the results are usually chock-full of errors, logic mistakes, and artificial limits on the long-term development of the application. Hastily cobbled-together code tends to include hard-to-use data structures created on an ad hoc basis. Sometimes developers even forget components — such as security systems! Time spent planning an application before coding is time well spent.

Books on formal application design and methodology abound, but most ideas on the subject can be summed up in a simple series of rules:

1. Define the objectives, or specifications, of the application.
2. Create the data structures needed to fulfill the objectives.
3. Outline the logic, or flow, of the application.
4. Design the user interface.
5. Implement the design in code.
6. Test the application against the specification and correct any problems.

These steps are general outlines but should suffice for the types of applications you'll be building with ColdFusion. You'll thank us later for making you go through all this work now.

Mission possible

Creating a ColdFusion application may be the effort of a single coder or a team of developers, but in all cases the project should involve careful planning. The easiest way to keep a project on track is to start with the following:

- ✔ A broadly defined idea of what the application does (a *mission statement*)
- ✔ A list of specific objectives for the application to accomplish

You've probably suffered through tedious mission-statement meetings that help define the role of a department or some other organization. But trust us — creating a clear mission statement for an application is crucial. The mission statement should include a list of specific objectives for the application to help guide the development process.

More sophisticated applications should undergo a formal specification process, but a mission statement and list of objectives is a good start.

For example, suppose you want to build an application to track your CD collection. You have the nucleus of the mission statement — "track my CD collection," but it's too broad. What specific functions should the application be capable of performing? These objectives, in concert with the mission statement, should guide the development of your application.

One possible set of objectives includes the following:

- ✔ Insert information about a CD
- ✔ Edit and update data records
- ✔ Delete records
- ✔ Search records for specific information on CDs or specific CF tracks

Your application may have different functions, but the point is that you should clearly list those functions before you start. Looking at such a list could help you realize that you left out certain functions or that you really don't need functions you thought were crucial. The design process is mostly brainstorming at this step, so it's common to revisit this step several times.

Data structure 101

After you sketch out the objectives of the application, it's time to determine what type of data is necessary to meet those objectives. This process starts with a simple list of needed data items, but eventually turns into a specification that includes the types, sizes, and allowable values for individual data fields. Because almost all ColdFusion applications include some sort of database, this step is often either based on an existing database or forms the beginning of the database design process.

Consider the CD collection example. What information do you want to track in your collection of CDs? I bet your list is different from ours. Here's some information we might want to include:

- ✔ Title, artist, and publication date for the CD
- ✔ Name of each track on the CD, as well as the length in seconds (or minutes)
- ✔ Individual artists on each track (especially on jazz or classical tracks)
- ✔ Musical genre information by album and track
- ✔ Location of the CD (such as which storage rack or loaned to which friend)
- ✔ Artist information (birth, death, biography)
- ✔ Frequency of play by CD and track names
- ✔ Person who entered, updated, or deleted the CD record

It should be clear by now that a wide range of "correct" data structures exists for any specific application. Your mission statement and list of objectives should help you focus on the data necessary to accomplish the goals of your application. For our CD collection example, we include artist and title information for each track and CD as well as genre information. The other data items would be interesting, but not that relevant to our objectives for this application.

If our data collection didn't already exist, the next step would be to design and create the database. This is a crucial and potentially difficult task that you should not take lightly. Good design has a substantial effect on both the integrity of your data and the ease of application development.

Database design is beyond the scope of this book, but as you embark on a new application, consult any one of the many good books on the subject — or better still, consult with someone with such experience.

One great book on database design is *Database Design for Mere Mortals: A Hands-On Guide to Relational Database Design* by Michael Hernandez.

Running the data flow rapids

After you determine the objectives of the application and map the data structures, your next step is to think about the application itself. The easiest way to do this is to create a diagram, or flowchart, of the functions of the application. This flowchart helps you create the navigation paths for users, which is essential in the design step that follows.

Our CD collection application is a standard drill-down database application. Figure 14-1 outlines the basic flow of the application.

Savvy readers probably notice that the diagram has some duplication (such as the search path for both searching and updating records), but that's okay — we can combine similar features later. For example, in the final application, the add and update forms will be handled by the same templates, as will the drill-down searches for finding and updating records. For now, however, it's better to sketch the individual functions of the application clearly instead of building a complex (and unreadable) diagram!

Make it pretty and usable

After the basics of the application design are handled, you may want to spend time making the user interface pretty and consistent. Although we don't focus on either subject in this book, Chapter 13 has some fancy CFFORM tags that you can use to create some spiffy user interfaces for database-oriented Web pages.

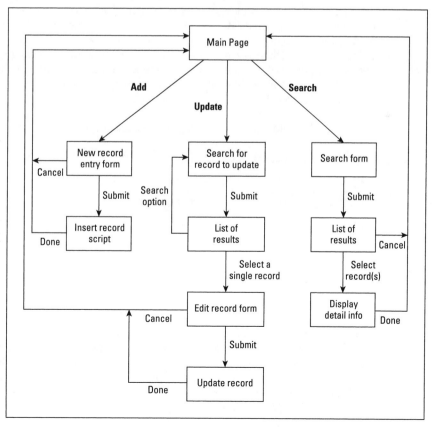

Figure 14-1: Diagramming the logic of an application makes it much easier to understand how the application will be built.

Code monkeying around

After you lay out everything on paper, you can finally begin coding. We talk about programming a lot in this book (particularly in Chapter 9), so we won't belabor the point here. Remember, however, that documenting your code while you're building it is essential. Variable names, algorithms, and other code fragments that make perfect sense today may be incomprehensible next week.

Testing time

Finally! You've designed the application and coded the templates. Now comes the hard part: testing. You should take your new application through its paces. Make sure that it can handle each of the objectives outlined in the design steps. You should also subject it to improper use — such as entering text instead of numbers, entering URLs to access pages in the wrong order, using bookmarks to access a result page without going through the request form first, and anything else you can think of. If you don't find the ways to break your program, your users will.

When you find errors in your application (they're inevitable), you obviously need to correct them. First, read the error message carefully. Believe it or not, many people are inclined to just jump back into the code to correct the error, without reading the error message first. ColdFusion error messages are often very useful, and will even identify the line and column number of the code in error (although sometimes the identified line of code might not be the real source of the error).

Check for the following first when you encounter an error message:

- Typos, especially in tag names
- Missing opening or closing brackets on a tag
- Mismatched opening and closing tags
- Missing closing tags
- Mismatched variable names (such as `temp` in one expression, but `tmp` in another)
- Missing required attributes for a tag
- Incorrect attributes for a tag

These errors are responsible for the majority of bugs in typical applications. If you check these and still have problems, the next step is to get in and see what's going on in your application. Debugging procedures can help shed light on the inner workings of your application and help you identify subtle and frustrating errors. The rest of this chapter is focused on techniques for finding and dealing with coding errors.

Designing for bugs

Regardless of how well you design an application, you'll almost certainly have to deal with bugs. An unfortunate truth is that your users will probably find them! You have two good ways to design your ColdFusion applications to gracefully handle bugs: the CFERROR tag and the CFTRY/CFCATCH tag pair. Both approaches make errors less startling to the user than the default ColdFusion error behavior.

CFERROR is used to create default error pages for two generic errors: template problems and data validation problems. These error pages can provide a look that's in keeping with the design of your site and can provide a single apology message and information for contacting technical support.

See the documentation (and Chapter 11) for more on the CFERRORs tag.

The CFTRY/CFCATCH set of tags is used for more sophisticated error trapping in your code. You execute a block of code, and the tags catch the resulting error, if one exists, and trigger another block of code. For example, you could use a try/catch block to try to update a database record and catch the error condition of the table being locked by another user. Then you could either create a custom error message or write some code that handles the problem (maybe by delaying a few seconds and trying again). This is a bit beyond the scope of this book, but is thoroughly discussed in the ColdFusion documentation.

ColdFusion Studio has features that can help you avoid common errors. The Edit Tag command and tag insight features are good ways to avoid missing or incorrect tag parameters. The Validator helps make sure you use tags correctly. And you can check for matching tags by pressing Ctrl+M, which finds the mate of any tag. See Chapter 3 for more information on these and other ColdFusion Studio features. Note also that Studio can jump to the line number reported in the error message; just use the Edit⇨Goto Line command.

Quick-and-Dirty Debugging

Although sophisticated debugging methods are available, sometimes you just need to solve an unexpected problem quickly, such as moments before the presentation of your application to upper management. In these emergencies or when other debugging methods are unavailable, use the following systematic approach to debugging your templates:

- ✔ Ensure that you have no trivial mistakes, such as misspellings, typos, or missing attributes.
- ✔ Double-check the values of variables, counters, and constants.
- ✔ Isolate the problematic pages into pieces.
- ✔ Make the code simpler and try again.

We leave the first step to you, because between this book and the online information from Allaire, you should have everything you need to ensure proper CFML spelling and grammar in your templates. The additional debugging steps require either new ColdFusion tags or interesting uses of existing ones. Rest assured we cover them all here.

Make a list and check it twice (or more)

The first step in debugging an application is to make sure that all variable and constant values you use in the application are the values you think they should be. The most common problems with values in an application follow, in order of decreasing likelihood:

- ✔ Referring to a nonexistent value
- ✔ Confusing two values (often with similar names)
- ✔ Incorrectly calculating the value of a variable

ColdFusion prevents you from using a variable that isn't defined. The error screen in Figure 14-2 shows what happens when you use an undefined variable in an expression. ColdFusion Server catches the problem and even points out helpful solutions. You'll find that the suggestions ColdFusion generates cover most typical situations that could cause that particular error.

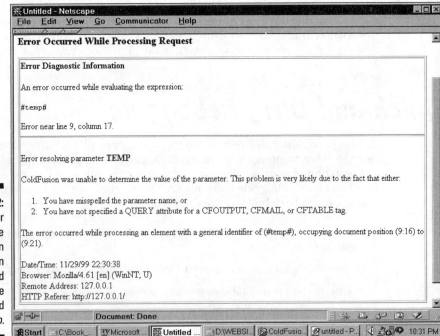

Figure 14-2:
Error
message
screen
for an
undefined
variable
named
temp.

A nonexistent variable may be caused by executing a page without properly passing the expected `form` or `url` variables. It's so easy for users to bookmark a page expecting to be able to return to it. But that bookmark doesn't contain the form information and might not contain the necessary URL information, and thus will create a problem. It's imperative that you design any page that expects to be passed form or URL data so that it fails gracefully if that data is not passed in.

For variables that do exist in your application, errors might occur if you confuse two values with similar names or functions. For example, suppose you use the `count1` and `count2` variables to keep track of different values in an application. A simple typo could change one into the other and cause all sorts of weird behavior in your application:

```
<CFIF form.count1 GT form.count2>
    count1 is bigger!
<CFELSE>
    count2 is still the champion!
</CFIF>
```

Seems straightforward, right? If `form.count1=15` and `form.count2=10`, we should get the `count1 is bigger` message. But now we add a typo — pretend you don't notice it:

```
<CFIF form.count2 GT form.count1>
    count1 is bigger
<CFELSE>
    count2 is still the champion
</CFIF>
```

The result of this code for the same values (`form.count1=15` and `form.count2=10`) is `count2 is still the champion`, which is clearly wrong. You should be able to catch this problem, but suppose you're on your 30th straight hour of coding, in a Mountain Dew caffeine haze, and not sure whether your code or the form contains the troublesome `count1` and `count2` variables. How can you check the values of `count1` and `count2`? With our old friend CFOUTPUT!

The following quick-and-dirty modification to your code helps track down the error:

```
<CFOUTPUT>
count1=#form.count1#<BR>
count2=#form.count2#<BR>
</CFOUTPUT>
<CFIF form.count2 GT form.count1>
    count1 is bigger
<CFELSE>
    count2 is still the champion
</CFIF>
```

The resulting Web page prints the values for `count1` and `count2` so that you can verify their value. Here, it's clear that the values are correct, so the code that does the processing on this page must be wrong. You kick yourself for missing the obvious and correct the CFIF statement. You can then remove the CFOUTPUT block of tags because they no longer have a purpose.

You might want to correct the use of such similar names by replacing them using Studio's Find and Replace features. And be careful to avoid such potential mistakes in the future.

Anytime you need to verify the values of variables, use temporary CFOUTPUT tags. This method is particularly useful for determining the values of session and client ColdFusion variables. You can get some of the same results with ColdFusion Server debug information and with the ColdFusion Studio interactive debugger, but this simpler method works just as well.

Putting the bugs in isolation

Programmers notice immediately one particular difference between ColdFusion and many other application platforms: ColdFusion Server executes ColdFusion templates in an all-or-nothing manner. ColdFusion Server processes the entire template, and the results are piped to the Web server and on to the browser window.

Most other programming languages allow developers to insert pauses in the code so that they can examine portions of a program as it executes. This technique is useful because programmers can isolate various sections until they find the problematic one. You do, however, have two ways to isolate portions of CFML code in a template: CFML comments and the CFABORT tag.

ColdFusion Studio includes special debugging tools that change the behavior of ColdFusion Server, allowing breaks, pauses, and even stepwise execution through a ColdFusion template line by line. These tools are discussed later in the chapter.

You can use ColdFusion comment tags to quickly turn large blocks of code on or off. Comment tags delineate text in the file that should be ignored — the text is solely for the benefit of someone trying to understand the contents of the template. The ColdFusion comment tag follows:

```
<!-- comment -->
```

where *comment* can be a single character or lines of text. This tag is the same as the HTML version, except HTML uses two hyphens instead of three.

The standard HTML comment tag,

```
<!-- comment -->,
```

will not prevent CFML code from being processed. ColdFusion Server pre-processes CFML code and inserts the resulting HTML into the Web page for delivery to the Web server. ColdFusion ignores the comments just like it ignores any other HTML tag. HTML comment tags are useful only for turning off sections of HTML in a template.

You can use the comment tag to quickly "comment out" a portion of a page. Suppose you have a complex but problematic bit of code that performs one of two sets of manipulations on some variables based on the results of a CFIF statement. One quick way to isolate the problem is to turn off all the manipulations and make sure that the correct portion of the CFIF statement is being executed. Then you can insert some temporary debugging statements to trace the execution of the program. The resulting CFML fragment would look something like Listing 14-1.

Listing 14-1:   Commenting out sections of CFML code.

```
<CFIF Session.code GTE 10>
IF Clause<BR>
<!--
<CFSET x=2*sin(x)+tan(x)>
<CFSET y=x/arctan(theta)>
<CFSET z=x+y>

-->
<CFELSE>
ELSE Clause<BR>
<!--
<CFSET x=2*sin(x)+tan(x)>
<CFSET y=x/arctan(theta)>
<CFSET z=x+y>
-->
</CFIF>
```

The complex processing code is skipped and the output is simply IF Clause or ELSE Clause, which indicates how the template is being executed. After you verify that the CFIF statement is working properly, you can remove the comment tags and the temporary debugging statements.

In addition to commenting out your code, another approach is to use Studio's Edit⇨Cut command to remove the problematic code, save the resulting template, run it, and see if the problem goes away. Then you can use Edit⇨Paste to put the code back. The default setup of Studio Release 4.5 enables the use of undo and redo to access changes after a file has been saved. The default setting of Release 4.0, however, is the opposite. You can change the default setup by choosing Options⇨Settings⇨Edit⇨Allow Undo After Save, and checking the check box to turn this feature on.

But what if the results of the complex processing code are wrong after you debug the CFIF statement? Well, odds are that your processing code is wrong.

How can you isolate the problematic line of code? Use CFOUTPUT to display the value of each variable at some appropriate starting point and after each step, as shown in the following:

```
<CFOUTPUT>
initial x=x<BR>
<CFSET x=2*sin(x)+tan(x)>
modified x=x<BR>
<CFSET y=x/arctan(theta)>
modified y=y
<CFSET z=x+y>
modified z=z
</CFOUTPUT>
```

Another way to isolate portions of code is to use the CFABORT tag to stop the processing of a template at a certain point. This is similar to using a BREAK statement in many other programming languages, but unfortunately you have no direct way to access the value of variables after you abort processing.

One typical use of CFABORT is to isolate destructive SQL queries (UPDATE or DELETE commands) so that you can run tests on that section without harming the database. You can test the logic of the delete capabilities of your ColdFusion database application by inserting CFABORT before the CFQUERY tag that contains the deletion commands.

The following code fragment confirms — without running the deletion command — that the appropriate portion of the template is called:

```
<CFIF URL.mode EQ "Delete>
    Delete code block reached<BR>
    <CFABORT>
    <CFQUERY datasource="datasource" name="delete_info">
        DELETE FROM Customers WHERE CustomerID=#URL.CustID#
    </CFQUERY>
</CFIF>
```

Achieving a simpler life

The final step in tracking down problems in code is to simplify. Previously in this section, you saw the value of commenting out large blocks of code in a template to focus on the behavior of the program. In this section, we point out that if complex code still isn't working after your best debug attempts, you might want to simplify the code.

Some programmers find beauty in sophisticated algorithms and the elegant use of variables, code, and decision structures. Other people try to do the job quickly and on time with brute-force approaches. Most programmers have shades of both extremes, but as a deadline approaches, the simplest methods start to win out over complicated and elegant designs.

If your complex, multistep calculation on a variable isn't working, try a simple calculation (such as 2+2) until you get the code working, and then insert the more complex expression. If your on-the-fly cascading style sheet generation isn't working, try plain-vanilla HTML. After the application's logic is working smoothly, you can revise the application's behavior; trying to debug both at the same time can be an exercise in both frustration and futility.

Interpreting ColdFusion Server Debug Information

Do you have a static IP address and a good working relationship with your ColdFusion administrator? Or are you a Studio user running the Single User Edition of ColdFusion Server? If so, you have a much easier way to handle debugging tasks quickly and easily. The ColdFusion Server software can automatically generate useful debugging information, assuming the ColdFusion Administrator application is configured to enable this feature. (See Chapter 4 for more on setting up the Administrator application.)

By turning on server debugging information, each execution of a ColdFusion template will display dozens of lines of information at the bottom of the page. The administrator can control both the kind of information presented as well as to whom the information is presented.

In the following, we list the most useful options to generate debugging.

Option	*What It Does*
Show Variables	Displays the names and values of every CGI, URL, form, and cookie variable on the page
Show Processing Time	Displays the total processing time for the page, measured in milliseconds
Show SQL and Datasource Name	Allows error messages to appear with the data source name and SQL code

Show Query Information	Displays the record count, processing time, and SQL code for each query on the page
Display the Template Path in Error Messages	Displays the template file name in error messages

The Administrator Debugging setup screen has a few more options, including enabling NT performance monitoring and controlling whether sensitive file name information is displayed and whether certain tracing information is tracked. See the administrator or Allaire's documentation for further details.

Server debug information appears to each user when he or she executes each ColdFusion template, unless otherwise indicated on the Administrator Debug setup page. ColdFusion Administrator can choose to limit to only users with specific IP addresses. After ColdFusion Administrator identifies at least one IP address to receive the debugging information, only those on the list will see it.

The information generated by the Enable Performance Monitoring option is not available to most users and is important only for higher-end performance tuning, so we won't discuss it here. The Show Processing Time option provides more usable performance information, but is of limited usefulness because it generates only the total processing time for a page.

You can use the timing information from the Show Query Information option with the Show Processing Time option to calculate the processing time for the page without the queries. You can then comment out blocks of code to get a rough idea of the bottlenecks in the page that has the inordinately large processing time. In most cases, however, queries take longer to process than any other page element.

You've seen how you can use the CFOUTPUT tag to display variable values on a page. Using the Show Variables option is far easier and less obtrusive for some debugging. It displays any form, CGI, and URL variables generated by the processing of a page. This information makes it easy to ensure that every such variable on a page has the value you expect it to have.

You still have to use CFOUTPUT to display the values of other types of variables for an application, such as local, session, cookie, client, application, and server variables.

Query debug information is as straightforward as variable information: For each query on a page, ColdFusion Server can display the data source, the time for the query (in milliseconds), the number of records, and the SQL code. The Show Query Information and Show SQL and Datasource Name options allow ColdFusion Administrator to control what query-related debugging information will be displayed. This debugging information is especially useful if you use CFIF statements to trigger dynamic SQL clauses based on user input because you can see what the generated SQL code looks like. Figure 14-3 shows an example of the query debug information generated by ColdFusion.

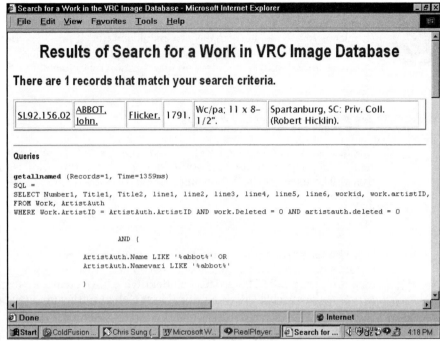

Results of Search for a Work in VRC Image Database

There are 1 records that match your search criteria.

SL92.156.02	ABBOT, John.	Flicker.	1791.	Wc/pa; 11 x 8- 1/2".	Spartanburg, SC: Priv. Coll. (Robert Hicklin).

Queries

```
getallnamed (Records=1, Time=1359ms)
SQL =
SELECT Number1, Title1, Title2, line1, line2, line3, line4, line5, line6, workid, work.artistID,
FROM Work, ArtistAuth
WHERE Work.ArtistID = ArtistAuth.ArtistID AND work.Deleted = 0 AND artistauth.deleted = 0

              AND (

        ArtistAuth.Name LIKE '%abbot%' OR
        ArtistAuth.Namevari LIKE '%abbot%'

        )
```

Figure 14-3:
Debugging
information
for query of
an art
database.

ColdFusion Studio Debugger

ColdFusion Studio is often called an *integrated development environment* (IDE) because, like traditional programming environments, it includes a number of tools to make developing Web applications a snap (see Chapters 2 and 3 for more). The query builder is great, the RDS server access is wonderful, and the automatic tag completion is a dream — but for getting working applications on the Web, nothing beats the integrated debugger that comes with ColdFusion Studio 4.5.

A debugger is simply a tool to assist in debugging an application. Although we have seen that Server error messages can be useful, and we have shown clever ways to modify your code to identify values and comment out code, a debugger is much more sophisticated and useful.

Debuggers typically include tools to watch or view values as the program executes (and even change them on the fly), step through code a line at a time, trace how functions and subroutines are called, and insert breakpoints that pause execution, which can be continued later. ColdFusion Studio Debugger includes all these standard features plus a few of its own, including the capability to debug over several pages in an application. Although figuring out how to use the debugger takes some time, the time it can save you makes the effort worthwhile.

In Chapter 16, we discuss the CF_DEBUG tag, which can drastically improve your debugging capabilities by tracking variable values and execution times for chunks of your code. It's also easy to install and free! It provides much (but not all) of the functionality of the server-side debugging options discussed here. But more importantly, it requires no intervention by ColdFusion Administrator.

Preparing to debug

The first step in debugging a ColdFusion application is to properly define the relationship between the page you're debugging and the ColdFusion server that will be used for the debugging session. Unlike a traditional self-contained C++ application, for instance, a ColdFusion template typically requires access to data sources and other services that are server-specific (such as e-mail or LDAP).

More importantly, a ColdFusion template must be executed by the ColdFusion server and its results displayed in a browser by way of its calling an appropriate URL. The process of identifying how a template maps to a server and a specific URL is a critical first step in setting up debugging.

The process for setting up a debugging session using ColdFusion Studio is fairly simple and starts with the same development mapping process discussed in Chapter 2:

1. **From the ColdFusion Studio menu, choose Debug⇨Development Mappings.**

   You can also call up this dialog box by choosing Options⇨Settings⇨Browse⇨Development Mappings or pressing Alt+M. The Remote Development Settings dialog box appears, as shown in Figure 14-4.

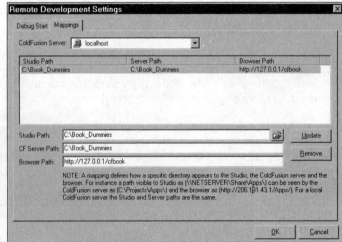

Figure 14-4: Configuring a debugging session in ColdFusion Studio.

2. **From the ColdFusion Server drop-down list, choose the server you want to use to debug the pages.**

   Only RDS-capable ColdFusion servers (as we discuss in Chapter 2) can run debugging sessions. In other words, you cannot debug using a server whose files you connect to through FTP. Also, you must be granted RDS access to that server. This involves being given the single Studio password for the server, unless Advanced Security was implemented on that server, in which case your user ID and password must have been granted access under RDS Security. Note that you may be able to debug a template more easily by installing the single-user version of ColdFusion on your workstation.

3. **Map the Studio path, CF Server path, and Browser path to the debug files.**

   The Studio Path is the path to the template as you've opened it in Studio. You might be opening a file on your own local drive, on a network-mapped drive, or even on an RDS-connected server. The first field simply asks you to identify the method you used. To browse the directory structure and indicate the path to the templates you are editing and want to debug, you can click the File Open icon, which is next to the Studio Path entry field.

   The CF Server Path is the path to those same templates, but as they would be found on the server on which they will execute.

   If you're developing on a local machine (running the Single User version of ColdFusion Server, for example), the Studio and CF Server Paths are usually the same. Otherwise, the Studio Path is the network path to the file, and the CF Server Path is the directory *as seen locally by the server*. For example, if you map D:\me to the network path \\MyMachine\users\me, the former is the Studio Path and the latter is the CF Server Path.

   Finally, the Browser Path is simply the URL with which you would request execution of the template.

   In all three paths, it's best to enter the most generic path possible. In other words, if all your files and their subdirectories are under the Inetpub\WWWRoot directory, define the paths pointing there without bothering to indicate any further subdirectory on the paths. This way, all directories under that path can now be browsed (and debugged).

4. **Click Add (or Update if you are changing a mapping).**

   Make sure you follow this step; it's easy to forget it and instead click OK. If you do that, however, you lose the changes you just entered.

5. **Click OK to continue.**

   You have now created a mapping for the templates, which enables you to browse as well as debug templates. Before proceeding, you may want to attempt to browse a template using the Browse tab in Studio (or the F12 keyboard shortcut) before attempting to debug it. If you can't browse it, you won't be able to debug it!

6. **Click the Debug Start tab in the Remote Development Settings dialog box.**

You can start the debugger also by choosing Debug⇨Start or by pressing Ctrl+F5 shortcut. The dialog box in Figure 14-5 appears.

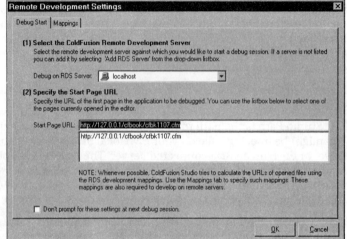

Figure 14-5:
Selecting
the start
page for a
debugging
session in
ColdFusion
Studio.

7. **In the Debug on RDS Server box, select the RDS Server hosting the template you want to execute.**

If you have several RDS servers defined in your Studio environment, the first one in the list is selected by default. Pay attention because if you unintentionally accept the default, you'll have problems getting the debugger to execute properly.

8. **In the Start Page URL box, select or type the URL to the page you're debugging.**

Studio offers a URL by default, which it determines using the mapping specified previously. But it's often an incorrect guess. Note that alternative URLs are often offered in the list. If none are the correct one, simply type the correct URL yourself.

9. **Click OK.**

The mappings you create stay active, so after you map the directory for an application, you can use the Debug Start tab to select various starting pages for working through your application. Read on to discover more about the practice of debugging a ColdFusion application.

Using the debugger

The debugger enables you to do two basic tasks:

✔ Control (stop, start, or pause) the execution of a template on a line-by-line basis

✔ Examine (and in some cases modify) the state of the template and its associated variables, database record sets, and tags processed so far whenever template execution is stopped or paused

To find errors in your code, the debugger takes the same basic approach we discussed in the quick-and-dirty debugging section earlier: isolate the problem areas and list the variable values.

Using the debugger is superior to quick-and-dirty debugging methods, however, because you need not modify the code to see the debugging information. More importantly, the debugging session is unique to you. You need not worry about having any effect on other users of the template while debugging. You can't get that with the quick-and-dirty approach.

One serious problem of using the quick-and-dirty debugging methods presented earlier is that it is *very* easy to forget about debugging code you added — at least until a user or client points it out. And because debugging messages to yourself are often cryptic, profane, or both, it is probably a good idea to find out how to use the interactive debugger instead!

The Debug toolbar, which is shown in Figure 14-6, appears along the bottom of the ColdFusion Studio workspace. Along with the buttons for controlling the processing of a page, the toolbar contains a number of icons that trigger the Debug pane, which is a tabbed display of the debugging information available after you pause an application.

Figure 14-6:
The Debug
toolbar.

The Debug toolbar is a floating toolbar that's docked in the lower left of the Studio environment by default. You can dock or undock the toolbar by simply dragging it to or away from, respectively, the lower-left corner of Studio.

Figure 14-7 shows a sample of the Variables tab of the Debug pane for a ColdFusion template. Note that this pane shows essentially the same information provided by the server-side debugging settings discussed previously in the chapter, but it also adds the many variable types not listed there. You see more about the information presented in the debugging pane, as well as how to manipulate the debugger, in a moment.

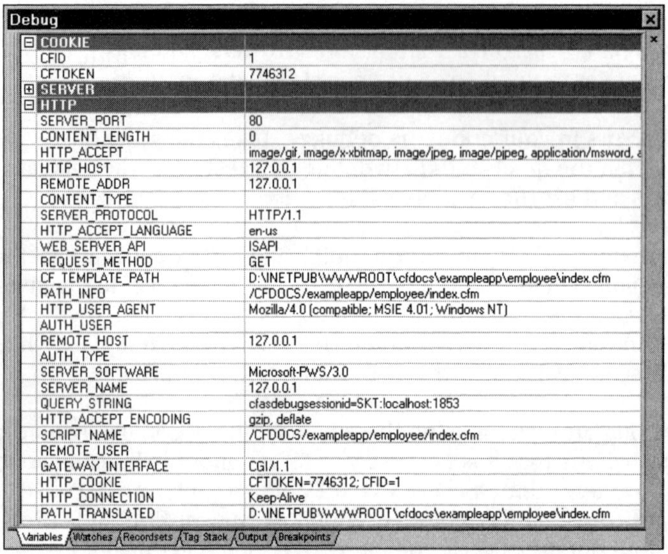

Figure 14-7:
Cookie and
CGI (HTTP)
variable
values in the
Debug pane
of
ColdFusion
Studio.

It's much easier to see how the ColdFusion Studio debugging process works with an example. Refer to the simple application in Listing 14-2 as we discuss how you can use the ColdFusion Studio debugger to deal with coding problems.

Listing 14-2   A simple application to demonstrate debugging techniques.

```
<CFSET testvar="test">
<CFQUERY datasource="CFexamples" name="SearchResults">
SELECT      EmpEmployees.*, EmpDepartments.*
FROM        EmpEmployees, EmpDepartments
WHERE EmpEmployees.DepartmentID=EmpDepartments.DepartmentID
</CFQUERY>

<H1>Debugging Example</H1>
<TABLE BORDER>
<CFOUTPUT query="SearchResults">
<TR>
<TD>#Firstname# #Lastname#</TD>
</TR>
</CFOUTPUT>
```

The basic function of the template in the listing is to perform a query on the EmpEmployees database table from the CFExamples database, the results of which are then made into an HTML table. (The CFExamples database ships with ColdFusion Server and is automatically installed if you install the documentation and example applications.)

This application works just fine, but we're going to use ColdFusion Studio Debugger anyway to follow the action so you can see how the template is being processed:

1. **Prepare for debugging by adding a breakpoint(s) to the template.**

   To add a breakpoint, click just to the left of the line number of the desired breakpoint in ColdFusion Studio. (If you don't see the line number displayed, click the 5th and 6th icons displayed just to the left of the code-editing window in Studio.) The line is highlighted in red and a stop sign icon appears where the line number was located. If you've ever turned this on by mistake and wondered why the line turned red, now you know!

   You can set a breakpoint only on a line of code that includes a ColdFusion tag or an expression (variable). Although the interface will let you set a breakpoint on a line with just HTML, for example, the debugger will not stop on that line. (Note also that you can set breakpoints by choosing Debug⇨Toggle Breakpoints or by pressing Ctrl+X.)

2. **Create the development mappings, if needed.**

   For more information, check out the steps in the "Preparing to debug" section.

3. **Choose Debug⇨Start/Continue.**

   If your attempt to debug the application fails for any reason, it's likely a problem with setup. See the previous section, "Preparing to debug," for more information on common mistakes.

   When the execution of the template reaches the first breakpoint, the Debug pane pops up and you can look at what's going on. The specific results vary depending on your environment, but note the following:

   • The Variables tab contains the CFQUERY.EXECUTIONTIME variable, which indicates the time spent on the SearchResults query. The tab also has the value of the testvar variable from CFSET.

   • The Recordsets tab has one query, SearchResults, which had 7 records returned. The SQL command is displayed as well.

   • The Output tab has the resulting HTML page up to the breakpoint, which is the point where ColdFusion Server paused execution.

4. **Click Debug⇨Start/Continue to continue to the next breakpoint, or click Debug⇨End to end the session.**

You could also choose to step to the next line of code, using Debug⇨Step Into, as well as several other forms of stepping over lines of code. You can even go back to the Edit window (using the editor's Edit tab) and set yet another break-point. When in debugging mode, the editor's Browse tab doesn't start browsing a page but rather simply returns to the debugging session where you left it.

There's other cool stuff you can do with the Debug pane, too! Use the Watches tab to evaluate the current value of a variable — type `testvar` in the input box and click the Evaluate button. The current value of that vari-able is displayed.

You can even enter an assignment expression to reset the value of most vari-ables. You can also set a watch so that the current value of the variable is evaluated and waiting for you in the Watches pane after *every* break. This fea-ture is a great way to track the value of a variable that's causing problems.

The Tag Stack tab provides a way to get a feel for the structure of complex pages, particularly ones that call or include other pages of custom tags. You probably won't need it a whole lot right now, though.

The Breakpoints tab lists all current breakpoints in the application and lets you manage them. Along with creating and deleting breakpoints, you can modify breakpoints so that they trigger only when a certain condition is met. This is a powerful feature when you know that some variable taking on some value is triggering a problem, but you don't know where the problem occurs.

For example, you can take a variable that's somehow becoming too large during a loop and trigger a break whenever that variable exceeds a threshold value. This makes it easy to find not only where the error occurs but also when, which can be complicated to determine in a loop or other structure.

To enable such conditional, or wildcard, breakpoints, get to the Breakpoints tab of the Debug pane. Then right-click in the pane and choose Add Wildcard Breakpoints. Enter your wildcard condition in the form of a valid ColdFusion expression (`form.variable IS "whatever"` rather than `form.variable= "whatever"`).

Two final important points to note about how the debugger relates to the per-sistence of debugging settings. First, after you set a breakpoint, it remains set until you remove it. This persistence even spans multiple Studio sessions. It can trip you up if a wildcard condition is turned on and stops when you're not expecting it. (The wildcards are not tied to a particular template.)

That leads to the final important point about persistence: After the debugger is turned on, it remains turned on until you turn it off. It does not terminate after the debugged template terminates. This is valuable, especially in the case of doing wildcard breakpoints. You can simply keep running the applica-tion until the breakpoint condition occurs, even if it's several templates deep into the application. Very cool!

The debugger is a powerful but often misunderstood or incorrectly configured tool. The time it takes to figure out how to use it, however, will *drastically* cut down on the time you spend correcting bugs — and probably improve the quality of your coding as well.

Server Configuration Problems

Even if you manage to create bug-free code using the techniques in this chapter, you can still run into problems running your application, particularly if you have to move it from one server (such as a test machine) to another (such as a staging or deployment server). One common problem is an incorrectly configured server. The information in Chapter 4 on configuring ColdFusion Server should solve most server configuration problems.

In this section, we outline the major issues of server configuration so you know how to properly configure your server or what to complain to your server administrator about!

Configuration problems are common if you're running ColdFusion Server on your personal development machine because most of us are not experienced server administrators.

Directory permissions

The two basic types of directory permission problems with ColdFusion are normal HTML read problems and ColdFusion template execution problems.

If you get the following error message:

```
HTTP/1.0 403 Access Forbidden
```

most likely Read permission has not been granted for Internet users accessing your directory. The system administrator or Webmaster can handle this by setting Read permission for the directory to True in the Web server administration application (typically the IIS or PWS Administrator).

In addition, ColdFusion scripts can run only if Execute permission is given to the directory where they reside. One indicator that this has not been accomplished is when you get a file download dialog box while trying to access a ColdFusion template. Another indicator is when the page appears but does not seem to be executing the ColdFusion tags on the server; they are simply passed to the browser (which you can see using the browser's view source command or equivalent). The system administrator or Webmaster can correct this problem by setting the Execute permission for the directory to True in the Web server administration application.

We've all heard the story of the person who complains something is not working, only to find out that it was simply not plugged in. The same can happen to ColdFusion developers who don't realize that problems might be caused because ColdFusion Server service simply hasn't been started.

A related problem, though not really one that's a server configuration error, is trying to execute a ColdFusion template by specifying just the file name (or choosing File⇨Open). ColdFusion templates must be executed by way of a Web server, so the URL must start with HTTP://servername/ or HTTP://ipaddress/ followed by the directory, or template name, or both.

ODBC drivers and data sources

Because ColdFusion's forte is database access, almost all ColdFusion applications require a database. For ODBC access, setting up database access means creating a data source.

The most common reason for data source errors is that the data source has not been registered. Other problems include the following:

- ✔ Mismatches between the type of database and the driver being used (for example, using a FoxPro driver with an Access database)
- ✔ Version mismatches between ODBC drivers (for example, using an Access 95 driver with an Access 97 database)
- ✔ Confusion about password-protected databases (such as forgetting to provide the security information or the garbled entry of security information)
- ✔ Incorrect path information in the data source entry (perhaps because you or the administrator moved the database to a different directory)

These problems can be corrected only by ColdFusion Administrator or by a system administrator who is familiar with ODBC.

Other common problems

Several other problems often trip up beginning (and even experienced) ColdFusion developers. Chapter 15 describes ten of the most common coding mistakes.

ColdFusion Administrator can correct almost all other server-based problems with ColdFusion. Typical problems and their causes are listed next. In general, an improperly configured ColdFusion Server causes the majority of these problems.

Problem	Cause	Solution
Mail problems	No mail server address in the Mail tab in ColdFusion Administrator	Add the name of the mail server to the Mail tab in ColdFusion Administrator
	Wrong port	Add the port of the mail server to the Mail tab in ColdFusion Administrator
No debug information	Debug options not checked	Activate debugging in ColdFusion Administrator
Debug information on each page	Debug information is not being filtered by IP address	Add debugging IP addresses in ColdFusion Administrator or turn off debugging
Problems with client/ session variables	Variables are disabled on the server	Enable the variables or discuss options with your ColdFusion administrator
Problems with client/ session variable duration	The timeout is set improperly	Check the maximum timeout values and revise your application

When All Else Fails

In a few cases, ColdFusion itself is causing the problem. All software has bugs — and ColdFusion is no exception. But before you blame Allaire, make sure you have thoroughly debugged your application.

In most cases, the problem is with your code, the design, the databases, your application logic, or the server. Consider checking with Allaire only after you can rule out these problems with 100 percent certainty.

Chapter 15 lists some resources for troubleshooting your code. In addition, the Allaire ColdFusion Support Forums are a particularly useful place to get a second opinion on the problems you have with your code. The URL is

```
http://forums.allaire.com
```

Although Allaire's support staff often visit and participate in the forums, this is not an official support resource.

Allaire also has a knowledge base of ColdFusion issues and runs a Developer's Zone filled with information on Web technology in general and ColdFusion in particular. All these resources are on the main Allaire Web site.

Another similar discussion forum is the CF-Talk mailing list, which you can find at `www.houseoffusion.com`

Allaire does offer fee-based support, as well as free support for problems with installation of ColdFusion Server. Also note that Allaire provides periodic maintenance releases containing major and minor bug fixes to the current version of ColdFusion Server. For more information, check out Allaire's Web site: `www.allaire.com`

Part V
The Part of Tens

The 5th Wave
By Rich Tennant

Now take your time and see if you can identify the person who attacked you on e-mail.

In this part . . .

Why do *For Dummies* books save so much good stuff for the end?

The list of common coding mistakes in Chapter 15 are the result of years of, well, making coding mistakes — mistakes you can now avoid! Before you post your code to the Allaire Support Forum in hopes that some kind soul will untangle it for you, run through this list and make sure you aren't making one of the listed mistakes.

The lists of functions in Chapter 16 are the result of years of ColdFusion development, consulting, and teaching experience. You may read through these today and think you'll never need to find a city and state based on a zip code or have your site communicate with CyberCash. But pick up this book in a year, and see whether you don't find something on these lists that saves you a week or more of work!

The last chapter contains a list of the custom tags we find most useful. Custom tags are the secret weapon in the experienced ColdFusion developer's bag of tricks. Why write, test, and debug code to do a specific task when someone has already performed the work for you? One of the reasons ColdFusion developers are so productive is that many commonly needed functions are available in custom tags for free or for a song.

Chapter 15

Ten Common Coding Mistakes

*E*veryone makes mistakes when they build ColdFusion applications. We made a lot at the beginning and fewer as we became more experienced. Chapter 14 discusses the process of debugging your applications, but some mistakes are so common that we describe them here as well.

A lot of the mistakes described in this chapter are more common for newer users of ColdFusion, but even pros get confused every once in a while!

Data Source Not Found

When you create a CFQUERY, CFINSERT, or CFUPDATE tag, one of the required components is the `datasource` name attribute:

```
DATASOURCE=""
```

Hardly anyone forgets the attribute, but it's not unusual to get so excited about doing the query that you use the name of the data table instead of the data source.

Suppose you have a data source named CDCollection with data tables named Artists and Albums. The `datasource` attribute for a CFQUERY should be `"CDCollection"`. If you're doing a query on the Artists table, for example, you might accidentally use the table name `"Artists"` instead.

This mistake isn't as crazy as you may think because in the very next line of your application, you write something like the following:

```
SELECT Name FROM Artists WHERE Name LIKE '#Form.Name#%'
```

Your mind is on that Artists table, not the name of the entire database. (Similarly, you need to refer to the name of the data source, not the name of the database. They are often, but not always, the same value.)

Wrong Field Name

Even if you use the correct data source name in a CFQUERY, it's easy to use the wrong field name, especially in complex databases with many tables and fields. The best way to avoid this mistake is to use ColdFusion Studio. Its Database tab lets you view the structure of the database, including field names and data types. You can drag and drop table or column names into your code to prevent typing mistakes.

To further reduce errors, you can use the integrated Query Builder to make sure your SQL code works before you put it into CFQUERY.

In some unusual and rare instances, you can have an incorrect field name because the database field name is not valid as a ColdFusion variable. For instance, some database engines allow spaces within the name of a column, but ColdFusion does not allow spaces within variable names. Database engines can also be confused when you use a reserved word (such as `date`) as the name of a database field. In these situations, use the SQL AS keyword, as in:

```
SELECT First Name AS FirstName FROM Artists
```

This SQL code would take an improper field name in the database (First Name) and turn it into a field named Firstname, which ColdFusion can manipulate. When you're designing from scratch, you should just avoid using strange database field names, but sometimes you have no choice when dealing with an existing database. The AS SQL keyword is a lifesaver in those situations!

Missing CFOUTPUT

Suppose you lovingly craft a beautiful page, test it, and see something like the following:

```
Welcome to the website, #Username#. We haven't seen you here
            since #query.lastvisit#!
```

When you see pound signs in your browser output, you've likely made a mistake. This type of incorrect output can occur also if you're using the quick-and-dirty debugging methods in Chapter 14.

In either case, you've likely left out a pair of CFOUTPUT tags. ColdFusion knows that any text in the format

```
#text#
```

should be interpreted as a ColdFusion variable. But ColdFusion Server will display only the value of such a variable if specified inside CFOUTPUT tags!

Problems with Single Quotes and SQL

Most of this book is about CFML, but you can't help but discover a little bit about SQL because it's essential to the operation of databases. The problem is that you probably don't know SQL well enough to create blocks of code instinctively. Many of you probably can create HTML pretty easily, however, and that can cause one big problem for your SQL that has to do with quotes and double quotes.

SQL *always* uses single quotes. HTML normally requires double quotes. CFML commands can often take either. To make your code more consistent, make sure you always use double quotes — except inside a block of SQL in a CFQUERY. Inside CFQUERY is the *only* time you need to use single quotes.

Some databases, including Microsoft SQL Server, technically do permit double quotes. To write the most portable code, however, use single quotes for SQL string values.

You can also have a more subtle problem with apostrophes in CFQUERY tags when part of the WHERE clause is coming directly from user input. Suppose you have a simple name-searching application from an employee phonebook. What if your user searches for the last name O'Brien? The SQL might look something like this:

```
SELECT * From Employees WHERE Name LIKE '#form.name#%'
```

This becomes

```
SELECT * From Employees WHERE Name LIKE 'O'Brien%'
```

which is interpreted by the database as a syntax error due to the extra (unmatched) single quote. This interpretation is certainly *not* what you intended. One quick way to address the problem is to use the CFML PreserveSingleQuotes() function, which ensures that single quotes are interpreted as the single quote character inside a SQL query instead of as the special signal to end a string.

Problems in CFIF

It's late, a deadline is looming, and you're coding like a maniac. Suddenly, you get an invalid parser construct in your CFIF statement. You check it by reading aloud to yourself . "If x = 5, do this block of code. Looks right to me."

If you were a little less sleep-deprived, however, you may see the problem immediately. Inside a CFIF statement, you always use the text equivalents of comparison operators, not the symbols themselves. Table 15-1 lists the operators and their equivalents to refresh your memory.

Table 15-1   Comparison Operators and Their Text Equivalents

Symbol	Text Equivalent	What It Means
=	EQ	Equal to
<>	NEQ	Not equal to
>	GT	Greater than
>=	GTE	Greater than or equal to
<	LT	Less than
<=	LTE	Less than or equal to

You must use text equivalents inside a ColdFusion tag (such as CFIF) because the angle brackets would confuse the code parser. The following example should make the problem clear:

```
<CFIF X>5 OR X<10>
```

The parser thinks that the CFML tag is <CFIF X> and then has trouble with the tag <10>. Using the text equivalents of the symbols corrects that problem. See Chapter 9 for more.

Mistakes in a SQL WHERE Clause

Developing SQL code is a significant but typically smaller portion of your development time when building a ColdFusion application. With the languages thus intertwined, you can forget that they have different rules. In our experience, the difference that causes the most problems is that SQL requires comparison operators to be symbols, not the text equivalents used in ColdFusion (discussed in the preceding section).

After creating a few dozen CFIF statements on a page, momentum can sometimes keep your fingers going so that you write a block of SQL that looks like this:

```
SELECT * FROM Employees WHERE X GT 0
```

That sort of comparison is required in a CFIF, but SQL has no clue what GT means. As far as the SQL engine is concerned, it's a nonsense word. In the SQL code inside the CFQUERY tags, you must always use symbols.

The most confusing part of symbols-versus-text errors is that you often embed CFIF clauses in CFQUERY. That can lead to code like the following:

```
<CFQUERY datasource="Company" name="GetInfo">
SELECT * FROM Employees WHERE Status='Active'
<CFIF form.Sales GT 100,000>
    AND sales > 1000,000
</CFIF>
and so on...
```

which is perfectly acceptable, but the rapid shift back and forth from SQL to CFML can easily lead to comparison operator errors.

Problems with URL Variables

Variables are often passed from one page to another using URL variables, but it's easy to run into problems with this technique if you're not careful. The HTTP specification states what can and can't be used in a URL string — and forbids the use of most special characters, including spaces and most punctuation.

The following are all examples of poorly formed URL variables:

```
page.cfm?CourseName=Math 101
page.cfm?Address=1100 Main St.
page.cfm?Name=O'Brien
```

Using an improper URL variable will often result in a "500 Error" in the browser (or the data following a space or a special character will simply be cut off), although recent versions of Internet Explorer are more forgiving.

The easiest solution to this problem is to avoid creating any URL variables that contain problematic characters. However, you do have another alternative. The ColdFusion function URLEncodedFormat() takes a string value and converts any values that are not allowed in a URL string to a special code that *is* allowed.

The following listing shows the problematic URL variables from the preceding example converted into URL-safe variables. Spaces have been replaced by the expression %20; other special characters have similar codes:

```
page.cfm?CourseName=Math%20101
page.cfm?Address=1100%20Main%20St%2E
page.cfm?Name=O%27Brien
```

The URLEncodedFormat() function makes it easy to address this problem without knowing a lot of complex HTTP information. This technique makes it safe to pass most arbitrary variables using URL variables.

Improperly Scoped Variables

While building an application, beginning developers are typically free in their use of variables. Many times, variables are no longer needed but remain on a page because the developer doesn't remove them. These parasitic variables are a particular danger when developers are lazy about scoping their variables. You often don't have to specify the context, but if you don't, you are taking a risk.

Scoping a variable means giving it a context. Typical contexts in CFML are application, form, client, session, CGI, URL, and local variable contexts. See Chapter 10 for more on variables and scoping.

A common example of an improperly scoped variable occurs when a dummy name is used for a ColdFusion variable. You might pass a URL variable named X, set a client variable you forgot about named X, and need to create a local variable on the page called X. What happens when you use CFOUTPUT to display the value of X? Good question!

ColdFusion looks up variables in this order:

- Local variables created using CFSET and CFQUERY
- CGI variables
- File variables

✔ URL variables

✔ Form variables

✔ Cookie variables

✔ Client variables

Continuing our example, if you simply refer to the variable as X, and forget that you have the local value, you'll notice that the value of your URL-based X variable is not what you expected because ColdFusion Server is confusing the local X and the URL-based X, with the local value winning because of the scoping rules. (Note that application, session, and server variables are not in the "look up scope" chain. To use such variables, you must specify their scope prefix.)

As with most of the problems mentioned in this chapter, you can solve the problem easily. In this case, you should fully qualify your variables. *Qualifying* a variable simply means that you always include the context. If you want the URL variable named X, refer to it as `URL.X`; if you need the client variable X, ask for `Client.X`. Doing so requires a little more typing, but it saves a lot of headaches in the debugging process.

The qualifier for local variables is `variables.` but because it's the first scope in the lookup of scopes, many developers simply leave it off. It's wise to scope all other types of variables, even when it's not necessary, if only to make your code more self-documenting.

Using HTML Comments instead of CFML Comments

Many developers comment their code so that they and others can understand the logic of their application. One problem with ColdFusion templates is that some of the comments shouldn't be on the resulting Web page sent to users, but should be available to other ColdFusion developers. Comments are also used, as we mention in Chapter 14, to temporarily stop some code from executing.

The trick to commenting the ColdFusion portion of your code is to make sure you use CFML comments

```
<!--- comment --->
```

for comments that shouldn't be sent to the end-user's browser or for code that you don't want ColdFusion Server to execute.

Uncommented Code

Not commenting your code isn't an error per se. But it certainly causes no end of problems for you and others who have to work with your code, so we think it should be treated like any other common code error.

You need to comment your code! It's as simple as that. You'll forget how the algorithm works, what the values passed to a function do, and what the page was supposed to do in the first place.

Documenting your code is easy. Many developers have a standard template they include at the beginning of each page that includes spots for basic information about the application and page. Listing 15-1 shows an example of such a template.

Listing 15-1	An Example of Standard Comments Included in an Application

```
<!---
AUTHOR:
VERSION:
DATE:
PAGES CALLED BY TEMPLATE:
PAGES CALLING TEMPLATE:
INCLUDES:
DESCRIPTION:
HISTORY:
PLANS/FIXES:
--->
```

You can modify the default template in ColdFusion Studio to include this information. That way, you are always reminded to document your code. See the menu command File➪Save As Template for more information.

Chapter 16

Ten of the Best ColdFusion Custom Tags

*1*n other chapters, we may have given you the impression that CFML will let you do just about anything in your applications. We're pretty close to right! The 75 tags and 230 functions in ColdFusion 4.5 provide just about any possible feature you could want . . . or do they?

Do you need a tag to validate Brazilian social security numbers? How about implementing strong encryption on your text? Or maybe you need to count down the time until your death (based on actuarial tables)? From the mundane to the sublime, ColdFusion developers have created more than 750 customized ColdFusion tags to handle features not found in standard CFML.

Building ColdFusion Tags for Fun and Profit

One of the most powerful features of ColdFusion is the capability to write your own ColdFusion tags. Allaire introduced a ColdFusion API that made it possible for advanced users to write their own tags in C++. These custom tags, identified by the CFX_*tagname*.dll file name, are implemented as Windows dynamic linking libraries (DLLs) or UNIX shared objects.

Later, Allaire added the capability to write custom tags in CFML, which are generally executed by the CF_*tagname* tag format or the CFMODULE tag. Because CFML is much easier to program in than C++, it's now much easier to customize ColdFusion.

The best place to find custom tags is the Allaire Developer's Exchange (formerly the Tag Gallery). More than 750 custom tags and other components are available. These tags can be freeware, shareware, or commercial products that can cost up to several hundred dollars, but most are free or less than $25.

Some tags duplicate typical Perl scripts (such as a guestbook) or build JavaScript routines for you (such as mouseovers or the determination of browser type and version), but many extend the capabilities of ColdFusion in a useful manner or improve existing CFML tags.

You can find the Allaire Developer's Exchange at

```
http://www.allaire.com/developer/gallery.cfm
```

You can also go to the main Allaire site, choose the Developer option, and then choose ColdFusion DevCenter.

Although most tags address specific issues, some are essentially full-blown applications wrapped up in a CFML tag interface. To handle the security and intellectual property issues involved in selling and distributing third-party tags, Allaire includes a utility in ColdFusion that puts a custom tag through an encoding algorithm (using the /cfusion/bin/cfcrypt.exe command-line utility), making it no longer readable by humans. Many custom tags, even the free ones, are encoded so that the source code can't be easily used to develop similar tags.

Often the source code is available for an additional fee. Check the documentation that comes with the tag.

This encoding capability was previously referred to as *encryption*, but it was simply an encoding process. Late in 1999, someone reverse-engineered the algorithm and created an unencrypting program, thus eliminating the intended protection from this encoding. In Release 4.5, the CFCRYPT program has been renamed CFENCODE. You should not rely on CFENCODE to provide complete security.

If you design a tag that you think would be useful to others, whether it's freeware or shareware, the Allaire Developer's Exchange is the best way to distribute it.

New tags are added frequently, so if you have a coding problem, it's a good idea to check in and see whether your problem has been solved before undertaking the effort to design a new tag. You'll find a number of similar tags in the Developer's Exchange — these are usually updated or free versions of tags that require a registration fee.

Installing Custom Tags

Custom tags built using CFML are simple to install. Basically, you just put the tag in the server's CFUSION\CUSTOMTAGS directory or the directory of the application calling the custom tag — the server will find it. More sophisticated tags written in other programming languages require that an administrator register them in the ColdFusion Administrator application. These custom tags are then available to any ColdFusion application on the server.

Installing custom tags built using C++ is more complex. These tags typically have a name starting with CFX_ to indicate that they are an extension of the basic ColdFusion functionality. These tags are more difficult to work with because they must be installed by an administrator using the ColdFusion Administrator application. This is not a problem if you run your ColdFusion servers in-house, but can be a big problem if you use an ISP.

Ten Useful ColdFusion Custom Tags

After looking at all available custom tags, we've chosen ten that we consider quite useful. We limited the playing field to custom tags that are free and tried to focus on CFML tags because they don't require intervention by the ColdFusion administrator.

These tags should give you an idea of the broad range of additional functionality that can be designed into a tag as well as provide you with a few useful tags for your own application development.

We did include a few really useful CFX tags to flesh out the wide variety of custom tags that are available.

All these tags (except one) are included on the accompanying *ColdFusion 4 For Dummies* CD-ROM. They're in the CustomTags directory, with each tag in its own folder named after the tag name.

CF_HTMLCONVERT

One common Web page function is gathering user comments, maybe in a guestbook application. But what happens if users embed HTML in their comments? You don't want their HTML to change the layout of your page (maybe because they added an extra </TR>, for example), but you do want them to be able to include an image tag as well as text formatting.

CF_HTMLCONVERT comes to the rescue! This custom CFML tag by Rick Root (rroot@koz.com) allows lots of flexibility in what type of HTML (and CFML) tags are allowed in a text string. The syntax is

```
<CF_HTMLCONVERT
      converttext="text"
      allow_html="Yes|No"
      allow_images="Yes|No"
      allow_tables="Yes|No"
      allow_cfml="Yes|No"
      allow_script="Yes|No"
      allow_embed="Yes|No"
      paragraph_format="Yes|No">
```

You can find the tag at the following URL:

```
http://www.allaire.com/developer/gallery/
        index.cfm?Objectid=11464
```

CF_USPS_LookupCityFromZIP

Nate Weiss (nweiss@icesinc.com) developed a custom CFML tag that uses the United States Postal Service Web site to look up city and state information based on a zip code. The tag returns a value for the city and state that you can use to validate the shipping information going into the database. This is a great example of using ColdFusion to incorporate Web data from other sites into an existing application. It's almost essential if you're building online order systems or anything else that requires a mailing address.

A typo in the version at the Allaire Web site generates an error message about duplicate methods. To correct the mistake, remove the extra `method="POST"` statement in line 46. Fortunately, the tag isn't encrypted, so it's easy to correct! The version of the tag on the *ColdFusion 4 For Dummies* CD has been corrected.

The syntax for the tag is

```
<CF_USPS_LookupCityFromZIP zip="zipcode">
```

You can find the tag at the following URL:

```
http://www.allaire.com/developer/gallery/
          index.cfm?Objectid=6950
```

If you do a lot of work with sites that deal with mail and shipping, you might want to check out CF_UPSPrice (which calculates UPS shipping charges using the UPS Web site) and CF_SHIPTRACKER (which can tap into the tracking systems of FedEx, UPS, and DHL).

CF_ BrowserCheck

Many ColdFusion developers have encapsulated common JavaScript functionality into a CFML wrapper to make the coding process easier. One of the most popular uses of JavaScript is to *sniff* the browser — determining which manufacturer and version of the software is being used so that pages can be customized for various popular browsers.

Spotted Antelope, Inc. developed a custom tag that enables you to use JavaScript browser sniffing through a ColdFusion tag. The syntax is

```
<CF_BrowserCheck agent="">
```

To check out the tag, go to the following URL:

```
http://www.allaire.com/developer/gallery/
          index.cfm?Objectid=6980
```

If you leave the `agent=` attribute blank, the current `HTTP.USER_AGENT` CGI variable is used, which sniffs the current user's browser. The tag returns a set of values indicating the user's browser and version number, the operating system used on the browser's machine, the complete version string for the browser, and which levels of JavaScript are supported by the current browser (1.0, 1.1, 1.2).

Other good examples of CFML tags used to generate JavaScript functions are CF_EscapeFrame, which breaks your pages out of external framesets, CF_Alert, which generates JavaScript alert boxes, and CF_SendOnce, which allows the submit button to be clicked only once.

CF_LoadTest

Brian Shin at Allaire (who wrote another tag in this chapter) developed a miniapplication that you can use for basic load testing of a ColdFusion template. First you must install it; this requires that the ColdFusion administrator create a data source and map a virtual directory (see Chapter 4). Then you simply type the URL for the page to test, the number of sessions, and the number of repeats for each of the sessions, and watch what happens.

This tag provides a basic way to simulate — without user input — a large number of hits on Web pages. The tag is most useful for pages with dynamically generated content (such as an online magazine). It's also a good start for those who need to develop more sophisticated load-testing software for their applications.

By the way, main commercial load-testing programs for Web sites can easily cost 10 to 50 thousand dollars. (This price is usually justified because the art of load testing is more complicated than the effect achieved by this useful but rather simple approach!)

The syntax follows:

```
http://servername/load/loadtest.cfm
```

The tag is embedded in the loadtest.cfm template, which is part of the custom tag. It will take a little concentration to figure out exactly how to get this tag to work for your custom code, but it's worth the effort and the price is right!

The tag itself is at the following URL:

```
http://www.allaire.com/developer/gallery/
        index.cfm?Objectid=6962
```

CF_IntlChar

When Jen Hartnett of NMP, Inc. had problems with international (high-ASCII) characters and an Oracle ODBC driver that interfaced with a ColdFusion application database, he turned to ColdFusion custom tags for a solution. His tag strips the international characters from a string and replaces them with

ANSI standard codes (é becomes the HTML entity é). This is an excellent example of solving real-world problems using custom tags. It's also a great example of how to build a custom tag because it's written in CFML and is unencrypted.

The syntax is

```
<CF_IntlChar string="string">
```

You can find the tag at the following URL:

```
http://www.allaire.com/developer/gallery/
            index.cfm?Objectid=7484
```

CF_DEBUG

Dan Switzer of PengoWorks developed an outstanding tool that generates debugging information for a Web page, including local, cookie, application, server, and session variables as well as execution time. One particularly cool feature of this tag is that you can call it multiple times on the same page — this lets you see how variables change at different points as well as determine the execution time of individual blocks of code.

This tag should be in everyone's toolbox because not everyone has access to server-based debugging information or Studio Interactive Debugger, which requires an RDS connection to ColdFusion Server. (See Chapter 14 for more on that sort of debugging.) The syntax is

```
<CF_DEBUG>
```

This tag is at the following URL:

```
http://www.allaire.com/developer/gallery/
            index.cfm?Objectid=7167
```

CF_Excite

Allaire custom tag wizard Brian Shin is responsible for a number of custom ColdFusion tags. CF_Excite is a great example of using ColdFusion to gather content from another page for inclusion or further processing in the ColdFusion template. This tag basically allows you to create an Excite.com search in your site. If you use some type of variable as the search string (such as the contents of a form text box), you can generate the results of an Excite search directly from your page, which is much cooler than simply linking to the search engine.

Brian is responsible for a dozen tags. He wrote the popular CF_CoolLink as well as CF_Banner, CF_Calculator, CF_RollMenu, CF_SQLexecute, CF_Stockmaster, CF_TimeDate, CF_TimeForm, CF_WebChat, and CFX_QueryDump, which is a useful tag for easily displaying all the results of a CFQUERY. And in addition to CF_Excite, he wrote the CF_LoadTest application/custom tag mentioned previously.

The syntax follows:

```
<CF_Excite search1="search term(s)">
```

This tag is at the following URL:

```
http://www.allaire.com/developer/gallery/
            index.cfm?Objectid=6848
```

A number of other CF_ tags include the contents of other Web pages in a ColdFusion page. Some of the most useful are CF_DIRECTIONS (directions from MapQuest), several stock quote and weather forecast tags, and CF_USPS_LookupCityFromZIP.

CF_IMG

S. Martin and P. Murphy of Cathalys Ltd. decided that they would like to make it easier to handle the HTML <IMG> tags in their applications by automatically calculating and including the height and width dimensions of the image file, a task that is tedious to do by hand. (Including the dimensions of an image file greatly speeds up page rendering in the browser.)

CFX_ tags enable developers to extend ColdFusion's functionality by using API calls to the server. Although CF_IMG is named like a CFML-based tag, it's really a CFX_ tag and must be installed by the ColdFusion administrator.

The tag takes the file name of the image as the SRC argument (just like HTML's <IMG> tag), determines the file size, and inserts the HEIGHT and WIDTH attributes into the HTML tag that it builds for you. Any additional attributes are ignored by ColdFusion Server, which means they are passed through to the generated HTML and are interpreted normally by the browser. Here's the syntax:

```
<CF_IMG src="filename" [optional standard HTML IMG
            attributes]>
```

You can find the tag at the following URL:

```
http://www.allaire.com/developer/gallery/
            index.cfm?Objectid=7467
```

ColdFusion and Java, a new relationship

In mid-1999, Allaire acquired Live Software, makers of the JRun Java servlet engine. This product is simply the most advanced technology for developing server-side Java applications, including database-oriented applications. This Java-database access was provided by a technology known as Java Server Pages (JSP).

Although it might seem as if JRun and JSP could be competitors to Allaire ColdFusion, they provide an excellent synergy. ColdFusion code can be quickly prototyped and developed; Java code can be optimized for high-performance and speed. The integration of these products over the next few years should provide an excellent platform for building Web applications using the best technology available.

CFX_CyberCash

Allaire has made e-commerce application building much easier with the release of the CFX_CyberCash custom tag for integrating CyberCash online payment systems into ColdFusion applications. The tag is a wrapper for sending API calls directly to the CyberCash cash register. If you already work with CyberCash, the tag's syntax should be a piece of cake. Otherwise, you should look into the CyberCash system to see whether it meets your online transaction needs. The syntax is meaningless unless you understand CyberCash, so we'll skip it.

Point your browser to the following URL to see the tag:

```
http://www.allaire.com/developer/gallery/
          index.cfm?Objectid=9368
```

 For those using the OpenMarket system, Allaire has created a similar tag called, you guessed it, CFX_OpenMarket. In addition, a few other tags deal with iCat stores.

CFX_J

Allaire recently released CFX_J, which is actually a framework for incorporating Java applications as custom CFX_ tags. This large (12MB+) framework has everything you need to get started programming the ColdFusion API with Java. Java is far beyond the scope of this book, but it's worth knowing especially if you're integrating ColdFusion and Java in the same Web projects.

To find the tag, point your browser to the following:

```
http://www.allaire.com/developer/gallery/
          index.cfm?Objectid=9322
```

Chapter 17

Ten of the Best ColdFusion Functions

· ·

· ·

*I*n this chapter, we focus on ten of the most useful functions for ColdFusion application development. Several hundred CFML functions are available, so this list only skims the surface. Check out the documentation to see what other functions are available; many of them will save you time and energy.

We tried to spread our choices over the thirteen categories of ColdFusion functions. You probably won't be surprised to find, however, that some categories are far more useful than others. We also included a few useful tags related to each of the ten functions we chose.

CreateODBCDate ( ) Function

The ODBC date format is strange to the uninitiated. It's also a bit weird to database pros. But dates must be formatted using the rules of ODBC if you're going to put them in a database connected using an ODBC driver. The following example shows a typical date and its ODBC equivalent (you'll know which is which!):

```
6/6/1970
{ts '1970-06-06 00:00:00'}
```

Clearly, you don't want to create date conversion routines yourself! ColdFusion has a function that handles the conversion for you. The CreateODBCDate( ) function takes typical standard date formats as input and produces ODBC-formatted dates as output. The usage is

```
<CFSET Birthdate=CreateODBCDate(Form.Date)>
```

If you validated the Form.Date input on the input form (using one of the techniques we discuss in Chapter 12, for example), the human-centric date is converted to the proper ODBC format.

A family of tags handles ODBC data conversions. CreateODBCTime and CreateODBCDateTime handle time values and date and time values, respectively.

Now ( ) Function

A common requirement in many database applications is the inclusion of a timestamp with a new or updated record. ColdFusion does this quickly and easily with the Now( ) function. The usage is simple:

```
<CFSET UpdateTime=Now()>
```

ColdFusion formats this date in a format required by ODBC.

If you want to display it in a more usable format, use the DateFormat( ) function. See Allaire's *CFML Language Reference* for more on formatting dates and times.

URLEncodedFormat ( ) Function

A common ColdFusion practice is to pass variables to another page using the URL. However, URLs shouldn't include spaces and other special characters, so passing user-supplied text can be a problem. The URLEncodedFormat( ) function corrects this problem by properly formatting any characters in a given string for use in the URL line. The syntax is

```
URLEncodedFormat(string)
```

The following code shows an example of using this function in a template that builds a URL:

```
<CFOUTPUT>
<A
HREF="do_search.cfm?search=#URLEncodedFormat(form.name)#">
</CFOUTPUT>
```

This tag corrects the string for URL presentation by replacing spaces and all special characters with their hex code equivalents. The result takes a string such as

```
"This will look weird!!!"
```

and turns it into

```
"This%20will%20look%20weird%21%21%21"
```

Replace ( ) Function

Manipulating strings is a fundamental requirement in many Web applications. A few dozen ColdFusion functions work with strings. We chose the Replace() function because it's neat and related to many other useful functions.

The function searches a string and replaces a specific substring with another substring. You can modify the function to replace either the first occurrence of the substring or all of them (the default is one). The result is the modified string:

```
Replace(string, substring1, substring2[, ONE|ALL])
```

Replace() is a useful function for replacing abbreviations stored in a database text field with the real word (for display) stored in an abbreviation translation table. In this way, text containing a lot of acronyms, such as medical records, would be a bit easier to read.

The Replace() function is case sensitive. If you want to do a replace that is not case sensitive replace, use ReplaceNoCase(). Other useful string manipulation functions include regular-expression-based replacement with the REReplace() function, functions to chop portions of the string — Left(), Right(), and Mid() — and functions that trim extra white space from the string — RTrim(), LTrim(), and Trim().

Regular expressions are statements that you can use to search for structured text. In the Find dialog box in Windows, for example, you've probably used the * character in a search for a word starting with a specific letter followed by any other letters (such as m* to find Mr. or Ms.) ColdFusion can handle far more sophisticated regular expressions using standard regular-expression syntax. You can use them not only with the REReplace() function but also in Studio features such as Extended Find.

ListFind ( ) Function

Many types of form processing require dealing with lists of values, such as a set of check boxes on an entry form. Suppose you have a list of favorite musical genres on a Web page. It wouldn't be unreasonable to create a set of check boxes with the name Genre and values corresponding to different types of music (that way you can store the list of values in a text or memo field). Now suppose you want to find out whether the user clicked the Genre check box for Jazz. You could create very complicated code using the CFIF tag, or you could use the ListFind( ) function.

ListFind( ) requires a list, the (case-sensitive) value to look for, and an optional value for the delimiter in the list (which defaults to the comma). If the value is found in the list, the function returns a number representing the position of the value in the list. If the value does not exist, the function returns 0.

To implement our check for users expressing a preference for Jazz, we could use the following code fragment:

```
<CFIF ListFind(Form.Genre,"Jazz") NEQ 0>
      User likes jazz
</CFIF>
```

A number of other functions work with lists, including ListFindNoCase( ), ListSort( ), and ListLen( ). The *CFML Language Reference* has information on these and other list-oriented functions.

FileExists ( ) Function

If you're using ColdFusion to work with files on the server, you need to know about a number of useful functions. Probably the single most important one is FileExists( ). This function simply checks for the existence of a file, which is something you should do before creating one to prevent overwrites.

The function is simple, returning a TRUE value if the specific file exists. It accepts an absolute file path as an argument. The typical use is in a CFIF statement:

```
<CFIF FileExists(Form.filepath)>
    That file exists, please choose another
<CFELSE>
    That is a new filename
</CFIF>
```

Other related functions include DirectoryExists( ) and ExpandPath( ). If you do a lot of work with file manipulation, you should certainly take a look at these functions.

IsDefined ( ) Function

My vote for the single best ColdFusion function is the incredibly useful IsDefined( ) function. The argument of the function is a variable name, and the result is a value of TRUE or FALSE. This technique is perfect for testing the existence of a variable before attempting to use it, to prevent errors and enable some sophisticated coding.

Suppose you want to use the same input form for both inserting new database records and updating existing database records. You could create two pages that are almost identical, or you could get fancy with the IsDefined( ) function. It's common to use URL values to pass — from the search results page to the detailed information page — the key field of the record to be updated. A new record, however, does not have a key value. We can use this distinction to make the input form serve double-duty through the IsDefined( ) function.

The basic idea follows:

```
<CFIF IsDefined("URL.RecordID")>
it's an update, so query to get info to update
<CFELSE>
you're inserting a new record
initialize all the values of inputs to their defaults
</CFIF>
build the input form
```

This way, based on the existence of the key field in the URL, it's clear when you're in update mode or insert mode.

The variable that's the argument of the IsDefined( ) function must be in double quotation marks, without pound signs.

A similar function exists for each specific data type: IsDate( ), IsNumber( ), IsTime( ), and so on. These functions are useful when you're dealing with a data field that can accept multiple types of data and you need to determine the format the user used.

HTMLCodeFormat ( ) Function

It's not unusual to create a Web page about creating Web pages. One problem, however, is getting HTML code to appear without being rendered by the browser as HTML for formatting. You can accomplish this task by replacing all special characters with their HTML character entity equivalents. For example, < becomes < and > becomes >.

This is a pain to do manually! ColdFusion has a function that can do the conversion for you. The syntax is

```
HTMLCodeFormat(string)
```

The string is also returned enclosed in PRE and end-PRE tags so that the formatting stays consistent. Any extra carriage returns are removed as well. If you don't need preformatting, you can use the related HTML EditFormat tag instead.

NumberFormat ( ) Function

Numeric data comes in all sorts of formats. For example, currency data could be entered in several different formats (such as $5, 5.01, 5.0125, $5.01) intended for display in a single column of data. The application displaying the data looks more polished if the values all have the same format, such as the currency symbol and two decimal places. This common format also ensures that columns of numbers line up with the decimal.

Although ColdFusion has a simple function that can do that formatting — the DollarFormat( ) function — if you need even more control over formatting numbers, use the NumberFormat( ) function. It uses masks for numeric data so that the data can be displayed in a common format, regardless of the underlying structure. The format of the tag is

```
NumberFormat(number[, "mask"])
```

The mask is generated using the characters in Table 17-1, and should be surrounded by quotes.

Table 17-1   Mask Characters for the NumberFormat() Function

Character	What It Is
_ (underscore)	Optional digit placeholder.
9	Optional digit placeholder. Same as _, but shows decimal places more clearly.

Character	What It Is
.	Specifies the location of a mandatory decimal point.
0	Located to the left or right of a mandatory decimal point, forces padding with zeros.
( )	Places parentheses around the mask if the number is less than 0.
+	Places + in front of positive numbers or – (minus sign) in front of negative numbers.
-	Places a space in front of positive numbers or – (minus sign) in front of negative numbers.
,	Separates thousands with commas.
L,C	Specifies to left justify or center justify a number within the width of the mask column. L or C must appear as the first character of the mask. By default, numbers are right justified.
$	Places a dollar sign in front of the formatted number. $ must appear as the first character of the mask.
^	Separates left formatting from right formatting.

The following code fragments and their results for the same numeric value might make this clearer:

```
NumberFormat(5.01,"$____.__")        $  5.01
NumberFormat(5.01,"_$___.__")        $5.01
```

Note that if you use NumberFormat( ) without a mask, it removes any decimal places, rounding the number to the nearest integer, and displays commas in appropriate places.

A number of related formatting functions, such as TimeFormat( ), ParagraphFormat( ), and DollarFormat( ), as well as a wide range of international formatting functions, are also available.

IIf( ) Function

The most underused timesaver in ColdFusion might be the IIf( ) function. This function is basically a full IF-ELSE logic block condensed into a single function. The basic format is

```
IIf(condition, expression_if_true, expression_if_false)
```

which replaces

```
<CFIF condition>
    <CFSET result=Evaluate(expression_if_true)>
<CFELSE>
    <CFSET result=Evaluate(expression_if_true)>
</CFIF>
```

For example, suppose you have the following expression:

```
<CFSET Bonus=IIF(Sales GTE 10000, Sales*0.10, 0)>
```

The Bonus variable is assigned either the value of 0 if sales are less than $10,000 or the value of 10% of sales if sales are greater than or equal to $10,000.

Appendix

About the CD

*Y*ou'll find the following on the CD-ROM:

- ✔ ColdFusion Studio, a 30-day trial version of the rapid-application development environment for ColdFusion (translation: a fast way to develop your CFML using wizards and dialog boxes)
- ✔ ColdFusion Express, the new, free application server that never expires
- ✔ ColdFusion Enterprise, a 30-day trial of the application server for Windows NT Server
- ✔ HomeSite, a 30-day trial of a Web-development tool by Allaire that's a great value and includes dialog boxes for CFML development

System Requirements

Make sure that your computer meets the minimum system requirements listed next. If your computer doesn't match up to most of these requirements, you may have problems using the contents of the CD.

- ✔ A PC with a 486 or faster processor (Pentium recommended).
- ✔ Microsoft Windows 95, 98, or NT. NT Server with Service Pack 3 is required for ColdFusion Enterprise and ColdFusion Express.
- ✔ Required RAM depends on the software you install:

    ColdFusion Enterprise: 64MB RAM (128MB recommended)

    ColdFusion Express: 32MB RAM (64MB recommended)

    ColdFusion Studio: 24MB RAM (32MB recommended)

    HomeSite: 16MB RAM

✔ Hard drive space required depends on the software you install:

> ColdFusion Enterprise: 70MB
>
> ColdFusion Express: 50MB
>
> ColdFusion Studio: 25MB
>
> HomeSite: 10MB

✔ A CD-ROM drive — double-speed ($2x$) or faster.

If you need more information on the basics, check out *PCs For Dummies,* 7th Edition, by Dan Gookin; *Windows 98 For Dummies* or *Windows 95 For Dummies,* 2nd Edition, both by Andy Rathbone (all published by IDG Books Worldwide, Inc.).

Using the CD

To install the items from the CD to your hard drive, follow these steps.

1. **Insert the CD into your computer's CD-ROM drive.**

2. **Click Start⇨Run.**

3. **In the dialog box that appears, type** D:\SETUP.EXE.

   Replace *D* with the proper drive letter if your CD-ROM drive uses a different letter. (If you don't know the letter, see how your CD-ROM drive is listed under My Computer or Windows Explorer.)

4. **Click OK.**

   A License Agreement window appears.

5. **Read through the license agreement, nod your head, and then click the Accept button if you want to use the CD — after you click Accept, you'll never be bothered by the License Agreement window again.**

   The CD interface Welcome screen appears. The interface is a little program that shows you what's on the CD and coordinates installing the programs and running the demos. The interface basically enables you to click a button or two to make things happen.

6. **Click anywhere on the Welcome screen to enter the interface.**

   Now you're getting to the action. This next screen lists categories for the software on the CD.

7. **To view the items within a category, just click the category's name.**

   A list of programs in the category appears.

8. **For more information about a program, click the program's name.**

   Be sure to read the information that appears. Sometimes a program has its own system requirements or requires you to do a few tricks on your computer before you can install or run the program, and this screen tells you what you might need to do, if necessary.

9. **If you don't want to install the program, click the Go Back button to return to the previous screen.**

   You can always return to the previous screen by clicking the Go Back button. This feature allows you to browse the different categories and products and decide what you want to install.

10. **To install a program, click the appropriate Install button.**

    The CD interface drops to the background while the CD installs the program you chose.

11. **To install other items, repeat Steps 7 through 10.**

12. **When you've finished installing programs, click the Quit button to close the interface.**

    You can eject the CD now. Carefully place it back in the plastic jacket of the book for safekeeping.

What You'll Find

Here's a summary of the software on this CD. The CD interface helps you install software easily. (If you have no idea what we're talking about when we say "CD interface," check out the preceding section, "Using the CD.")

ColdFusion Studio

Evaluation copy from Allaire. For Windows 95, 98, and NT.

The rapid-application development environment — a spiffy desktop tool for developing CFML in a jiffy — that offers wizards to create sophisticated Web applications using HTML, CFML, and your own database. This is a 30-day evaluation copy. To purchase a copy, visit Allaire at www.allaire.com.

ColdFusion Express

Fully functional, licensed copy from Allaire. For Windows NT Server.

ColdFusion Express is the new, free application server that allows you to do most of what's covered in this book. This version will never expire.

Express is a limited functionality version of ColdFusion Server. Details of the limitations in ColdFusion Express are at the Allaire Web site.

ColdFusion Server, Enterprise version

Evaluation copy from Allaire. For Windows NT Server.

The Enterprise version of ColdFusion Server is the Web application server that everyone's talking about. This is a 30-day evaluation copy. You may purchase a licensed copy from Allaire. If your Web server runs on Solaris or HP-UX, download the evaluation version from the Allaire Web site.

HomeSite

Evaluation copy from Allaire. For Windows 95, 98, and NT.

HomeSite is an award-winning Web development tool that also includes some limited hooks for CFML. This is a 30-day evaluation copy of the original Allaire HTML editing tool from which Studio was born (it lacks the CF-specific application development features that Studio adds). The commercial copy is only $89 by download from Allaire.

If You Have Problems of the CD Kind

We tried our best to compile programs that work on most computers with the minimum system requirements. Alas, your computer may differ, and some programs may not work properly for some reason.

The two likeliest problems are that you don't have enough memory (RAM) for the programs you want to use, or you have other programs running that are affecting installation or running of a program. If you get error messages like `Not enough memory` or `Setup cannot continue`, try one or more of these methods and then try using the software again:

✔ **Turn off any antivirus software that you have on your computer.** Installers sometimes mimic virus activity and may make your computer incorrectly believe that a virus is infecting it.

✔ **Close all running programs.** The more programs you're running, the less memory is available to other programs. Installers also typically update files and programs; if you keep other programs running, installation may not work properly.

✔ **Close the CD interface and run demos or installations directly from My Computer or Windows Explorer.** The interface itself can tie up system memory or even conflict with certain kinds of interactive demos. Use My Computer or Windows Explorer to browse the files on the CD and launch installers or demos.

✔ **Have your local computer store add more RAM to your computer.** This is, admittedly, a drastic and somewhat expensive step. If you have a Windows 95 PC, however, adding more memory can really help the speed of your computer and enable more programs to run at the same time.

Also, Allaire provides free installation support to registered users. This is discussed at the Allaire Web site's support section, which you can get to by clicking the installation support link. This support is limited to getting past the following problems:

✔ **ColdFusion Server and ColdFusion Express:** Unable to successfully run the Test your ColdFusion Installation utility or unable to launch the ColdFusion Administrator page

✔ **ColdFusion Studio:** Unable to open and edit a local file; unable to make an RDS connection to localhost; unable to view the cfsnipets and cfexamples data sources provided with ColdFusion; or unable to use the internal browser to browse local files

✔ **HomeSite:** Unable to successfully complete the installation without experiencing error messages; unable to start HomeSite without experiencing error messages; or unable to use design mode with Internet Explorer

If you still have trouble installing the items from the CD, please call the IDG Books Worldwide Customer Service phone number: 800-762-2974 (outside the United States: 317-572-3000; extension 3994).

Index

• *Q* •

• *y* •

• *Z* •

IDG Books Worldwide, Inc., End-User License Agreement

READ THIS. You should carefully read these terms and conditions before opening the software packet(s) included with this book ("Book"). This is a license agreement ("Agreement") between you and IDG Books Worldwide, Inc. ("IDGB"). By opening the accompanying software packet(s), you acknowledge that you have read and accept the following terms and conditions. If you do not agree and do not want to be bound by such terms and conditions, promptly return the Book and the unopened software packet(s) to the place you obtained them for a full refund.

1. **License Grant.** IDGB grants to you (either an individual or entity) a nonexclusive license to use one copy of the enclosed software program(s) (collectively, the "Software") solely for your own personal or business purposes on a single computer (whether a standard computer or a workstation component of a multiuser network). The Software is in use on a computer when it is loaded into temporary memory (RAM) or installed into permanent memory (hard disk, CD-ROM, or other storage device). IDGB reserves all rights not expressly granted herein.

2. **Ownership.** IDGB is the owner of all right, title, and interest, including copyright, in and to the compilation of the Software recorded on the disk(s) or CD-ROM ("Software Media"). Copyright to the individual programs recorded on the Software Media is owned by the author or other authorized copyright owner of each program. Ownership of the Software and all proprietary rights relating thereto remain with IDGB and its licensers.

3. **Restrictions on Use and Transfer.**

    (a) You may only (i) make one copy of the Software for backup or archival purposes, or (ii) transfer the Software to a single hard disk, provided that you keep the original for backup or archival purposes. You may not (i) rent or lease the Software, (ii) copy or reproduce the Software through a LAN or other network system or through any computer subscriber system or bulletin-board system, or (iii) modify, adapt, or create derivative works based on the Software.

    (b) You may not reverse engineer, decompile, or disassemble the Software. You may transfer the Software and user documentation on a permanent basis, provided that the transferee agrees to accept the terms and conditions of this Agreement and you retain no copies. If the Software is an update or has been updated, any transfer must include the most recent update and all prior versions.

4. **Restrictions on Use of Individual Programs.** You must follow the individual requirements and restrictions detailed for each individual program in the "About the CD" appendix of this Book. These limitations are also contained in the individual license agreements recorded on the Software Media. These limitations may include a requirement that after using the program for a specified period of time, the user must pay a registration fee or discontinue use. By opening the Software packet(s), you will be agreeing to abide by the licenses and restrictions for these individual programs that are detailed in the "About the CD" appendix and on the Software Media. None of the material on this Software Media or listed in this Book may ever be redistributed, in original or modified form, for commercial purposes.

IDG BOOKS WORLDWIDE
BOOK REGISTRATION

We want to hear from you!

Visit **http://my2cents.dummies.com** to register this book and tell us how you liked it!

- ✔ Get entered in our monthly prize giveaway.

- ✔ Give us feedback about this book — tell us what you like best, what you like least, or maybe what you'd like to ask the author and us to change!

- ✔ Let us know any other ...*For Dummies*® topics that interest you.

Your feedback helps us determine what books to publish, tells us what coverage to add as we revise our books, and lets us know whether we're meeting your needs as a ...*For Dummies* reader. You're our most valuable resource, and what you have to say is important to us!

Not on the Web yet? It's easy to get started with *Dummies 101*®: *The Internet For Windows*® *98* or *The Internet For Dummies*,® 6th Edition, at local retailers everywhere.

Or let us know what you think by sending us a letter at the following address:

...*For Dummies* Book Registration
Dummies Press
10475 Crosspoint Blvd.
Indianapolis, IN 46256

BESTSELLING
BOOK SERIES

Installation Instructions

The *ColdFusion 4 For Dummies* CD offers valuable information that you won't want to miss. To install the items from the CD to your hard drive, follow these steps.

1. **Insert the CD into your computer's CD-ROM drive, and click Start⇨Run.**

2. **In the dialog box that appears, type** D:\SETUP.EXE **and then click OK.**

   Replace *D* with the proper drive letter if your CD-ROM drive uses a different letter.

3. **Read through the license agreement, nod your head, and then click the Accept button if you want to use the CD.**

   The CD interface Welcome screen appears.

4. **Click anywhere on the Welcome screen to enter the interface.**

   Now you're getting to the action. This next screen lists categories for the software on the CD.

5. **To view the items within a category, just click the category's name.**

   A list of programs in the category appears.

6. **For more information about a program, click the program's name.**

7. **If you don't want to install the program, click the Back button to return to the previous screen.**

8. **To install a program, click the appropriate Install button.**

   The CD interface drops to the background while the CD installs the program you chose.

9. **To install other items, repeat Steps 5 – 8.**

10. **After you've finished installing programs, click the Quit button to close the interface.**

    You can eject the CD now.

For more information, see the "About the CD" appendix.